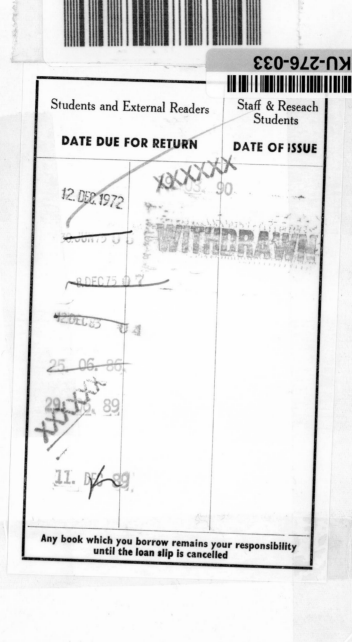

Students and External Readers	Staff & Reseach Students
DATE DUE FOR RETURN	**DATE OF ISSUE**

xxxxxx 03. 90

12. DEC. 1972

WITHDRAWN

8 DEC 75

12 DEC 83

25. 06. 86

29. 89

11. DEC 89

DRAMATIC THEORY

AND

THE RHYMED HEROIC PLAY

DRAMATIC THEORY
AND THE
RHYMED HEROIC PLAY

CECIL V. DEANE

FRANK CASS & CO. LTD.
1967

Published by
FRANK CASS AND COMPANY LIMITED
67 Great Russell Street, London WC1
by arrangement with Oxford University Press

First edition   1931
New impression   1967

C

Printed in Great Britain by
Thomas Nelson (Printers) Ltd., London and Edinburgh

PREFACE

THE study of the literature of an age of transition is always interesting, and it is liable to be particularly instructive when the period is one of English assimilation of foreign influences. The specific purpose of my inquiry is to determine how far the heroic play observed the neo-classic 'Rules' of the drama as expounded by the French theorists and as somewhat freely adapted by English critics, but the book may also be regarded more generally as an attempt—not, I hope, over-obscured by documentation—to throw fresh light on the somewhat elusive process whereby the English genius almost always contrives to impose its native individuality on forms borrowed from abroad. With the advance of literary studies it becomes increasingly clear that our non-indigenous literary and artistic movements must be considered less as the retarded northern offshoots of European culture than as periods of creative enterprise, during which new ideas and fashions from a variety of sources are welcomed for purposes of experiment.

The heroic play is a particularly good example of a product of this kind of activity. At the Restoration a new form of drama was needed, and playwrights did not hesitate to graft on to the old stock whatever likely material came their way. The species which resulted, although artificial in essence and grandiose and extravagant in effect, somehow possesses a life and vigour of its own and an arrogant assurance that tends to sweep censure aside. Something similar may be said in behalf of the theoretical criticism of the time. Its pedantry and dogmatism are apt to be oppressive, but behind much of this may be discerned a keen interest in dramatic reform, together with a zealous spirit of inquiry not unlike that which animated the contemporarily founded Royal Society. Moreover, the much-reviled 'Rules', as far as they applied to the heroic play, were intended less as restrictions than as aids to the establishment of a formal and highly specialized type of drama.

In tracing the connexions between theory and practice I have found it necessary to bring together the conclusions of the principal French and English critics on a number of selected topics; I hope that this in itself has done something to exhibit more clearly the trend of critical opinion. Further, the account of the influence of contemporary thought on the heroic play may be said to break fresh ground, while, so far as I am aware, the reasoned survey of the variations of Dryden's critical opinions has not before been so systematically undertaken.

The book was begun as a Ph.D. thesis at Cambridge, where I was enabled to carry out the task by being awarded the Adelaide Stoll Research Scholarship at Christ's College and, later, the Emmanuel College Research Studentship. The further award of a Sterling Research Fellowship at Yale gave me the opportunity of revising and enlarging my work and of bringing it to its present form. I wish to express my sincerest thanks to Mr. B. W. Downs of Christ's College for the unfailing help and many valuable suggestions he gave me while the work was in progress. I also desire to express my gratitude to the Master and Fellows of Emmanuel College for assisting me with the publication of this book. To Professor J. R. Crawford of Yale I am indebted for encouragement and practical help, while I wish thankfully to acknowledge the advice given me on various occasions by Professor G .H. Nettleton of Yale and by Professor Allardyce Nicoll.

COLCHESTER,   C. V. D.
January, 1931.

CONTENTS

CHAPTER ONE

INTRODUCTION

1. INTRODUCTORY

DURING the Restoration theoretical criticism was taken more seriously and occupied the attention of a larger number of people than at any previous period of English literature. Nearly every play had its preface; literary controversies often arose out of these prefaces, and were either published separately or else embodied in the subsequent plays of the authors concerned. Moreover, a fair proportion of the audiences at the Theatre Royal, or the Duke's Theatre in Lincoln's Inn Fields, may be accounted to consist of playwrights, actual or potential, whose critical faculties were kept alert by jealousy or desire to emulate. Charles's interest in and influence on the drama was considerable, and the cult of the literary discussion spread from the court to the coffee-house, whose reign had just begun. The *Essay of Dramatic Poesy* imitates the form of the Socratic dialogue, yet it may be presumed that it also reproduces a type of actual conversation not uncommon at that time,[1] both in England and on the Continent.

With regard to the Continent, it may be safely averred that whatever the 'influence' of France on the more creative forms of literature in England, it certainly originated the increased respect for criticism here, the commendable assumption that a familiarity with traditional guiding principles and 'tests' of art was part of the normal equipment of men of education and social position. The critical activity of the Restoration period had been preceded in France by the same thing in an intensified form. The founding of the Académie, the dispute over *Le Cid*, the

[1] Cf. Pepys's *Diary*, 1 Sept. 1660.

numerous *Poétiques* and *Examens* which appeared during
the thirty years before the Restoration; all these could not
but serve to impress Englishmen (especially those in France
as refugees) with the prestige which formal criticism had
attained, and to encourage them to practise it more extensively and in a more scientific manner themselves. The
dialectical set pieces of Dryden, Sir Robert Howard, and
D'Avenant, then, besides some of the lesser criticisms to
be found in prefaces, prologues, and epilogues of individual
dramatists, largely owe their origin to French example.

This body of English criticism has been frequently
weighed and analysed on its merits as a separate depart-
ment of letters, but its practical bearings have not, perhaps,
been sufficiently considered. Few writers on the history
of literary criticism would go so far as to say that criticism
after the Restoration was no more than an abstract
intellectual diversion, keeping in view the fact that the
problem of the rehabilitation of the national drama was
a pressing one. Yet though this may be admitted, none
(so far as I am aware) has troubled to investigate with
any thoroughness the question of what fruit all this talk
bore, of how far these much discussed principles were
embodied in the form in which we should most expect to
find them, namely the English heroic play. There is no
doubt that in France the effect of theory on the drama was
profound. The outstanding instance of it is *Horace*, whose
straitened plan Corneille carefully excogitated as a result
of the strictures of the Académie on *Le Cid*. In *Horace* he
not only excluded all episodic characters and incidents,
took his story from classical Rome rather than romantic
Spain, and strictly adhered to the Unities, but he also chose
a theme the reverse of what Richelieu, the absolutist, had
censured in *Le Cid* (which had shown natural affection
triumphing over the claims of the state).

Possibly because there is nothing approaching such direct influence in England, it becomes all the more interesting to inquire how much theory counted for here; especially when other elements which helped to model the heroic play—such as the needs of the contemporary audience, and the persistence of certain traits of the Jacobean and Caroline drama—have also to be taken into account.

Those who like to stress the continuity of English drama, and who maintain that the Restoration play, both tragedy and comedy, was above all a natural development of the Beaumont and Fletcher romantic tragicomedy on the one hand, and of the Jonson comedy of humours on the other, are likely to overlook the fact that even if the Elizabethan was the predominant influence, there were so many different types of drama at hand—ancient, or of the last age, English or foreign—so many recent successes in totally distinct *genres*, that the selection by Restoration playwrights, for the foundation of their work, of any one of these types savours of something conscious or revivalistic, something far removed from the spontaneous growth of the Elizabethan drama.

While pursuing our investigations we may expect to find three rather indeterminate stages in the relation of theory to practice. The first heroic plays are likely to be those which show the impress of the French school of criticism most clearly. Next comes a period in which the plays are affected by French theory as interpreted and slightly modified by the growing school of English criticism. Finally, as the latter reaches maturity and comparative independence, so the play widens its scope; it deals with less stereotyped situations and even seeks to appeal to emotions different from those usually evoked. The last phase more or less coincides with the return to blank verse, i.e. from about 1678 onwards; therefore, since our study is confined to the rhymed heroic play, we shall not be much concerned with the latter phase, except in so far as the early work of Lee and Otway foreshadows the change. It was the rhymed heroic play which received the fullest impact of critical theory, and which will yield most in the way of deliberate acceptance or rejection of the 'Rules'. I propose to start by discussing points of importance gathered from the chief works of the most prominent critics of the period,[1] both French and English, taking the remarks as far as possible in chronological order. It will be convenient, however, to take the French writers before the English, since the former (with one or two important exceptions) stand in relation to the latter somewhat as legislators to lawyers. Moreover, as has already been indicated, much English criticism directly owes its origin to French work. *The Essay of Dramatic Poesy* itself Dryden called 'A little discourse in dialogue, for the most part borrowed from the observations of others'.[2] W. P. Ker,[3] commenting on this passage, quotes from a letter[4] of one Martin Clifford, a Master of the Charterhouse: 'I was about 6 years since a little acquainted with a namesake and Countryman of yours, *who pilfered out of Monsieur Hedelin, Menardière and Corneille* an Essay of Dramatic Poesy, wherein he tells us another Tale.'

It will be found while surveying the critical material that discussions of certain mainly Aristotelean principles (the Unities, the Happy Ending, Tragic Diction, and so forth) recur in almost every writer of the two nations.

---

[1] Boileau, Rapin, and Le Bossu are excluded, since their vogue in England came too late to affect the rhymed heroic play. Dryden first mentions the first two in his essay on *Heroic Poetry and Poetic Licence* (1677), and Le Bossu in his essay on *The Grounds of Criticism in Tragedy* (1679).   [2] *Defence of the Essay of Dramatic Poesy.*
[3] *Essays of John Dryden*, vol. i, p. 305.   [4] Written in 1674.

A choice of the most relevant among these will provide the necessary equipment for our inquiry. I propose, in fact, with their aid to conduct *Examens* of some representative plays of the chief heroic dramatists, very much in the contemporary manner; but with a different end in view, and in a different spirit, including in the treatment of each play a verdict on how far it thrives or suffers as a work of art by adhering to or departing from the 'Laws of Good Sense.'

But before embarking on our main project, it will be well to clear the ground a little by discussing briefly the literary and other origins of the heroic play. And this may not be superfluous, for while the ancestry of each aspect of that highly composite product has been worked out at one time or another, a reasoned summary of the results of these analyses is less often come by.

The chief forces which were at work in determining the characteristics of the heroic play I take to have consisted first of general European factors, comprising (*a*) the Literary Ideal, (*b*) the fame of the French classical drama, and (*c*) the Rationalist movement in contemporary thought; secondly, of purely national elements, which included the inheritance from the Elizabethan drama, and the requirements of the Restoration audience.

2. THE LITERARY IDEAL

The *locus classicus* for the first of these points, the Literary Ideal, is Dryden's *Essay of Heroic Plays*.[1] In it, seeking to improve on the type of drama which D'Avenant had inaugurated, he decided that 'An Heroick Play ought to be an imitation, in little, of an Heroick Poem, and, consequently, Love and Valour ought to be the subject of it.'[2]

---

[1] 1672. Prefixed to *The Conquest of Granada*.

[2] Whether or not Dryden in thus defining the scope of the heroic play was, as Mr. W. S. Clark maintains (in *The Review of English*

The heroic play, in other words, was to be yet another ramification of the attempts of the literatures of many countries after the Renaissance to reproduce the classical epic in mo.ʾern guise. How abstract this conception of the epic was, can be estimated as much by the astonishing variety of compositions which were supposed to fulfil its requirements and reproduce its spirit—ranging from Tasso's *Gerusalemme* to *Gondibert*,[1] from *The Faery Queen* to *Le Grand Cyrus*—as by the diversity of aim with which such works were undertaken: best illustrated by placing the first twenty-six lines of *Paradise Lost* by the side of Chapelain's preface to his execrable *La Pucelle*, in which he states that his knowledge of the theory of epic poetry should be sufficient to produce a successful epic 'without any great elevation of mind'.

Dryden, indeed, is concerned to find a precedent for Almanzor's extravagances in the conduct of Achilles, but that the affiliation of the heroic play to the heroic poem is not confined to *The Conquest of Granada* receives an illustration in his *The State of Innocence and Fall of Man*

Studies, vol. iv, 1928), chiefly concerned in defending *The Conquest of Granada* from the ridicule cast on it by the recent *Rehearsal*, it would still seem that in this phrase he succeeded in succinctly expressing a literary aim of the heroic play which had been hitherto only vaguely realized. The correspondence between the two forms had been stated, but not dwelt on, by Thomas Hobbes in 1650 in his Answer to D'Avenant's Preface to *Gondibert*: 'For the Heroique Poem narrative, such as is yours, is called an Epique Poem. The Heroique Poem Dramatique is Tragedy.'

[1] D'Avenant's idea of an heroic poem was that it should be 'Dressed in a more familiar and easy shape . . . than was done by the Ancients or Moderns'. Accordingly he based his structure of *Gondibert* on the English (pre-Restoration) drama, and 'Proportioned five Books to five Acts, and Cantos to Scenes'. (Preface to *Gondibert*, written in Paris in 1650.) 'But this', Dryden objected, 'is rather a play in narration than an heroic poem.' Chamberlayne's heroic poem *Pharonnida* is divided into five books, and the poem has affinities with Dryden's play *Aureng-Zebe*.

(1677), which is *Paradise Lost* turned, it is true, into opera, but probably in furtherance of the same theory. How close was the approximation in the case of *The Conquest of Granada* is well pointed out by Mr. B. J. Pendlebury (*Dryden's Heroic Plays*): 'The most striking resemblance to the epic is the unity given to *The Conquest of Granada* by the dominating figure of Almanzor. The play is not the study of a tragic conflict, but a representation of a triumphant career. Almanzor is rather more exclusively the centre of interest in Dryden's play than are Achilles and Aeneas in their respective epics.' Again, the bombast which became such a marked feature of many of Dryden's heroic plays and those of his followers, from *Tyrannic Love* onwards, was largely an attempt to reproduce the supposed grandeur of epic speech.[1] Bouts of inflated dialogue are occasionally to be found in the French heroic poems, from which, rather than the classical epic, Dryden probably derived his own variety. The following passage, a speech of Pharaoh from Saint Amant's *Moyse Sauvé*, Part iv (1653), is not far below the level of Maximin:

> Quel est, dit-il, ce Dieu, cet arbitre du monde,
> Ce souverain du ciel, de la terre et de l'onde,
> Dont vous venez ycy me chanter la grandeur?
> Quoy donc! cet univers, en sa vaste rondeur,
> Connoist-il quelque roy, sçait-il quelque puissance
> Qui ne rende à mon sceptre entière obeïssance?
> Et le clair œil du jour voit-il quelque mortel
> Qui ne doive à mon nom ériger un autel?
> Ha! c'est moy, c'est moy seul qu'il faut que l'on adore.
> Au bout de vos labeurs vous n'estes pas encore,
> Infames circoncis: je les augmenteray.

---

[1] W. S. Clark (loc. cit.) has made this clear by giving due prominence to a passage in the preface to that play. It is probable that Dryden was also indebted to Tasso's theory of heroic poetry (*Opere*, ed. Rosini, vol. xii. 20) for the evolution of his Maximins and Almanzors.

In asserting that it was the duty of the heroic play to depict
'Love and Valour', Dryden was actuated by a desire to
find an illustrious backing in antiquity for a contemporary
fashion. Saint-Evremond, from different motives, argued
to this effect [1]—Love is our brilliant new addition to the
Tragic Art, ridding us of the dark terrors and superstitions
employed by the ancient drama. No passion excites us
more to deeds of nobility and generosity than an honest
love, &c. Actually the love and valour themes derived
from Beaumont and Fletcher on the one hand,[2] and from
the French heroic romances on the other. The latter
source may be advantageously considered here for a
moment, the former we will reserve for treatment when
considering the influence of the Elizabethan drama on the
heroic play. The romances were regarded as prose epics,[3]
and hence their composition was eagerly undertaken by
many authors whose ambitions exceeded their talents.
Their popularity spread to England, especially during the
Commonwealth, when there was a dearth of livelier forms
of polite entertainment, and translations were soon followed
by native imitations, such as Orrery's *Parthenissa*.[4] The

---

[1] *De la Tragédie Ancienne et Moderne*, 1672.

[2] W. S. Clark (loc. cit.) minimizes the importance of the resemblance
of the heroic plays to those of Beaumont and Fletcher. It is true, as he
says, that Beaumont and Fletcher drew on European prose romances
for many of their situations and incidents; so that the romances may
be considered the ultimate source of nearly all of the love and honour
themes. But the fact that these themes had been successfully embodied in a popular type of English drama before the heroic dramatists
began to write should be taken into account in determining influences.
The romantic tragicomedies of Beaumont and Fletcher were eagerly
revived during the early Restoration period, and it is most probable
that while the playwrights of the time drew chiefly on the contemporary French romances and heroic poems for their plots and characters, they derived many suggestions from Beaumont and Fletcher as
to the dramatization of them.

[3] Georges de Scudéry so terms them in his preface to his heroic
poem *Alaric*.   [4] Published in 1654, in 6 vols.

most obvious indebtedness of the heroic plays to these romances is in their plots. The several plays which deal with Solyman and his family—such as *The Siege of Rhodes*, Settle's *Ibrahim*, and Orrery's *Mustapha*—derive in greater or less degree from de Scudéry's *Ibrahim où l'Illustre Bassa* (1641), while Dryden plundered *Le Grand Cyrus* for many incidents, and Lee filched the material of *Theodosius* from La Calprenède's *Faramond* (1662) and that of *The Rival Queens* from the same author's *Cassandre* (1642). But 'the story is the least part' of their debt, in spite of Dryden's contrary implications. Professor Saintsbury's account of the general characteristics of the French heroic romance [1] will serve to show some striking similarities between the two forms. In the first place, both share that intricacy of design which was the age's substitute for amplitude, and which imperilled, while it changed the course of many arts—as can be seen in the overloaded frescoes of Luca Giordano and Solimena, the senseless roulades and cadenzas of Italian operatic music, and the oppressive ornamentation of Baroque architecture. Again, in both the love story is in the forefront, in both the happy ending is common, and in both the characterization is abstract and lifeless. Later I shall deal with an important cause of the last-named defect, under a separate heading. Furthermore, interminable discussions hamper the course of their action; [2] this may partly derive from some mistaken notion of epic stateliness, which would also account for the notable absence of a sense of humour in both forms. [3]

[1] *History of the French Novel*, vol. i, cap. viii.

[2] Buckingham, had he burlesqued the heroic romance as well as the heroic play, would not have let escape the Gilbertian twenty times repeated exchange of ships in the ferocious naval engagement in *Le Grand Cyrus*, cited by Professor Saintsbury.

[3] 'There are endless episodes . . . but none absolutely disconnected from the main design' (Saintsbury, loc. cit.). On the whole this is also

Lastly, valour of the utterly superhuman order is common in the plays (especially Dryden's), and is almost invariably present in the romances. The incident in *Le Grand Cyrus*[1] of the trial by battle of two hundred a side from which Artamène emerges the sole survivor gives the type.

These correspondences are enough to suggest that playwrights who wished to share in the exalted movement towards expressing epic grandeur thus found a pleasantly modernized, not too austere source close at hand from which to draw their example.

Before leaving this subject, however, something remains to be said concerning the early history and growth of heroic sentiment in England. Heroic sentiment may be claimed to have originated in the salon of the Marquise de Rambouillet, and to have found its first permanent expression in D'Urfé's pastoral romance, *Astrée*.[2] It is true that the points of similarity between the *Astrée* and a play such as *The Conquest of Granada* are few and comparatively unimportant, so strongly had the fully developed heroic play been influenced by a variety of outside forces. But there is little doubt that the school of Platonic Love, which was fostered at the court of Charles I from 1635 to 1642 by Queen Henrietta Maria, was responsible for the introduction into the drama of much of the peculiar artificiality of character, sentiment, and situation which we find in the heroic play. In the *Astrée*, courtiers disguised as shepherds and shepherdesses spend their time in debating the various implications of their esoteric cult of passionless love. The merits of constancy, the inadmissibility of jealousy, the validity or otherwise of 'fruition in

true of the heroic plays, which can rarely be convicted of violating the Unity of Action in any narrowly technical sense.

[1] Part I, vols. i. and ii.

[2] Part I was printed in 1607, II in 1610, III in 1619, IV and V in 1627.

love', these and similar themes provide the characters with endless scope for testing the efficacy of their code, and for toying with the *précieuse* love-imagery of flames, streams, ice, tears, and the like. By 1620 an English translation had appeared, and under the influence of the queen the new mode of social etiquette became established at court. Its success was primarily due to its superficial qualities, to the opportunities which it afforded for a new elegance of speech and grace of compliment. From Marmion's comedy, *The Antiquary* (1636), we learn that the habit of the fashionable gallant of the time is to 'lie a-bed, and expound Astraea, and digest him into compliments; and when he is up, accost his mistress with what he had read in the morning'. The Cavalier Poets were not slow to embellish their verses with the new conceits which the cult engendered, and in their hands (particularly in Suckling's) the *Astrée* type of sentiment lost some of its vapidity, and became infused with something of the debonair Cavalier spirit.

The royal taste also favoured the inclusion of the cult in the drama, but here, owing to the more extensive treatment involved, the task could not be undertaken so lightly, and dramatists found themselves obliged to make a thorough study of the new doctrines. As semi-official laureate, D'Avenant was expected to lead the way in this direction, and industriously he set out to do so, though he was temperamentally unsuited to the undertaking, and at first unable fully to grasp the meaning of the creed, as may be seen from his prologue to *The Platonic Lovers* (1635):

'Tis worth my smiles to think what enforc'd ways
And shifts, each poet hath to help his Plays.
Ours now believes the Title needs must cause,
From the indulgent Court a kind applause,
Since there he learnt it first, and had command
T'interpret what he scarce doth understand.

His other productions of this period, *Love and Honour*
(1634), *The Fair Favourite, The Unfortunate Lovers* (1638),
and *The Distresses* (1639), are all expositions of the Platonic
cult, and contain the conventional features of frigid abstract discussions, ideal attachments undefiled by thoughts
of possession, and magnanimous recognitions of the claims
of rivals. One of the chief points of the Platonic belief is
the rejection of jealousy as unworthy to play any part in an
ideal love. A portion of dialogue from *The Fair Favourite*
gives a fair illustration of this tenet:

King. Are you not weary of your virtue yet?
Queen. Nor of your love unto my rival, Sir.
   If it were low and sinful love, I should
   Not think it worth my envy or my fear;
   If pure and noble, as my strictest faith
   Believes, it is too great a treasure to
   Be made particular and own'd by me
   Alone, since what is good doth still encrease
   In merit of that name by being most
   Communative.
King. This doctrine, Madam, will
   Be new, and much unwelcome to your sex.
Queen. True love admits no jealousy.[1]

D'Avenant's example was followed by a number of other
dramatists, among whom Lodowick Carlell, with his emphasis on the conflicting claims of love and friendship, and
William Cartwright, with his highly formalized, skilfully-
patterned dialogue, attain prominence, but Suckling is the
most notable of these playwrights on account of the fluency
and inventiveness which he brings to the mannered style
then in demand. As an added refinement in the drama,
Suckling evidently welcomed warmly the conventions of
the new love-code. In *Aglaura* (1637) he enjoys pitting

[1] Act IV.

'Platonics' and 'anti-Platonics' against each other, and assigning the victory in discussion to the ladies, who are all staunch supporters of the former persuasion. The constant interplay of similes, with which his characters conduct their arguments, exhibits his ingenuity in no small degree, while the abundance of duels, amorous intrigues, and political conspiracies with which he enlivens his plots both reflects on his own character and environment and points forward to the adventure-laden scenarios of the heroic play.

These sophisticated pleasures and delightful abstractions were rudely broken in upon by the Civil War, which put an end to court entertainments. Yet to some extent the *précieuse* tradition managed to survive in non-dramatic literature. Cowley's collection of love poems, *The Mistress* (1647), employs many of the themes which Suckling used in his Platonic lyrics, while Mrs. Katherine Philips, 'The Matchless Orinda', produced a succession of poems celebrating 'Friendship' in the Platonic manner. But it was chiefly the translations of French heroic romances, of which we have spoken, that kept interest in the Platonic convention alive during the Commonwealth period. It is natural, therefore, that the early heroic plays should have taken over some of the familiar Platonic elements. In *The Siege of Rhodes* the formalized loftiness of the characters, the abstract debates, and the unfailingly magnanimous motives derive in part from Platonic sources, while the plays of Orrery with their unselfish rival lovers—such as the King and Tudor in *Henry V* and the brothers Mustapha and Zanger in *Mustapha*—show the same influence to a more marked extent.

We must beware, however, of discovering too close a connexion between the heroic drama and the Platonic plays of the court of Charles I. Miss Lynch, to whose interesting

study, *The Social Mode of Restoration Comedy*,[1] I am indebted for several suggestions, does not recognize the
diversity of influences (e.g. those of the French classical
drama, Elizabethan romantic tragicomedy, the heroic
poem, and Cartesian philosophy) which helped to mould
the heroic plays; and to term the first examples of these
'Platonic tragedies and tragicomedies' is arbitrary and
misleading. In the interval between 1642 and 1660 the
Platonic strain had not only become diluted with the many
other influences which converged on the heroic play, but
had undergone a change itself. The disturbances and
excitements in France of the Fronde insurrection had their
effect on polite literature, and these years mark the period
of transition from the *roman berger* to the *roman héroïque*,
from the passive Platonism of the pastoral novel to the
Platonism translated into action of the pseudo-historical
novel of heroism and gallantry. Though in *Le Grand
Cyrus* jealousy and possession are still held to be inconsistent with the ideal of true love, yet in other prose
romances a tendency to depart from these austere standards is discernible. These changes are reflected in the first
group of heroic plays. Love is frequently accompanied by
jealousy in them [2] and possession is nearly always implied,
if it does not actually take place. The plots, moreover, are
mazes of exciting adventure, and the heroes are models of
courage and military prowess.

Nevertheless, the characters remain too strictly bound
by scruples of honour to be distinct as individuals. It is
true that during the course of its history the heroic play
seldom succeeded in creating characters which were

[1] New York, 1926.
[2] Cf. Alphonso in *The Seige of Rhodes* and Zempoalla in *The Indian
Queen*. The plot of the latter play is drawn from Gomberville's heroic
romance, *Polexandre*.

credible as human beings; this, however, was really foreign to its purpose. Yet Dryden, while he shunned realistic characterization, was more averse to the colourlessness and uniform uprightness which the Platonic system imposed on the characters of fiction and drama; and though content for dramatic purposes to retain several of the Platonic *motifs* (e.g. the abstract debates, the conventional poetic imagery, and the exalted magnanimity of the 'sympathetic' characters), he led the revolt both in his plays and his criticism [1] against the good-mannered school of drama, being encouraged to do so by the example in France of the heroic poem, which favoured a more formidable and unscrupulous type of heroism than had prevailed hitherto. Concerning Dryden's part in thus invigorating and re-orientating the heroic play we shall have more to say later. Meanwhile we may conclude that, as regards the phases of 'Platonic' influence on the English serious drama, the affinities of the court drama of Charles I were with the *roman berger*, those of the early heroic play were with the *roman héroïque*, and those of the fully-developed heroic play were with the French heroic poem.

3. INFLUENCE OF THE FRENCH CLASSICAL DRAMA

We must now turn to the most important of the foreign influences; that of the French classical drama. Many writers of heroic plays had been in France during the Commonwealth, and a reliable indication of how far the contemporary classical drama impressed them is provided by the wave of enthusiasm for translations of the plays of the two Corneilles and Racine which swept over England shortly before and after the Restoration.

[1] *Tyrannick Love* (1669) was the first of his plays in which the villain-hero becomes the centre of interest, and the first in which extreme bombast appears. *The Essay of Heroic Plays* (1672) contains his chief protest against the restrictions and pedantry of the *précieuse* code.

Pierre Corneille was—and had been since the production (before Charles I and his French queen) of Joseph Rutter's *Cid* in 1637—by far the most popular of the three. Eight translations of his plays, as against three of Thos. Corneille's and two of Racine's, appeared in the period between Rutter's *Cid* and 1680. As Miss Canfield remarks in her able monograph on the subject,[1] 'Corneille's fire and spirit and heroic strength were much more likely to excuse the limitations of French Tragedy than Racine's melting passion, to English minds'. And it is, perhaps, Corneille's drama to which the heroic play more nearly approximates than that of any other foreign author. It is curious to note—in view of what the heroic drama afterwards became—that Rutter in his preface, while approving of the 'Conveyance and Oeconomy' of *Le Cid*, bestows special praise on its absence of 'Hyperboles, which is the wit in fashion'. He can hardly, however, be taken to have ignored such outbursts as the famous 'Paraissez, Navarrais, Mores et Castillans', and must be referring to the fact that its style is not 'pestered with metaphors', as was the English drama of the time. It is no accident that the years most productive of these translations (1663–7) coincided with the formative period of the heroic play. The Earl of Orrery's plays, with their *confidentes*, and *héros raisonneurs* dominated by a single idea, in their restricted sphere of action and fairly conscientious following of the 'Rules', are visibly influenced by those of Corneille. And it is significant that it was Orrery—at a time when he had already written (though not published) one or two of his plays—who by his backing, personal, literary, and financial, was chiefly responsible for the production [2] of the

[1] *Corneille and Racine in England* (ch. i).

[2] In Dublin, February, 1663. A rhymed translation of Corneille's *La mort de Pompée*.

Pompey of 'The Matchless Orinda' (Mrs. Katharine Philips), the earliest and one of the best of the post-Restoration translators.

Before long, however, there came a change. If the National drama was to be a living entity, it could not hope to become so by means of the somewhat frigid translations and imitations of French classical plays on the part of authors who, when all is said, chiefly wished to be modish, and had little perception of the true greatness of Corneille and Racine.

Indications of dissatisfaction are apparent from the first. Dryden, in the *Essay of Dramatic Poesy*, complaining of the monotonous uniformity of tone of the French plays, defends the English mixture of comic and tragic as a means for securing the necessary variety of action. 'It has the same effect upon us which our music has between the acts'.

Now at 'Orinda's' special request there were songs between the acts in the Dublin production of her *Pompey*. Dances were given after the songs, and a Grand Masque was presented at the conclusion. Her translation of *Horace* when performed before their majesties in 1668 was also enlivened by *entr'actes* of songs, dances, and shows.[1] Charles Cotton, too, put lyrics of his own between the acts of his translation of *Horace* (1665). The success of Lodowick Carlell's *Heraclius* (1664)—it is not considered one of Corneille's best plays—was chiefly due to its intricate plot, whose series of short shocks, and 'the garments like Romans very well' which Pepys noted, combined to hold the attention of the audience.

[1] Evelyn (Diary, 4 Feb.) was present at the above-mentioned performance. Pepys saw it on 19 Jan. 1668/9. 'As to the dances, only some Dutchmen come out of the mouth and tail of a Hamburgh sow.' He speaks disparagingly of the play.

All these instances are either unconscious or tacit admissions of what Dryden later openly declared;[1] 'The feast is too dull and solemn without the fiddles'.

Later on, these transplanters of the French classical plays were no longer content with providing varied entertainment between the acts, but must need tamper with the plays themselves. A notable instance of this is provided by John Crowne's *Andromache* (1675), the first of Racine's plays to be translated. In his somewhat meretricious preface Crowne remarks that in his version 'There is all that is in the French play, and something more, as may be seen in the last Act, where what is only dully recited in the French play is there represented'. Oreste's narrative provided him with the opportunity of a spectacular scene—a temple, with processions and hymns. Pyrrhus is killed on the stage, and his body is dragged 'off' by the Greeks. Though amply shown in the English heroic plays themselves, the taste for spectacle and violent action could not receive better illustration than here. In spite of this gaudy treatment the play was a failure, and though its main cause was the ineptitude of Crowne's translation, there is some truth in his excuse, 'Had it been acted in the good well-meaning times when *Le Cid*, *Heraclius*, and other French plays met such applause, this would have passed very well; but since our audiences have tasted so plentifully the firm English wit, these thin Regalios will not down'.[2]

It needed an Otway to make Racine palatable to

---

[1] Arguing on behalf of Tragicomedy (which 'fiddles' metaphorically represented) in the Epistle Dedicatory to *The Spanish Friar*, 1681.

[2] The enthusiastic reception, in 1712, of the same play competently translated (*The Distrest Mother*, by Ambrose Philips) showed that English audiences, after an even longer familiarity with 'the firm English wit', possessed a more catholic taste than Crowne had allowed them.

Restoration audiences. His own passion and pathos enabled
him in translation to bring out the same qualities in Racine,
and his *Titus and Berenice* [1] reveals in many ways his
ability to reproduce the spirit of the original. Even Otway,
however, adapts rather than translates, and the tilt towards
the happy ending in his version betrays an acquiescence
in the stereotyped poetic justice which the English playwrights (appreciably influenced by Corneille's practice)
deemed inseparable from the interplay of heroism and
honour.

But besides the indications afforded by these translations, we have some valuable direct acknowledgements by
English authors of the influence of the French classical
drama on their plays. *The Siege of Rhodes* [2] has long been
considered the first heroic play, and if we are right in
maintaining that the French drama had most effect on the
earliest plays of the type, we might hope to find some contemporary recognition of French influence on this play.
It is provided by the Preface to *The Conquest of Granada*,
wherein Dryden, having remarked that D'Avenant's play
was the first of the species, that D'Avenant [3] was compelled to introduce in it 'examples of moral virtue written
in verse' and to produce it as an opera because of the Puri-
tans' objection to play-acting, adds: 'But he heightened
his characters (as I may probably imagine) from the
example of Corneille and some French poets'. Corneille's
name occurs in D'Avenant's *Address to the Reader* prefixed

[1] 1677, from Racine's *Bérénice*.
[2] Part I was first acted in 1656, at Rutland House. Part II, with the
revised Part I, was first acted in 1661, at the new theatre in Lincoln's
Inn Fields.
[3] D'Avenant, in his dedication of the play to the Lord Chancellor
(the Earl of Clarendon), complaining of Puritan hostility, says, 'And
yet while those virtuous enemies deny *Heroic Plays* to the gentry, they
entertain the people with a seditious farce of their own counterfeit
gravity'.

to the 1656 version of the play. Nor is there doubt that the play derives in part from this source. Our coming analysis will show more fully what must here be barely stated; that the 'Rules' are conscientiously observed, that versified disputations are much in evidence, that the theme is the rival claims of love and honour, with a fortunate issue, and that though the hero (Alphonso) does not dominate the action to the extent of his counterpart in the plays of Corneille and Dryden, he is far more formidably endowed than any of D'Avenant's previous heroes, whose affinities are with the slightly effeminate type popularized by Fletcher.

Moreover, Dryden, in the same essay, praises D'Avenant as an innovator, but says that his play 'lacked fullness of plot and variety of characters'. The French classical dramatists, following ancient example, reduced the number of their dramatis personae to the strict minimum required by the logical needs of the plot. A glance at the lists of dramatis personae of heroic plays will show how much fewer were the characters employed than in the Elizabethan drama. Shakespeare's *Henry the Fifth* contains thirty-four characters besides supernumeraries, as against twenty without supernumeraries in Orrery's *Henry the Fifth*, while *The Siege of Rhodes*, though it consists of two parts, employs two or three fewer persons for the whole than D'Avenant's *Love and Honour*, written in 1634. There is (as is generally admitted) a lack of individuality about Corneille's characters, and this is true of the characters in *The Siege of Rhodes*, while those of Dryden seem clearly differentiated one from the other in comparison. As regards 'fullness of plot'', though there are several exciting changes in the fortunes of war, the main outlines of the plot remain the same to the point of monotony. It has been pointed out, too, that Roxolana, the sultan's queen, is jealous of Ianthe, the heroine, but shows no affection for Alphonso.[1] Such restriction is probably due to emulation of French models.[2] With most heroic playwrights, however, intricacy of plot became an end in itself, and these wearisome diagonal amours (partly avoided in *The Siege of Rhodes*) recur in play after play.

Orrery was the next dramatist to take up the heroic play at all thoroughly. Dryden and Sir Robert Howard's *The Indian Queen* (acted Jan. 1663/4) had indeed appeared before the public before any of Orrery's heroic plays, the first of them to be performed—*Henry the Fifth*[3]—being in August 1664; but that his plays had been circulating in manuscript among friends previous to this (as Professor Nicoll thinks) is rendered probable both by Dryden's remarks in his *Epistle Dedicatory* (to the Earl of Orrery) of *The Rival Ladies*,[4] and by a letter of Orrery dated

[1] Professor J. W. Tupper, in his Introduction to D'Avenant's *Love and Honour* and *The Siege of Rhodes*, Boston 1909. It should be noted that D'Avenant himself excused the fewness of the dramatis personae on the grounds of the narrowness of the Rutland House stage, but this, of course, is applicable only to the first part of the play.

[2] Yet D'Avenant himself soon grew tired of this classical convention of chastened simplicity of plot—whose peculiar virtues English writers seemed incapable of transplanting, if not of perceiving—as is to be seen in Act I of his *The Play-House to be Lett*, 1662:

> The French convey their Arguments too much
> In Dialogue; their Speeches are too long,
> Such length of speeches seem not so unpleasing
> As the Contracted Walks of their Designs.

Cf. *infra*, p. 151, D'Aubignac on the subject of *tirades*.

[3] The plays of both authors were performed before they were printed. A case has been made out by Dr. F. W. Payne, in *The Review of English Studies* of April 1925, for a performance in 1663 of Orrery's *The Black Prince*, but the evidence seems inconclusive.

[4] Written in 1664. Speaking of Orrery's 'poems' (i.e. plays), he says, 'Plotting and writing in this kind are certainly more troublesome employments than many which signify more'; and 'All your heroes are more than your subjects, they are your creatures; and though they seem to move freely in all the sallies of their passions, yet you make

23 January 1661/2. The latter is chiefly important to us because it contains his acknowledgement of French influence. 'When I had the honour and happiness the last time to kiss his majesty's hand, he commanded me to write a play for him . . . and therefore, some months after, I presumed to lay at his majesty's feet a tragicomedy, all in ten-feet verse and rhyme . . . because I found his majesty relished rather the French fashion of writing plays than the English.' Charles continued to encourage this new elegance, and we hear of his approving of the unfinished *Black Prince* and conjuring its author, with mildly benevolent humour, 'to go on and complete it, which if he could not do until he had a fit of the gout, he wished him a fit presently'. Usual features of his plays are rigid standards of honour, forensic arguments in rhyme, sustained decorum, characters each the embodiment of one ruling idea, attention to the 'Rules', and the skilful use of the regular distich; and the conjunction of these strongly suggests an indebtedness to Corneille, for whose plays his tour abroad towards the end of Charles I's reign probably first fostered a taste.

When we come to Dryden himself, the position is different. His denunciation of 'the point of honour, so much magnified by the French, and so ridiculously aped by us',[1] his complaint of their lacking any feeling for historical atmosphere,[2] and his merciless attack on the 'barrenness of the French plots', their lengthy *tirades* and servile

destinies for them which they cannot shun . . . instead of an absolute power over their actions, they have only a wretched desire of doing that which they cannot choose but do'. The Fate element is prominent in *Mustapha* (cf. the scene between Mustapha and Zanger in Act IV) but is absent in the earlier-acted *Henry the Fifth*. Both Dryden, upholding the use of rhyme in plays, and Sir R. Howard attacking it, agree in praising Orrery's use of it.

[1] *Essay of Heroic Plays.*
[2] Preface to *Troilus and Cressida.*

adherence to the Unities,[1] are a few instances of his sustained hostility to French theory and practice in so far as
either might have been expected to have taken effect on
his own plays. Dryden, with his vigorous and independent
mind, realized that if the English drama were to be securely
re-established it must cease to be imitative. But by the
time he had written his first unaided heroic play,[2] certain
conventions of the French drama had been accepted and
incorporated in the English drama. Accordingly, starting
on a groundwork of these and working both in the service
of the national drama and in his own interests as a playwright seeking popularity, his object in his plays was to
bestow as individual a flavour as possible on the genre he
had adopted, and in his criticism ostentatiously to mini-
mize (even, on occasion, to deny) the original indebtedness
of the type to France. The virulence and the inconsistency
(his critical opinions like his political and religious views
were generally in a state of flux) of his assaults on French
theory and practice suggest that his plays were more
affected by them than he was willing to admit. Thus, in his
defence of 'following the new way' of writing plays in
rhyme,[3] his aversion to the idea of foreign influence
prompts him to contend that it is 'not so much a new way
as an old way revived',[4] but though he supports his argument by remarking that Spanish and Italian tragedies
are rhymed, he will have none of the French. 'For the
French, I do not name them, because it is the fate of our

[1] Neander, in the *Essay of Dramatic Poesy*.
[2] *The Indian Emperor*, 1665.
[3] Epistle dedicatory of *The Rival Ladies*.
[4] The revival which claimed only '*Queen*' *Gorboduc* (in blank verse)
as a forbear cannot have been a very searching one. It is interesting to
note, however, that some of the Senecan plays (such as Nuce's translation of Seneca's *Octavia*) in that earlier period of Neo-Classicism
(1559–67) were written in rhymed heroic couplets. It is unlikely that
they were known to Restoration dramatists.

countrymen to admit little of theirs among us but the basest of their men, the extravagances of their fashions, and the frippery of their merchandise.' As we have seen, both Charles II and Orrery considered rhyme an integral part of English plays composed 'in the French manner'.[1] Moreover, four years later, in the *Essay of Dramatic Poesy*, stung by Sir Robert Howard's pertinent attacks on rhyme,[2] Dryden was impelled to add France to his list of foreign countries where the rhymed drama was successfully practised. Much of Dryden's criticism, brilliant though it is, is little else than special pleading; and though his general sympathies were on the side of emancipation he could, when it suited his present purpose, own (as others had done) to drawing on French sources; as in the Prologue to *The Maiden Queen*:

> He who writ this, not without pains and thought
> From French and English theatres has brought
> The exactest rules by which a Play is wrought:
> The Unities of Action Place and Time;
> The Scenes Unbroken; and a mingled Chime
> Of Jonson's humour, with Corneille's rhyme.

The *Defence of the Epilogue* (to *The Conquest of Granada*) is a justification and expansion of the four following lines in the epilogue,

> If *Love and Honour* now are higher raised
> 'Tis not the poet, but the age is praised;
> Wit's now arriv'd to a more high degree,
> Our native language more refined and free.

The exuberance of Elizabethan poetic diction had been replaced by a more restricted vocabulary and stilted mode of utterance, which was felt to be the fit vehicle of expres-

---

[1] Cf. also Shadwell's Prologue to *The Squire of Alsatia* (1688):
   Infected by the French, you must have Rhime,
   Which long, to please the Ladies' Ears did chime.
[2] In the Preface to the 1665 Folio edition of his *Four New Plays*.

sion for the persons of exalted rank with whom tragedy
was exclusively concerned; the same holding good almost
to the same extent in comedy, from which anything
savouring of low life, of 'Cobb and Tib' was excluded.
Miss Lynch in her recent book, *The Social Mode of Restoration Comedy*, is occupied with showing that the comedy of
manners is primarily an emanation from altered social conditions, that 'the interest changes from the bourgeois aping
gentry [in Elizabethan times] to the bourgeois become
gentry and accepting a code of manners'. Although, as
I have tried to show, the change which spread over
tragedy at the Restoration was partly the outcome of a
literary programme, her theory would also help to account
for the diction and the always elevated rank of the characters of the tragedy. These, however, are also characteristics
of the French classical drama. Discussing diction [1] (in the
same essay) Dryden asks 'Whence is it that our conversation is so much refined?' He ascribes it to the court, and
particularly to the king's example. 'His own misfortunes
. . . afforded him an opportunity of travelling, and being
conversant in the most polished courts of Europe.' On his
return the English through his example were 'loosened
from their stiff forms of conversation'.[2]

[1] He discusses diction generally; conversation as a contributory
aspect.

[2] Dryden also expresses his satisfaction with the greater skill with
which courtly persons are depicted in plays in his 'polished age' than in
Elizabethan times. Mercutio, he says, was Shakespeare's nearest approach
to the desired type, an opinion which Dr. Johnson unwisely echoes.
John Wilmot, Earl of Rochester, in *An allusion to Horace* (*c.* 1678),
adversely comments on Dryden's censorious tone in this essay:

> But does not Dryden find ev'n Johnson dull?
> Fletcher and Beaumont uncorrect, and full
> Of lewd Lines, as he calls 'em? Shakespeare's stile
> Stiff and affected; to his own the while
> Allowing all the justness that his Pride
> So arrogantly had to these deny'd?

Many of the bourgeois 'became' gentry by serving the royal cause during the Commonwealth and by sharing the king's exile in France, and there is little doubt that the literary among them were responsible for the fashionable importation of the two features in question into the heroic play, as also that Dryden's remarks (properly interpreted) constitute another tacit admission of the influence of the French drama.

The rhymed heroic play started by borrowing many traits from the French drama, as we shall see when we come to deal with the plays (especially those of Orrery) in detail. But many of them were discarded after the reaction led by Dryden had set in. Only two which betoken undiluted French influence remained; the reduced number of dramatis personae and rhyme. There were, however, other permanent characteristics of the heroic play which were without doubt *partly* due to their presence also in the French classical drama. The artificially symmetrical grouping of characters, their criss-cross affections and rival predicaments of honour, are present, it is true, in the plays of Fletcher and his disciples, but not so intensively as in the French and later English drama. The characters themselves, devoid of personal idiosyncrasies and each the embodiment of a ruling abstract idea, largely owe their peculiarities to Corneille's men and women; their ultimate origin we will discuss shortly. The persistent happy endings certainly derive on one hand from the romantic tragicomedies of the 'thirties, but they can be amply paralleled in Corneille's plays.[1] And what there is of the Unities in the heroic play is due partly to the example of the French drama, though, of course,

[1] Corneille also defends the happy ending in his criticism. *Vide infra*, p. 76. Such endings were not, however, universal in either Corneille's drama or the English heroic drama.

principally to the *Poétiques* and *Examens*. Though no set of influences on the heroic play outweighs another set by much, it may be maintained that the drama of Corneille was almost the most potent force of all.[1]

4. THE INFLUENCE OF CONTEMPORARY THOUGHT

Let us now consider our third heading—the Rationalist movement in contemporary thought. It has been fairly well recognized that Cartesian Philosophy and the drama of Corneille have many points in common.[2] What is often lost sight of is the fact[3] that Corneille did not directly draw on the work of Descartes, since the famous *Traité des Passions* of the latter (which shows striking affinities with Corneille's plays) was published at a date (1649) when nearly all Corneille's masterpieces had already appeared.

It is, however, of considerable importance to us to realize that the philosophy of Descartes and his followers

[1] W. S. Clark, in *The Review of English Studies*, vol. iv, 1928, ably contends that the principal sources of the heroic play were the French heroic poems and romances, but he ignores a possible comparison of the type with the drama of Corneille. Such a comparison reveals a considerable indebtedness of the former to the latter; particularly on the part of the first group of rhymed heroic plays, before Dryden had somewhat altered the species with his innovation in *Tyrannic Love*. Contemporary recognition (in England) of this influence is not lacking, as I have shown. Cf. also Edward Phillips's account of Corneille, in his *Theatrum Poetarum* (1674): 'Corneille, the great Dramatic writer of France, wonderfully applauded by the present age, both among his own Country-men, and our Frenchly affected English, for the amorous intrigues, which if not there before, he commonly thrusts into his Tragedies and acted Histories; the Imitation whereof among us, and of the perpetual colloquy in Rhime, hath of late very much corrupted our English stage.' In his recently published *Playgoer's Handbook to Restoration Drama* (p. 17). Mr. Malcolm Elwin regards Corneille as 'the spiritual founder' of the heroic drama.

[2] The credit of originating the comparison belongs to Sainte-Beuve.

[3] First pointed out by M. Lanson in his essay on the subject in the *Revue d'Histoire littéraire de la France*, 1894.

constitutes precisely the *rationale* of many of the aspects of the wave of Neo-Classicism which spread over Europe at that time. Many of the conventions of the contemporary drama which strike us as fantastic or absurd become intelligible when referred to their origin in the prevailing mode of thought. In a sense, Drawcansir is the illegitimate offspring of Descartes. The peculiar forms which the idea of heroic valour, suffering, and sacrifice of love to honour took in the contemporary drama could only have been so popular among a society whose metaphysical notions favoured a rigid dualism of mind and matter (and thus a confidence in the superiority of mind over matter) such as that propounded by Descartes. Article 40 of the *Traité des Passions* states, 'Qu'il n'y a point d'âme si faible qu'elle ne puisse, étant bien conduite, acquérir un pouvoir absolu sur ses passions', and Article 49, 'Il y a fort peu d'hommes si faibles et irrésolus, qu'ils ne veuillent rien que ce que leur passion leur dicte'. Seldom do the chief characters of Corneille and Dryden quail in an emotional dilemma, their indomitable wills [1] are not harassed by sudden revulsions of feeling, rarely do they behave impulsively, seldom like human beings. It is noteworthy that whatever element of human impulsiveness was admitted into both philosophy and drama was so well ordered as to be barely recognizable as such. Descartes' theory becomes far from satisfactory when he has to account for the effect of bodily states upon the mind. He conveniently supposed the body to contain a subtle fluid which he termed 'animal spirits'; these he held existed independently of the mind, but could be controlled by the conscious exertion of its reasoning powers. In the *Traité des Passions* he prescribed for this purpose 'une excitation volontaire des passions contraires à celle qu'on veut ôter, par la représentation des choses qui y sont

[1] Cf. Almanzor's vaunt, 'But know that I alone am king of me.'

jointes'.[1] In the English heroic drama we usually become aware of the 'impulses' only by the argumentative efforts of the characters to overcome them; as, for example, in Mustapha's attitude to his recent declaration of love for the queen in Act II of *Mustapha*, or in Zempoalla's wrestling with pangs of love at the sight of Montezuma captive before her in Act III of *The Indian Queen*.

The austerely ontological nature of Cartesianism[2] was inimical to the principle of human individuality. Leibnitz's modification of it (the theory of 'monads') came too late to affect the characterization of the heroic drama. The very formula, *Cogito, ergo sum*, facilitates the idea that in order that a character may exist it is enough that he should reason. In one of Dryden's plays, indeed, the *Cogito* is directly introduced. Act II, sc. i of *The State of Innocence and Fall of Man* (1674) opens thus:—*A Champaign Country. Adam, as newly created, laid on a bed of moss and flowers, by a rock.*

Adam. What am I? or from whence? For that I am
  I know, because I think; but whence I came,
  Or how this frame of mine began to be,
  What other being can disclose to me?[3]

According to Descartes there was only one infallible kind of knowledge, namely, that 'clear and distinct perception'

[1] Lanson aptly points out how well Chimène, for instance, follows this advice. 'Son amour est si fort qu'elle a besoin d'exciter sans cesse en elle la représentation de son père mort, de ses plaies, de son sang, de tous les objets sensibles qui sont joints a l'idée de son devoir; c'est un moyen, comme on dit, de se fouetter, de produire en soi de la force pour l'action obligatoire et voulue.'

[2] 'Ontological' in the restricted sense of 'concerned solely with Being *in the abstract*'.

[3] This soliloquy, it is perhaps needless to say, is not derived from anything in *Paradise Lost*. It should be added that Dryden makes mention of Descartes' first principle in his *Discourse concerning the Origin and Progress of Satire* (1693).

which was uninfluenced by 'the fluctuating testimony of
the senses, and the misleading judgement that proceeds
from the blundering constructions of the imagination'. It
embraced both 'substances' and minds. Just as all the
attributes of a 'substance' most prized by the artist or poet
—such as rhythm, colour, warmth, and poise—were held
to obscure the 'clear and distinct knowledge' of its essential
quality, its mechanism;[1] so a mind properly constituted
could be summed up in abstract terms, and the summary
was believed to be all that was needed to provide a clear
and exact account of the person concerned. Undoubtedly
this attitude was in a large measure responsible for the
stereotyped characters of Corneille and of the English
heroic playwrights. Criticism fostered the idea by reitera-
ting the pseudo-Aristotelean rule of 'truth to type'. Dryden
enjoins its observance,[2] yet at the same time censures the
French tragedies for their lack of historical atmosphere,[3]
and complains that though Racine's Bajazet is bred at
Constantinople he has the manners of Versailles. (But the
difference in this respect between the characters of the
French and English drama is one between incongruity and
impossibility, for Dryden's flamboyant heroes are as un-
imaginable at the courts of Louis or Charles as at the
Indian or Roman camps and palaces to which they are
assigned.)

Descartes' views on Love throw some light on the
eternal love and honour conflicts of the heroic play. In

---

[1] See Descartes' *Principles of Philosophy*, Part I, lxvi–lxxii.

[2] Preface to *Troilus and Cressida*, 1679 (*The Grounds of Criticism in Tragedy*).

[3] He borrowed (without acknowledgement) this means of attack from Saint-Evremond, who in his observations on the *Alexandre* (1665) of Racine includes the remark 'tous ces héros, grecs ou indiens, parlent et sentent en gentilshommes français'. Several years later, in his *Character of M. St. Evremond*, Dryden praised Saint-Evremond's criticism of the *Alexandre*.

general, he maintains that true love between individuals is the mutual love of the good qualities of those persons; it is no unreasonable elusive emotion but conscious and voluntary; a moral debt which one pays to virtue.

The mechanical way in which heroism never fails to arouse love in the heroic play is notorious; and the honour conflict is merely a logical extension of the same attitude, for the more a person sacrifices his or her love concerns to honour, the more the additional heroism thereby acquired deserves—and, in the heroic play, usually receives—greater affection. Thus, in Dryden's *Tyrannick Love, or, the Royal Martyr*,[1] Berenice's insistence on remaining faithful to her criminal husband, whom she loathes, only renders her worthier of the love of the valorous Porphyrius, and only serves to increase Porphyrius' affection for her. Such sacrifices often take the form of what is called, in heroic terminology, 'losing and meriting the lover'; chiefly applicable to characters who vainly love persons of higher rank or prowess than themselves, or whose claims are outshone by those of some illustrious rival. This kind of renunciation frequently results in the death or suicide of the person who makes it, as with Valeria in *Tyrannic Love*, who 'loses and merits' Porphyrius and then dispatches herself; but where it does not, the recognition by the hitherto unresponsive person of the magnanimous act usually results in an abrupt bestowal of his or her complete affections on its author, the latter now being (conformably with Descartes' principle) irresistible as a lover because unrivalled in virtue.

A good instance of the latter situation is afforded by Dryden's *The Rival Ladies*, in which Gonsalvo, whose devotion to the fair Julia had borne the brunt of four acts of incessant intrigue, transfers his affection at the dénoue-

[1] II.

ment with astonishing ease to Honoria (who, disguised as a man, had been serving him through considerable perils) when it appears how her fidelity had survived all hopes of winning his heart. When it was possible to look on an emotional crisis much in the same light in which one approached a problem in mechanics,[1] it is not surprising that many of the 'divided soul' soliloquies of the contemporary drama ring false; we cannot share in predicaments whose issues are so obviously foregone conclusions.[2]

Though Descartes personally favoured the observance of Christian morals, he recognized that the 'intuitive' method of apprehending truth which he advocated involved, strictly speaking, the rejection of all moral precepts which did not receive the sanction of the individual mind. With regard to morality 'there would be as many reformers as heads, if any other save those whom God has established as sovereigns over his peoples, or those to whom he has given grace and zeal to be prophets, were permitted to attempt any change therein'.[3] It is easy to see that he set more store by the power of the will to accomplish altruistic actions than on the ethical quality of the actions themselves. At times, indeed, he comes near to identifying

[1] The vogue of which science, in Newton's age was, of course, great.

[2] In his *Principles of Philosophy*, Part IV, cxc, Descartes denied that there was any fundamental connexion between passion and intellectual love. '. . . other movements of the nerves produce other effects, as the feelings of love, hate, fear, anger, &c., as far as they are merely affections or passions of the mind; in other words, as far as they are confused thoughts which the mind has not from itself alone, but from its being closely joined to the body, from which it receives impressions; for there is the widest difference between these passions and the distinct thoughts which we have of what ought to be loved, or chosen, or shunned, &c., although these are often enough found together'. Clear and dispassionate reasoning was necessary to keep them apart. Philosophical warrant was not lacking, therefore, for the carefully-balanced soliloquies and debates of the contemporary drama.

[3] *Discours de la Méthode*, Pt. VI.

virtue with strength of will. Article 153 of the *Traité des Passions* states that a man should know, 'Qu'il n'y a rien qui véritablement lui appartienne que cette libre disposition de ses volontés ... qu'il sent en soi-même une ferme et constante résolution d'en bien user, c'est-à-dire de ne manquer jamais de volonté pour entreprendre et exécuter toutes les choses qu'il jugera être les meilleures; ce qui est suivre parfaitement la vertu'. Corneille's chief figures partake of the above characteristics. In his tragedies the incidents are disposed so as to bring out to the full the conflict between an overmastering will and the forces of Fate, but the interest centres on the dauntless endurance of the individual,[1] and there is little attempt to envisage or suggest the universal moral problem inherent in the nature of Tragedy, nor do his chief characters submit to ordinary morality; each is a law unto himself by virtue of his particular kind of heroism. In this respect Corneille's interpretation[2] of Aristotle's statement that character must be 'good', is instructive—it approximates, moreover, to the explanation of the dictum which is generally accepted today[3]—though its critical value is somewhat dimmed by Corneille's general preoccupation with shaping the 'Rules' of the *Poetics* to fit his own plays. 'Good', he says, cannot simply mean 'virtuous', for that would invalidate much of Ancient Tragedy, with its Medeas and Clytemnestras; its real implication is 'le caractère brillant et élevé d'une habitude vertueuse ou criminelle'. It is permissible to endow one's character with 'une grandeur d'âme qui a quelque chose de si haut, qu'en même temps qu'on déteste

[1] Cf. Medée's reply:
   'Dans un si grand revers que vous reste-t-il?' 'Moi!
   Moi, dis-je, et c'est assez!'
[2] *Discours du Poème Dramatique.*
[3] One which associates with the dictum the fact that its author considered a slave, i.e. a slave-like nature, worthless.

ses actions, on admire la source dont elles partent'. The satanic hero, it is true, was no newcomer to the drama, and Corneille may have been influenced by tradition, but it is not unlikely that the prevalent doctrine of the sufficiency of mind played its part in his emphatic justification of the type in this context.

There is little doubt that Dryden's formidable and unscrupulous characters—his Maximins, Zempoallas, and Almanzors—are similarly descended; if not directly, at least through the medium of Corneille. Yet (as with most of the traits of the heroic play) more than one influence was at work, and something must be allowed for the effect on characterization of the heroic poem,[1] as also for contemporary theatrical conditions and the influence of the Elizabethan dramatists—particularly of Marlowe. In the rhymed heroic play it is, as a rule, the unprincipled characters who indulge most freely in bombast, and this may be due to it having been thought necessary to display their indomitable wills in order to justify to some extent their conduct.

Thus Maximin, having tried to coerce Valeria into marriage with Porphyrius, and hearing her declare that her free will cannot be bound, orders her immediate imprisonment and exclaims:

> Free Will's a cheat in any one but me;
> In all but Kings 'tis willing slavery.
> An unseen Fate which forces the desire,
> The Will of Puppets danced upon a wire.

A monarch is

> The Spirit of the World in every mind
> He may match wolves to lambs, and make it kind.[2]

---

[1] Cf. Dryden on Almanzor in the *Essay of Heroic Plays*.
[2] *Tyrannick Love, or, The Royal Martyr*, IV.

As we have seen, the tendency of Cartesianism was to explain all phenomena in terms of geometry and mechanics, and in the heroic drama the absurdly symmetrical arrangement of conflicting loves and hates,[1] the regarding of the imbroglio as a problem to be worked out, may be a reflection of this. Correspondingly, the situations are nearly always observed from the outside, and the resulting lifelessness would appear at times to be as much due to a conscious effort at detachment as to an inability to objectify experience. Lastly, when we consider how abstract was the language needed to convey that 'clear and distinct knowledge' which was the ideal of Descartes, we are in a position to understand how the diction of the heroic play, second-hand and shorn of metaphor, was thought to be appropriate for its purpose.[2] The following quotation, a speech of Mustapha in Act III of Orrery's play, will serve to exemplify all the last-mentioned points:[3]

> Fortune did never in one day design
> For any heart, four torments great as mine;
> I to my Friend and Brother Rival am;
> She who did kindle, would put out my flame;
> I from my Father's anger must remove,
> And that does banish me from her I love.

It may be advisable, before leaving this subject, to indicate briefly to what extent the philosophy of Descartes made its influence felt in English thought at the time of the appearance of the heroic play, and also to inquire how far the leading English dramatist of the time is likely to have

---

[1] Most ignobly conspicuous in the adaptations of Shakespeare; as when Nahum Tate 'pairs off' Edgar and Cordelia in his *Lear* of 1680, or when D'Avenant (collaborating with Dryden) adds a man who had never seen a woman to *The Tempest*, 1667.

[2] 'Our native language more refined and free.' Dryden, see *ante*.

[3] i.e. the forced symmetry, the problem requiring solution, the externality of the situation, and the tameness of the diction.

encountered the new philosophy. With regard to the latter point, we cannot be positive that Dryden had any first-hand knowledge of Descartes' work. He makes, it appears, only two direct references to it, and these we have already quoted. But he could hardly have escaped coming into some kind of contact with it during two periods in his career; first as a student at Cambridge, and later as a member of the newly-formed Royal Society.

Dryden entered Trinity College in 1650; his tutor there was the Rev. John Templer, who, like Dryden, came from Northamptonshire. Templer's interest in contemporary thought is shown by his having written a Latin treatise in confutation of Hobbes; and Dryden may have acquired some of the rudiments of current philosophy from its author. More important were the activities of the Cambridge Platonists—Cudworth, More, Whichcote, and others—who were already prominent at this time. The common aim of these men was to prove that a spiritual world pervaded all physical phenomena, and to exhibit the universal operation of a 'plastic nature'—to use Cudworth's expression. They were vehemently opposed to the 'Mechanick' philosophy of Hobbes, with its denial of free will, its doctrine that the soul is material, and its ultimate reduction of all causes to a primary motion. But the element of idealism in Descartes' philosophy rendered the latter congenial to the Cambridge Platonists, and they were the more inclined to welcome it since it provided them with an intellectual weapon of unusual keenness wherewith to combat Hobbism. There were, however, certain essential differences which prevented any permanent accord between the ideas of Descartes and those of the Cambridge divines. The latter found it impossible, for instance, to reconcile the concept of a rigid separation of mind from matter with the notion of immanence.

Nevertheless, at first, the Cambridge writers wholly approved of Cartesianism; Cudworth praised it for rejecting the errors of pagan atomism, while More went so far as to urge that the reading of Descartes' works should be encouraged in all public schools and universities in order to fortify the Church against its 'proudest Deriders or Opposers'.[1]

Dryden, then, may well have heard something about the general principles of Cartesianism while he was still at the University. When, however, he became a member of the Royal Society, in November 1662, it is probable that Cartesianism came to his notice more closely, since it was one of the modern scientific theories which that body occupied itself with investigating. The Royal Society, though naturally more enthusiastic for the cause of science than the Cambridge Platonists, resembled them in adopting a critical, or 'sceptical', attitude towards the philosophic theories which were often built upon the latest scientific discoveries. Some of its members, moreover, such as Boyle and Glanvill, showed as much zeal as the theologians in guarding religion against the dogmatic materialism of Hobbes. It is highly probable that Dryden's interest in Hobbes's views (as is shown by various references to them in his essays and prefaces) was aroused by his association with these men. In a recent article of interest on the subject of 'Dryden, Hobbes, and the Royal Society'[2] Mr. L. I. Bredvold quotes a note from John Aubrey's *Brief Lives* to the effect that Dryden told the antiquary that he admired Hobbes and often made use of his doctrines in his plays. Mr. Bredvold refers to several

[1] It may be noted that in the Dedication to his *Treatise on Immortality of the Soul* More stated that he was indebted to Descartes' treatment of the passions.

[2] *Modern Philology*, vol. xxv, May 1928.

instances from the plays (some of them illustrating the problem of necessity and free will) which support Aubrey's statement, but justly remarks that it would be a mistake to conclude from them that Dryden personally favoured Hobbes's doctrines, and suggests that the presence of these passages in the plays is due either to rhetorical and dramatic considerations or simply to Dryden's fondness for reasoning in verse. We may surmise, in view of the religious leanings which he later displayed, that Dryden was more sympathetic to the outlook of Descartes than to that of Hobbes; but there is nothing in his work to imply that he was a disciple of either philosopher.

Unlike the passages in Dryden's plays which derive from Hobbes, the examples which we have brought forward from heroic plays to denote Cartesian influence do not suggest direct borrowings from philosophical writings; it could hardly be said, therefore, that they are merely the outcome of a search for dramatic material. For the most part, we may suspect, heroic playwrights were unaware that the traits of character with which they endowed their dramatis personae, and the sentiments which they made them utter, were subjects of discussion in contemporary philosophy.

The parallels which we have exhibited may be accounted for in two ways. To a certain extent it may be said that Descartes' work formulated and gave precise expression to what many men of the time were already thinking. This is the most satisfactory explanation of the presence of the Cartesian influence in Corneille's plays, which is generally admitted even where (as in the case of the *Traité des Passions*) it is impossible that Corneille can have borrowed from Descartes. But even where the ideas are attributable to Descartes alone, it would seem that Cartesianism affected the English heroic dramatists only after having been diffused through the consciousness of the age. Indeed, among them its influence was more pervasive for being indirect.

5. THE ELIZABETHAN LEGACY

We have now to consider English rather than foreign influences on the heroic play, and first in importance is the legacy from the Elizabethan drama. Unlike as is the post-Restoration drama to the pre-Commonwealth in quality, we must not forget that there was no complete severance between the two phases of dramatic activity; but there is nowadays less risk of overlooking this owing to valuable work on the subject by various recent writers.[1] We now possess abundant evidence to show that in spite of the proclamation of 2 September 1642 and of numerous successive ordinances prohibiting stage-plays, the latter took place frequently during the Commonwealth period, sometimes in quite an open and public manner. Thus, during the latter part of 1647 (when the war was regarded as at an end) and at the beginning of 1648, the players took advantage of the expiration of one of the ordinances to produce plays at the Cockpit, the Salisbury Court, and the Fortune. The actors of the Salisbury Court even went so far as to post up printed playbills announcing a performance of Beaumont and Fletcher's *A King and No King* for 6 October 1648. This excessive boldness, and probably the political implications of the title of the play, brought

[1] e.g. Professor Nicoll, op. cit. J. W. Tupper, *The Relation of the Romantic Plays of Beaumont and Fletcher to the Heroic Drama*, Modern Language Assoc. of America, 1905. Also the Introduction to his edition of D'Avenant's *Love and Honour* and *The Siege of Rhodes*, Boston, 1909. Hyder E. Rollins, *A Contribution to the History of the English Commonwealth Drama*, Studies in Philology, 1921. Leslie Hotson, *The Commonwealth and Restoration Stage*, Harvard Univ. Press, 1928.

about one of the many raids to which the actors were subjected during the Commonwealth period. The Lord Mayor
and the sheriffs surprised the players, broke up the performance, and made arrests. The risk of imprisonment,
fines, and confiscation of costumes, however, did not out-
weigh the material gains to be secured by the production
of favourite pieces. We hear of successful performances of
Fletcher's *Wit Without Money*, and of *Rollo, or, the Bloody
Brother*. People of fashion fearlessly drove in their coaches
to attend plays, rather than to hear sermons, and a contemporary news-sheet[1] states that where a dozen coaches
'tumble after Obadiah Sedgewick', seventy wheel to the
Cockpit.

Continued public interest in the drama during this
period is also shown by the writing and publication of
plays, designed both to atone for the lack of regular performances and to provide remuneration for the impover-
ished playwrights and acting companies. The Beaumont
and Fletcher Folio of 1647 was the most important venture
of this sort: and several editions of the plays of Richard
Brome and Sir Aston Cokayne were brought out at later
dates. D'Avenant's *Unfortunate Lovers* was printed in
1643, his *Love and Honour* in 1649; Shirley's *Triumph of
Beauty* appeared in 1646, and Quarles's *Virgin Widow*
(interesting on account of its early use of the heroic
couplet) in 1649. Professor Rollins has drawn attention
to the fact that there was a considerable sale for ballads
at this time, and that many of them utilized subjects
made familiar by the Elizabethan stage. Several of those
composed by the ex-actor Thomas Jordan were merely
versified plot-summaries of *Philaster*, *Much ado about
Nothing*, *The Merchant of Venice*, and other well-known
plays.

[1] *Mercurius Elencticus*, 16–19 Jan. 1648.

There came a time, however, when the public had to rely to a larger extent on the printed versions for their dramatic entertainment. In March 1649, soon after the execution of Charles I, the laws against acting were harshly enforced, and the interiors of the Fortune, the Cockpit, and the Salisbury Court were dismantled. The plight of the actors connected with these houses became precarious, and, according to Wright,[1] they took to acting surreptitiously in tennis courts and private houses, particularly at Hollands House, Kensington. The Red Bull managed to escape destruction, possibly on account of its inferior rank as a playhouse, and for seven years it remained the only public theatre in action. Ostensibly its programme consisted of fencing displays, juggling, and acrobatics, but it was soon found possible to intersperse these with 'drolls' —short racy scenes drawn from well-known comedies, with famous characters such as Falstaff and Bottom as the focus of interest. It was hoped, no doubt, that the slightness of these pieces would guarantee them against Puritan interference, and under the actor Robert Cox they certainly proved profitable, yet the Red Bull was by no means immune from the soldiers' raids. When sufficient warning was given, the actors ran away to save their costumes; but if caught they often defended their property with vigour. The frequency of the raids may be partly attributed to the trouble which beset the actors who occasionally presented entire plays at the tennis courts and private houses. Out of jealousy, actors often betrayed their rivals into the hands of the soldiers; and the players had as much to fear from traitors within as from spies without.

The history of the theatre during the Commonwealth may be divided into three periods; first, the period of surreptitious performances on a fairly extensive scale of

[1] *Historia Histrionica*, 1699.

plays from the old repertory; secondly, the barren phase lasting from 1649 to 1656, when dramatic activity was confined to the drolls and a few furtive performances in private houses, and, lastly, the period of D'Avenant's attempts to secure official tolerance for his 'Representations' and operatic entertainments, in spite of the Puritan laws. D'Avenant was the successor of Jonson in the laureateship,[1] and during the Commonwealth his thoughts often turned to the desirability of restoring the drama in England, as can be seen from his Preface to *Gondibert* (written in Paris in 1650), wherein, like Sidney, he attempts on moral grounds to justify the drama to Puritan readers; contending that public entertainments make the people contented with their lot, and that their performance savours of 'the wisdom of those, who to their Beasts that are much loaden, whistle all the day to encourage their Travail'; instancing how the wise Athenians devoted one-third of their revenue to plays and shows, and concluding with the time-worn quibble on the subject of Plato's banishment of poets from his Republic. Moreover, the first episode of his curious *The First Day's Entertainment at Rutland House, by Declamations and Music; after the manner of the Ancients*[2] (which was produced in London in 1656) is thus announced: 'A Concert of Instrumental Music, adapted to the sullen disposition of Diogenes, being heard

---

[1] We may qualify this statement by quoting from E. K. Broadus, *The Laureateship*, Oxford, 1921, ch. v; 'It is not until we reach the warrant for the appointment of John Dryden, on April 13, 1668, that we find any document in the Record Office with the significant endorsement on the margin: "To bee Poet Laureatt." But there is reason to believe that the cumulative force of the tradition which Jonson had helped to foster operated to give to D'Avenant a quasi-official, even if unrecorded, recognition as poet laureate.'

[2] It may be described as an embryonic 'English' opera (i.e. one without recitative); but it was purposely of an indeterminate species in order to evade the Puritan ban on play-acting.

awhile, the Curtains are suddenly opened, and in two gilded Rostras appear sitting, Diogenes the cynic, and Aristophanes the Poet, in Habits agreeable to their country and Professions: who declaim against and for Public Entertainment by Moral Representations.' The arguments in Aristophanes' declamation are almost identical with those of his author in the *Gondibert* preface. There is a touch of pathos in the regretful note of the Epilogue:

> Where you by Art learn joy, and when to mourn;
> To watch the Plot's swift change, and counterturn;
> When Time moves swifter than by nature taught;
> And by a chorus Miracles are wrought;
> Making an Infant instantly a Man;
> These were your Plays, but get them if you can.

Encouraged, perhaps, by the Government's condoning of a private performance [1] of Shirley's masque *Cupid and Death* on the occasion of the visit of the Portuguese Ambassador, D'Avenant had carefully prepared the ground for this enterprise by writing a letter to Thurloe, the Secretary of State, again using arguments similar to those propounded in his *Gondibert* preface. *The First Day's Entertainment* was evidently used as a stalking-horse; once it had received semi-official sanction, D'Avenant was emboldened to proceed much further in the direction of drama in his next undertaking, the production of the first part of *The Siege of Rhodes*, at Rutland House, in the autumn of the same year. Again he took preliminary precautions; this time enlisting the support of Bulstrode Whitelocke, the Lord Keeper, who in 1628 had been Master of the Revels for the Society of the Middle Temple. D'Avenant's chief concern, however, was for the reinstatement of public performances. Here the way was beset with difficulties, for open infringement of the law

[1] On 26 March 1653.

was involved. But he chose his moment well, at a time when war with Spain was imminent, and ingeniously obtained permission from Thurloe, the Secretary of State, to use the public stage for purposes of Government propaganda. Thus it came about that *The Cruelty of the Spaniards in Peru*, a series of tableaux accompanied by illustrative songs and dances, was presented at the Cockpit some time during the summer of 1658. The piece shows a retrogression from the path towards drama proper, yet this was scarcely avoidable under the circumstances. *Peru* stood in the same relation to publicly acted plays as *The First Day's Entertainment* to those acted semi-privately. *The History of Sir Francis Drake*,[1] the last of D'Avenant's pre-Restoration productions, marks a slight advance on the road to dramatic freedom; it, too, was mainly a musical entertainment, but it was not devoid of action or of plot. These public performances gave rise to a certain amount of Puritan censure, and on 23 December 1658/9 Richard Cromwell ordered an inquiry to be made, appointing a committee to examine by what authority they were presented. But before anything definite had been done the Restoration supervened, and the future of D'Avenant and of the drama was secure.

From this summary of D'Avenant's interregnum activities one consideration emerges which has a decided bearing on the question of the continuity of dramatic development. Whereas *The First Day's Entertainment*, *Peru*, and *Sir Francis Drake* were the outcome of D'Avenant's perseverance in getting the Government to permit some innocuous form of theatrical entertainment (in which pieces, we may add, the chief influence discernible is that of the masque), *The Siege of Rhodes*, in the form in which we have it, was written under no restraint other than that

[1] Acted at the Cockpit in the winter of 1658/9.

involved in fitting it to an operatic form, and in confining
it to the somewhat narrow stage-limits of Rutland House.
The Siege of Rhodes, then, is the only one of D'Avenant's
Commonwealth productions which affords us a reliable
indication of the way in which serious drama was develop-
ing; it alone enables us to estimate whether D'Avenant
was merely aiming at a modification of a previous type of
drama, or, as seems more probable, was reaching out to
something new and comparatively independent. In this
connexion Dryden's views ought to carry most weight,
since he not only brought the species to full growth himself, but was better aware than most of his contemporaries
of the extent of the inheritance from the Elizabethan
drama. In the *Essay of Heroic Plays* he lays stress on *The
Siege of Rhodes* as the first play of the new type:

'We are bound . . . to acknowledge what advantage we received from that excellent groundwork which he [D'Avenant]
laid: and, since it is an easy thing to add to what already is
invented, we ought all of us, without envy to him, or partiality
to ourselves, to yield him the precedence in it.'

Moreover, as regards 'influences', he considered (as we
have already seen) that D'Avenant had the music and
scenes from Italian opera, but the heightening of character
'from the example of Corneille and some French poets'.
There is a marked difference, too, between this play and
those which D'Avenant composed for the court of Queen
Henrietta Maria; the finicking sentiments and unreal
motives of his early pieces are no longer in the forefront
in *The Siege of Rhodes*, and, while the artificiality is still
present, it is coloured by a robuster type of heroism and
diversified by plenty of stirring action.

In dealing with the history of the drama during this
period, it is important to distinguish between two kinds
of continuity; first, in the literal sense of a sequence of

performances, and, secondly, in the more significant sense
of the perpetuation of a literary tradition. We have quoted
some instances out of many to show that during the
Commonwealth the Elizabethan drama was constantly
kept before the public eye in some form or another. The
serious drama of the Restoration, however, bears far less
resemblance to the popular Elizabethan play, with its
vigorous appeal to an unsophisticated audience, than to
the private performances with their specialized appeal and
foreign refinements—the 'Masques à la mode de France',
the highly fashionable love and honour themes, and the
operatic elements. These were designed to meet the tastes
of the nobility,[1] of whom a fair proportion returned to
London from France in the years after 1647, and they
represent a development, on original lines, of the court
drama of Charles I, which, as we have seen, owed much
to a literary fashion borrowed from France.

During the first few years after the theatres reopened,
most of the plays to be acted were those of Beaumont and
Fletcher, Shakespeare, and Jonson; and that care went to
their production and intelligence to their reception may
be gathered from many of the memoranda of the garrulous
Downes, who was prompter and book-keeper at the Lincoln's Inn Fields theatre under D'Avenant, of which the
following, concerning *Hamlet*, the third play to be produced there, is an interesting specimen: 'Hamlet being
performed by Mr. Betterton: Sir William D'Avenant
(hav ng seen Mr. Taylor of the Black-Fryars company act
it; who being instructed by the author Mr. Shakespeare)
taught Mr. Betterton in every particle of it; it gain'd him

[1] The attitude of 'persons of quality' to the Red Bull was frequently
one of disdain. In verses prefixed to Richard Brome's *Five New Plays*
(1653), Sir Aston Cockayne wrote that when a new government
decides to allow stage-plays, theatres will 'scorn the rustic Prose of
a Jack-pudding'.

esteem and reputation superlative to all other plays. . . .
No succeeding Tragedy for several years got more reputation or money to the company than this.'[1] Sir A. W. Ward
has labelled D'Avenant 'a limb of Fletcher'. This designation, however, really applies to him only in his earliest
phase of production, for when he resumed work as a
dramatist in 1634 with *Love and Honour*, after four years
of inactivity due to illness, his style underwent a marked
alteration, and that play, together with the subsequent
Platonick Lovers (1635), *The Fair Favourite* (1638), and
The Unfortunate Lover (1638), shows him a leading exponent of the cult of platonic love, as imposed on the court
by the queen. In general, it is doubtful whether the Beaumont and Fletcher romantic tragicomedy influenced the
heroic play as much as is sometimes maintained. Certainly
the two types have several points in common, such as the
uniformly exalted rank of the characters, the remotely
foreign settings and unreal atmosphere, the plots made up
of a series of sensations, and the tendency towards the
happy ending; but all these characteristics, it must be
remembered, are also present in the French heroic
romances.[2]

---

[1] *Roscius Anglicanus.*

[2] A possible instance, however, of *contemporary* recognition of the
derivation of the heroic play from Beaumont and Fletcher occurs in
Richard Flecknoe's *A Discourse on the English Stage* (1663): 'For
Playes, Shakespear was one of the first who inverted the Dramatick
Stile, from dull History to quick Comedy upon whom Jonson refined,
as Beaumont and Fletcher first writ in the Heroick Way, upon whom
Suckling and others endeavoured to refine agen.' But it is unlikely
that 'the Heroick Way' connotes all that is usually signified by the
term Heroic Play; for Flecknoe wrote at a time when neither the
Drydenesque nor the Orrery type of drama had been evolved. Sir
John Suckling's *Aglaura* (1637) and *Brennoralt* (printed 1646) somewhat resemble D'Avenant's transitional productions; and it is probable
that (together with *The Siege of Rhodes*) Flecknoe chiefly had these in
mind.

The plays of Beaumont and Fletcher, it is true, enjoyed a remarkable popularity during the greater part of Charles II's reign. Those of them which managed to get publicly performed during the Commonwealth—such as *The Scornful Lady*, *A King and No King*, and *Rollo*—were all favourites with Restoration audiences. In 1668 Dryden made his well-known observation, 'Their plays are the most . . . frequent entertainments of the stage, two of theirs being acted through the year for one of Shakespeare's or Jonson's'. By far the greatest number of revivals took place between the years 1663 and 1682, but, in his *Beaumont and Fletcher on the Restoration Stage*, Mr. A. C. Sprague computes that during the period 1660–1710 no less than thirty-nine of the plays were produced, of which ten 'seem to have enjoyed an almost uninterrupted popularity'. It is not without significance that Restoration audiences preferred on the whole the comedies to the tragedies and tragicomedies of these authors. The comedy of manners, for all its brilliance of spirit and essential originality, had securer roots in Elizabethan drama, and was less subjected to a complexity of outside influences than the heroic play. A play such as Fletcher's *The Wild Goose Chase* anticipates many of the characteristics of the comedy of manners, and the 'proviso-scenes' of Restoration comedy, though they derive ultimately from the light-hearted contract drawn up by Hylas and Stelle in the *Astrée*, had become completely naturalized in the comedies of Massinger, Fletcher, and Shirley. It is worthy of note that of the many Beaumont and Fletcher plays which were adapted for use during the Restoration, the comedies received mainly such alterations as were required to fit them for new stage conditions, whereas the serious plays were revised, fairly consistently, in accordance with the new dramatic criteria.

We may select one or two instances, to make the latter point clear.[1] In 1664 D'Avenant produced *The Rivals*, an adaptation of *The Two Noble Kinsmen* of Fletcher and a collaborator. The piece took well, according to Downes, and lasted nine days. The alterations tend to regularize the play, to impose on it symmetry of structure and artificiality of sentiment. Attention is paid to the Unities; the underplot of the gaoler's daughter is removed, the Theban scenes of the original are rejected in order to preserve the unity of place, and the duration of the action is reduced to four or five days. The chivalrous friendship of Palamon and Arcite is not much in evidence in the Restoration version; it is replaced by a conventionalized theme of rivalry in heroic love. D'Avenant introduces rhyme in some of the new scenes, noticeably where honourable scruples are bandied to and fro in the heroic way. Thus Philander (Palamon) argues:

> My heart did first Heraclia's captive prove,
> To her, I am oblig'd in bonds of love.
> Celania gave my person liberty
> To her by honour I shou'd grateful be,
> I owe myself to both, what shall I doe
> To be to Love, and yet to honour, true?[2]

The conclusion of the play is rewritten in conformity with contemporary taste. Theocles (Arcite) no longer meets his death by a fall from his horse, but survives to be wedded to Heraclia (Emilia). Celania, a subsidiary character in the original, is given a more prominent rôle in order to qualify her for the hand of Philander. To increase the symmetry, Cunopes, a low-comedy personage, is betrothed

---

[1] Here I am under some obligation to Mr. Sprague, who, in his work mentioned, has made a thorough comparison of each adaptation with its original.

[2] V. ii.

to Leucippe, and the happy ending is complete in every detail.

Rochester's version of Fletcher's *Valentinian* also displays characteristics of the new style of drama. By concluding the play with the death of the royal libertine, Rochester omits some subsequent material which is irrelevant to the main theme, and thus preserves the unity of action. Rhyme is occasionally introduced, and in one instance stanzas are used, when Maximus reflects on the problems of foreordination and the presence of evil in the world. As a lover, Valentinian soars to greater heights of grandiloquence than in the original, and when he lapses into the monster the bombast increases, and reaches its apex in the rant of the death scene. In keeping with the canons of artificial tragedy, the characterization is standardized, and Lucina's prudery and uprightness are stressed to the point of unreality in order to balance her against the incredibly villainous emperor. In its altered form the piece bears some resemblance to *Tyrannick Love*, and it is not unlikely that Rochester derived some suggestions from Dryden's play.

In Settle's version of *Philaster* (produced 1695) the heroic additions take the form of a heightening of the nobility and magnanimity of the hero, and a liberal supply of florid and extravagant sentiment. Dryden, in his *Defence of the Epilogue*, had complained that Fletcher 'neither understood correct plotting, nor that which they call the decorum of the stage', and gave as an instance 'Philaster wounding his mistress, and afterwards his boy, to save himself', which elsewhere he described as being 'contrary to the character of manhood'. In a version of *Philaster* entitled *The Restoration* (written in 1683, possibly by Buckingham) these irregularities are to some extent eliminated. Philaster (renamed Philander) wounds Arethusa

(Araminta) by accident, and later strikes a blow at his page in just anger, without any thought of self-preservation. Settle renders the hero of the play even more exemplary. In his version, Philaster, when he suspects the Princess of being guilty of an intrigue with Bellario, offers her his sword and begs her to take his life. To show her constancy to him she falls on it herself, but the wound she receives does not prove fatal. Convinced of her innocence and overwhelmed with remorse, he cries to the courtiers as they hurry in:

> Erect a Scaffold,
> High as the Clouds, and sound a Trump so loud,
> If possible, the Summon'd World may call:
> Invite 'em to a Feast, and gorge 'em all.

Later, Bellario's endeavours to save Philaster by a feigned confession of guilt evoke from him another turgid ebullition:

> If thou must die, such Truth, such Honour die,
> Let these Embraces be thy Executioners!
> These twining Arms, and stifling Kisses kill thee.

Finally, when the crown is offered him, he recoils at such an impious suggestion, and displays his unwavering loyalty by claiming that virtue is its own reward. Such unnatural faultlessness of character brings to mind the same author's Muly Labas, the impeccable hero of *The Empress of Morocco*, and the frequent resort to bombast recalls the wilder flights of Crimalhaz and the Empress in that play.

The adapters of Beaumont and Fletcher, then, evidently had before them the ideal of the heroic play, and felt that even the most popular plays of the old repertory fell short, in important particulars, of the new mode of dramatic composition. In the same way the imported French neo-classic plays were frequently found wanting as judged by the newly-established standards, and were adapted so as

to comply with the prevailing taste. It is instructive to
compare the alterations which each type of drama received; violent action on the stage, happy endings, and
comic or musical *entr'actes*—mainly English elements—
were foisted on to the French, while adherence to the
Unities, fixed characterization, rhyme, and the love and
honour strain—characteristics due to direct or inherited
Continental influence—were imposed on the plays of
Beaumont and Fletcher. But it was not the case that each
type of drama automatically bestowed on the heroic play
what the other lacked. The adapters of the Beaumont and
Fletcher plays did not set about their task mechanically;
they made changes, not merely because these were war-
ranted or suggested by French example, but because the
plays concerned fell short, in such-and-such particulars,
of the established synthesized product, a manifestation of
the peculiar consciousness of the new age. The same considerations apply, *mutatis mutandis*, to the revisers of the
plays of Corneille and Racine. It cannot be too often
insisted that the heroic play, while content to borrow much
from a variety of sources, yet achieves an independent
unity—a quality wholly its own.

What elements of the heroic play can be finally singled
out as showing an unmixed Elizabethan ancestry? It may
be said that the frequent scenes of violence enacted on the
stage in the heroic play—the murders, suicides, fights, and
deaths—show an essentially English proclivity,[1] for concerning violent action nearly all foreign neo-classic critics,
from Castelvetro to Boileau, echo with varying degrees of

---

[1] In the *Essay of Dramatic Poesy*, Neander, replying to the attacks
of Lisideius (who, with his stress on verisimilitude, represents the
orthodox French view), is constrained to admit the justice of his argument in principle, but pleads that the English love of tumult and combat on the stage is so great 'that they will scarce suffer combats and
other objects of horror to be taken from them'.

emphasis Horace's *incredulus odi*, while the French classical drama sternly avoids offending 'les bienséances' in this respect. Saint Evremond[1] recognized the origin of such scenes in 'les vieilles tragédies anglaises', while Dryden in his *Essay of Heroic Plays* defends the use of 'drums and trumpets and representations of battles' and pleads that Shakespeare used them frequently. Plays, however, which indulge much in scenes of blood and torture, such as those of Settle, derive from the Webster-Ford-Tourneur school rather than from the Romantic Tragicomedy.

We may say also that the frequent presence of the supernatural in the heroic play is a relic from the Elizabethan drama, in the sense that it points to a survival of certain aspects of the masque. A Restoration audience, that is to say, would have looked on the witch scenes in *Macbeth* (it was performed sometimes at the Lincoln's Inn Fields Theatre from 1661 to 1665) as a masque embodied in a tragedy. Dryden tries to find a precedent for his extravagances in this respect in *The Tempest*[2] and *A Midsummer Night's Dream*,[3] but the majority of Elizabethan dramatists, like Shakespeare, treated the supernatural as an organic part of the play. With the heroic playwrights, on the contrary, it was a mechanical accretion, and in more than one sense, since it was introduced purely as an opportunity for spectacle, for 'machines'. The incantation scene in *The Indian Queen*[4] and the 'Indian Cave' scene in *Tyrannick Love*[5] are attached by the slenderest threads to the main action of the plays in which they occur.

Dryden welcomed such episodes as providing fresh

[1] *Sur les caractères des Tragédies*, 1672.
[2] Preface to *Troilus and Cressida*, 1679.
[3] Essay on *Heroic Poetry and Heroic Licence*, 1677.
[4] III. The literary origin of this scene, however, is Part III of Gomberville's heroic romance *Polexandre*.
[5] VI.

fields for his verse to play in, and as opportunities for
song and show wherewith to enhance the popularity of his
plays, and so long as these two needs were satisfied he
concerned himself little with their dramatic appropriateness. But while there is little doubt of the Elizabethan
origin of these scenes,[1] the actual forms they took were
borrowed from contemporary stage settings in France and
Italy,[2] from that type of entertainment which nearest resembled the defunct masque, namely, the opera. The
'Scenes' and 'Machines' of the Italian Opera were famous
—they were copied by the French Opera[3] and transported
thence to England by Betterton[4] and others. Obviously
the more startling were the discoveries, disappearances,
and transformations which the machinist contrived, the
more frequently had the playwright to call in Apollo, Iris,

[1] 'Scenes and Machines . . . are no new invention, our Masks and
some of our Playes in former times (though not so ordinary) having
had as good, or rather better then any we have now.' Richard Flecknoe,
A Short Discourse of the English Stage, 1664.

[2] As at the Teatro di SS. Giovanni e Paolo, at Venice (built 1639),
where Torelli introduced his scenic innovations. A setting in what
must be either Wren's Theatre Royal, Drury Lane, or the Court
Theatre in Whitehall (more probably the latter, in view of Mr. W. J.
Lawrence's recent investigations on the subject—see *The Times Literary Supplement*, 26 Sept. 1929) is depicted in the frontispiece to the
opera of *Ariane* (1674) and shows close resemblances to one of
Torelli's scenic designs. Cf. also Sabbatini's *Pratica di fabricar Scene
e Macchini ne' Teatri* (1638).

[3] Torelli moved to Paris and worked there till 1660. He was
succeeded by Gaspare Vigarani, under whose direction arose the
Salle des Machines, the stage of which was constructed more than four
times as deep as it was wide, in order to accomodate the machines. The
abnormal depth in proportion to its width of the stage of the Dorset Garden Theatre (opened 1671), which more than other English
theatres produced operas and plays with spectacular effects, may have
been derived from the Salle des Machines.

[4] Cf. especially the elaborate scenic devices introduced by Betterton
in his operatic version of Fletcher's *The Island Princess* (renamed *The
Prophetess*).

and Neptune to account for the phenomena. This explains to some extent why contemporary English criticism occupied itself from time to time with discussing the place of the supernatural in dramatic art; for in this way spectacular licence was tacitly condoned without loss of critical prestige. In France, where classicism held greater sway, spectacular elements were generally excluded from the serious drama and confined to opera; it is possibly on this account that we hear little of the supernatural in French critical theory; what there is is hostile to it. Saint-Evremond condemns it—as we should expect, on the score of *vraisemblance*—'We should seek to depict extraordinary, though natural events. We should portray greatness, but it must be *human* greatness.' [1]

It was not until well after the commencement of the eighteenth century that this more chastened view of tragedy obtained in England,[2] and sensational scenic effects became restricted to opera, to the advantage of both forms.

The presence of the comic element in the heroic play may be regarded as the persistence of an Elizabethan trait, though here there is also a pronounced foreign influence to take into account. It is unlikely that any Restoration tragicomedies derive from those of the Hardy type in France, but it is otherwise with the Romantic drama of Spain. There are not a great number of English plays of mingled mirth and seriousness in the period 1660–78, but several of them are of the pattern of Tuke's *The Adventures of Five Hours* and Mrs. Behn's *The Dutch Lover*, and these plays are based on the Spanish drama of intrigue, the type perfected by Calderon and Moreto. In

---

[1] *De la Tragédie ancienne et moderne.*

[2] Charles Johnson, however (the 'play-a-year Johnson' of *The Dunciad*), made use of spectacular effects in his version of *Medea* (1730).

the 'Intrigue' play the principal action seldom rises to a
truly serious level, and, consequently, there is little cleav-
age between it and the comic portion. This is not the
case with plays such as Dryden's *The Spanish Friar* and
Crowne's *Juliana*, which show, rather, an attempt to follow
Elizabethan tragicomedy. Restoration playwrights were
struck by the sharp contrast between the tragic and comic
elements of the native drama, yet did not perceive that the
humorous scenes—such as those devoted to the servants
in *A Woman Killed with Kindness*, or to the porter in *Macbeth*
—were also necessary for a completer harmony of expression.[1] Like the supernatural, comic admixture in the
heroic play was treated as an inorganic element; it was
relegated to the same sphere as 'music between the acts'.
Dryden was fully aware of the neo-classic authorities'
prohibition of the intrusion of the comic into tragedy,
and to follow his critical tergiversations, as he skilfully
attempts to justify in his prefaces each tragicomedy, obviously designed mainly to catch the applause of the
moment, is both entertaining and instructive, as we
shall see.

Complexity of plot is another feature of the heroic play
which shows descent from the Elizabethan drama. Although, as we have seen, some heroic plays followed the
contemporary French drama in the matter of restricted
plots, the general tendency was to shun these in favour of
what D'Avenant termed 'the meanders of the English
stage'. Dryden emphasizes few points in his dramatic
essays so repeatedly as the need for preserving and promoting the 'variety and copiousness' of the English plots,

[1] It is true that D'Avenant rejected the porter, in his version of
Macbeth, just as Nahum Tate discharged the Fool, in his adaptation
of *King Lear*. The principle on which they acted was probably the
same as Rymer's, as set forth in his *Tragedies of the Last Age*. See p.
81, footnote 1.

and in the *Essay of Dramatic Poesy* he upholds *The Maid's Tragedy*, *The Alchemist*, and *The Silent Woman* as models in this respect. We have previously seen that Dryden's protestations of independence of French example cannot always be taken at their face value, and we have noted elsewhere that intricacy of plot is partly due to the influence of the French heroic romances; but in spite of this there is little doubt that the Elizabethan strain predominates. For a steady increase of this characteristic may be traced from the period in which Elizabethan drama was at its height, down to the era of flamboyant Love and Valour.

In the tragedy of Shakespeare and his fellows (with, of course, important exceptions) the texture is loose, though secure; the method is one of 'diffused lyricism' which permits a wealth of incident, yet is detrimental neither to clear characterization nor to unity of aim. Midway comes the drama of Beaumont and Fletcher; with them tragedy shows a decline in artistic integrity, the plot becomes more intricate and is conceived not as a whole but as a sequence of sensations. Two unfortunate effects of this (which appear also in the heroic play) are that the characters become submerged under the accumulation of incident, and that languid uncertainty takes the place of dramatic suspense. In the heroic play we but see the same process carried a step farther. Dryden and Sir Robert Howard's *The Indian Queen*, for example, shows clearly how fatal are the many artificial combinations of the conflicting loves and hates of the chief characters to any atmosphere of tragic inevitability. As regards the unity of action, indeed, many of the heroic playwrights obeyed the letter of law, but this did not prevent their productions from being overloaded with melodramatic incident.

6. INFLUENCE OF THEATRICAL CONDITIONS ON THE DRAMA

Much may be said of the heroic play that is derogatory, but no just estimate of it should fail to take into consideration the fact that the heroic playwrights worked under difficult theatrical conditions. There was, indeed, considerable enthusiasm for things of the theatre during the Restoration, but among the majority of spectators it was not serious enough to encourage the rise of great drama, and went little further than a desire for constant and varied entertainment.

Audiences were small. There was no theatre-going public like that of Elizabethan times; the theatre was virtually an adjunct to the court, and the middle classes neither desired nor were encouraged to attend performances. Whatever the effect on comedy, the effect on tragedy of plays which, furthered by a royalist censorship, mirrored only a small section of life could not but be deleterious. But apart from this, there were not even enough play-goers to fill the two small theatres which were in existence for the first twenty years of the Restoration. Numerous prologues and epilogues (besides the testimony of Pepys) concur in complaining how one theatre was deserted while a new play was being presented at the other. Wright is even more despondent:

'It is an argument of the Worth of the Plays and Actors of the last Age, and easily inferred that they were much beyond ours in this, to consider that they could support themselves merely from their own merit, the weight of the matter, and the goodness of the action; without scenes and machines. Whereas the present plays, with all their show, can hardly draw an audience.' [1]

[1] *Historia Histrionica*, 1699.

The regular drama also suffered somewhat owing to the competition of the puppet-shows, which drew many spectators (among them Betterton himself on one occasion) to Bartholomew Fair and other places in the city. In his *Apology*, Colley Cibber notes how they troubled the two patent theatres in early Restoration times: 'A famous Puppet-shew in Salisbury Change . . . so far distrest these two celebrated Companies that they were reduced to petition the King for Relief against it.'[1]

Many of the audience, moreover, evaded payment by means of the 'free act' custom. One can see, therefore, the economic reasons for the extremely short life of the average Restoration play, of which Professor Nicoll estimates that 'Many plays died on the first night; the majority of the others saw no more than three consecutive performances'.[2] To cope with the hankering for variety, new plays had to be manufactured at a speed unfavourable to the production of work of any value. Dryden's plea that *Tyrannick Love* was 'conceived and executed in seven weeks' was no idle excuse. It may be averred that similar conditions did not deter the Elizabethan dramatists from writing plays of permanent worth; but while it is true that the run of a play in Elizabethan times was not long, its duration—though it was rarely played on consecutive afternoons—quite doubled that of the Restoration play. Henslowe's diary shows us that his company brought out a new play or revived an old play about once a week: moreover, this output fell considerably during the winter

[1] For further details, see A. Thaler, *Shakspere to Sheridan*, Harvard, 1922, ch. i. From the *Diary*, we learn that Pepys attended puppet-shows on eighteen occasions. The most popular of the puppet plays was *Polichinello*, which was introduced from Italy by way of France soon after the Restoration. Pepys saw it no less than nine times.

[2] Pepys often saw as many as four different plays on four consecutive nights.

months when the open-air theatres were closed, whereas
the Restoration theatres remained open all the year round.

Characterization, amongst other things, suffered under
the rapidity with which heroic plays were written and
mounted; for even if the playwrights had been able to
create living characters under these conditions, the actors
hardly had time to identify themselves with the psychology
of their parts. As an inevitable result the characters were
designed to suit the actors: a pretentious bombastic rôle
was seldom absent from a play when Mohun was available,
nor a sprightly one when Nell Gwyn was of the company.[1]
We have assigned various reasons for the characters being
of stock types, but this is not the least important of them.
In time, audiences became so used to the idea of a particular actor in a particular part that we hear[2] of a play
being damned because a favourite actor was cast in an
unexpected rôle.

The heroic playwrights were precariously dependent
upon the whims of their audience; and it was not easy for
them to oppose the general preference for a stereotyped
drama, and to incur the risk involved in writing occasional
plays of a more individual flavour, in a way that would
have been possible had the clientèle been larger. How
sensitive the heroic play was to any hint of popular dissatisfaction, may be gathered from the tone of many a preface, but it is more directly illustrated by the fact, first
pointed out by Sir Walter Scott, that Dryden's *Marriage
à la Mode*[3] shows clear signs of having been hastily altered
from a serious heroic play to a serio-comic one, under
the impact of the recently-acted *Rehearsal*[4] which had

---

[1] The prevalence of the magnanimous hero may even be connected
with the fact that Betterton, with boundless opportunities for being
otherwise, was notably upright in private life; this, however, is con-
jectural.   [2] In Cibber's *Apology*.
[3] First acted May 1672.   [4] Dec. 1671.

ridiculed the extravagant solemnities of the regular Love and Honour play.

Not only were audiences scanty, they were frequently rowdy and ill-behaved as well. To many, the theatre served less as a place for witnessing plays than as a social rendezvous, like the Exchange or the Mall, where they might pursue their amours or quarrels. Wycherley's Country Wife, intent on visiting the playhouse only for the opportunities which it provided for amorous adventure, may be taken as representing a fair number of the regular patrons. Another, more offensive, section consisted of swaggering young gallants who to advertise their mettle drew their swords over a fabricated quarrel and so held up the play; Dryden complains of them in the prologue to *The Spanish Friar*:

> Now we set up for Tilting in the Pit,
> Where 'tis agreed by Bullies, chicken hearted,
> To fright the Ladies first, and then be parted.[1]

On several occasions, however, there were more serious affrays, and we hear of fatal duels among both actors and onlookers.

People not seldom treated the play as their toy, like the theatre. Thus Lady Castlemaine in 1669 induced Mrs. Corey, while acting Sempronia in *Catiline*, to give an imitation of Lady Harvey's peculiarities. The latter, enraged,

---

[1] The Hôtel de Bourgogne suffered from the same disorders in the period between the death of Richelieu and the complete establishment of the classical drama. D'Aubignac in his 'Project for Re-establishing the French Theatre' (appended to *La Pratique du Théâtre*) offers the following remedy: 'The King shall forbid all Pages and Footmen to enter the Playhouse upon pain of Death, and prohibit likewise all other persons, of what quality soever, to wear their swords there, nor any offensive arms, upon the same penalty . . . And for the greater conveniency of the spectators, the Pit shall be raised and filled with seats, that shall overlook the stage, which will hinder the quarrelling of the Hectors, there being not room for them to fight.'

managed to have the actress imprisoned, but the Royal
Mistress soon secured her release and caused her to act it
over again 'worse than ever, where the King himself was',
while the frantic Lady Harvey hired persons to hiss and to
throw oranges at the stage. How shallow the conception
of tragedy could be is also illustrated by the alternative
tragic and comic ending with which Sir Robert Howard
provided his *The Vestal Virgin* (1665).

In fact, the only things that could be counted upon to
hold the attention of the philandering, brawling audience
were the obscenity of comedy and the bombast[1] and
spectacle of the heroic play. Tragedy to win acceptance
had to 'elevate and surprise', as Johnson insists in *The
Rehearsal*.[2] To provide the element of surprise, scenic
effects were chiefly relied on,[3] but scenery was expensive[4]
and when once built could not be discarded after the short
run of the play for which it was designed was over.
Accordingly, just as parts were often composed simply to
suit the idiosyncrasies of the repertory company's actors,
so plots were frequently 'written round' its stock scenery.

The best example of this practice is provided by Dryden's *The Indian Emperor*,[5] which play, nominally *The
Sequeal of the Indian Queen*, has in reality very little con-

---

[1] The extravagant rants of the heroic play persisted in spite of the
ridicule cast on them by *The Rehearsal* and by many prologues and
epilogues.

One reason for their popularity is suggested by Addison: 'The Ladies
are wonderfully pleased to see a Man insulting Kings, or affronting the
Gods, in one scene, and throwing himself at the feet of his Mistress in
another. Let him behave insolently towards the Men and abjectly
towards the Fair One, and it is ten to one but he proves a favourite
with the Boxes. Dryden and Lee, in several of their Tragedies, have
practised this secret with good success.' (*Spectator*, No. 40; quoted
by Pendlebury.)

[2] I. i.   [3] Cf. Epilogue to *The Indian Queen*.

[4] Cf. Prologue to Part II of *The Siege of Rhodes*.

[5] Noted by Professor Nicoll.

nexion with it (so little that when it was produced a printed synopsis of intervening events had to be circulated amongst the audience) and was clearly written chiefly to re-exhibit the prison scene and the temple scene which had made the success of the earlier play.

These considerations are enough to show that we should in fairness attribute many of the crudities and blemishes of the heroic play as much to the effect of the light-headed, noisily fashionable audiences of the time as to the dramatists themselves, many of whom, indeed, may have felt as sorely as Edward Howard when he complained that 'Scenes, Habits, Dancing, or perhaps an Actress, take more with Spectators, than the best Dramatick wit'.[1]

Much the same may be said on behalf of some aspects of contemporary dramatic criticism. Several of its transparent artifices, as when it attempts authoritatively to justify some recent licence of the stage; many of its inconsistent lapses, as it approves some feature of the heroic play which it formerly condemned, or vice versa, are partly excusable when we consider how capricious and exacting were the demands of the public which it addressed. The end of the long controversy between Dryden and Sir Robert Howard as to the relative merits of Rhyme and Blank Verse comes unexpectedly with Dryden wearying of abstract principles and admitting, 'I am satisfied only if Rhyme cause delight; for delight is the chief, if not the only end of poesy. . . . For I confess my chief endeavours are to delight the age in which I live.'[2] In the same way, in the *Epistle Dedicatory* to *The Spanish Friar*, he tires of the laborious theoretical justification for comic admixture

---

[1] Preface to his *Six Days' Adventure*; acted 1671. We learn from Downes that Betterton, in order 'to gratify the desires and Fancies of the Nobility and Gentry', was obliged to procure the best singers and dancers from abroad, at great cost to himself and the Duke's company.

[2] *A Defence of an Essay of Dramatic Poesy.*

in the serious drama, and again resorts to the appeal to its popularity: 'For this time I satisfied my own humour, which was to tack two plays together; and to break a rule for the pleasure of variety. The truth is; the Audience are grown weary of continued melancholy scenes.' In spite of such obliquities, however, we may say that Criticism strove on the whole sincerely, and in the face of considerable difficulties, to formulate a lucid and reasonable Poetic.

We have brought out some points in extenuation of the heroic playwrights, yet it cannot be denied that they, too, partook of the shallowness of the age.

In the serious drama of the Restoration there is but a handful of plays of abiding merit. Though it is true in the main that an audience gets the kind of drama it deserves, at the same time had a dramatist of the first rank appeared in the period under review, it is probable that he would have produced a steady stream of plays of permanent worth, even while submitting to the unfavourable conditions and conventions of the theatre of his time.

CHAPTER TWO

CORNEILLE AND *LES SENTIMENTS*. TRAGICOMEDY

1. CORNEILLE AND *LES SENTIMENTS*

WE must now proceed to survey the 'written law' of the period as expounded by French critics, and as somewhat freely adapted by their English contemporaries. The French writers drew their tenets principally from the commentaries of the Italian critics of the sixteenth century; the *Poétique* of La Mesnardière, for example, is chiefly a point-by-point 'improvement' on the work of Castelvetro, though, unlike the majority of contemporary French critics, La Mesnardière interprets Aristotle in a more liberal spirit than his Italian predecessor.

In 1637 appeared the first considerable piece of French criticism embodying the neo-classic creed; the famous *Sentiments de L'Académie Française sur la tragicomédie du Cid*. The 'Rules' in France, however, had been fairly thoroughly established earlier than its publication, though informally, by way of discussions at the Hôtel de Rambouillet, and by letters passing between Georges de Scudéry, Chapelain, and their friends. By 1630 the twenty-four hour rule had been formulated; by the following year Corneille had become acquainted with the general terms of the Unities; in 1634 came Mairet's *Sophonisbe*—usually regarded as the first French classical tragedy—while by 1635 Cardinal Richelieu had been brought to regard the 'Rules' as law. Richelieu disapproved of *Le Cid* on account of its Spanish theme and its sanction of duelling, also, perhaps, because Rodrigue and Chimène put their own interests before those of the state. The controversy which arose after its production between Georges de Scudéry and the author gave Richelieu the opportunity of causing his censure to be felt, and he requested the recently-founded Academy (on which he could count to comply with his views) to judge between the disputants. Somewhat reluctantly it accepted the task, and entrusted most of the work to Chapelain, whose adverse opinions of the play were unfeigned. The *Sentiments*, which resulted, thus represents a genuine critical opinion, in spite of being made to order. For a piece of fault-finding it is moderate in tone, and the only trace of Richelieu's authority is its overjudicial manner, which was in any case a characteristic of most applied criticism of the time.

Corneille's full reply, the *Examen* of *Le Cid*, did not come till twenty-three years after, but in spite of the greater assurance which experience had brought him in the interval, he was still too respectful towards the Academy's findings to question them except in detail, and considered it necessary to tender the excuse that the age was uncritical when he wrote his play. In the *Trois Discours* (submissive in spirit though they may seem at times) he gives his judgement the freer rein which he had not had the boldness to allow to his plays. Thus it happens that the two most famous critical works of the period— the *Trois Discours* and the *Essay of Dramatic Poesy*—are emancipatory in outlook and do not truly represent the neo-classic creed.

To return to *Les Sentiments*. It is strange that Chapelain in his concluding remarks, when selecting merits of *Le Cid* to counterbalance the faults which he enumerated, should have praised its 'vehemence of passion'; since a recognition of this quality, it would be thought, would have invalidated his principal objection, which was directed against the 'mauvaises mœurs' of the story. In effect, he blamed the play for not being a totally different kind of play. *Le Cid*, for all its imposed formalities of design and treatment, is in essence a play of youthful romance and love. In Chapelain's view, to depict honourable lovers yielding to their emotions in a moral dilemma was to reject the nobility and restraint which it was the business of the serious play to extol. The elevated honour code of the romances was so widely known in society that it was impossible not to accuse the author of having deliberately avoided its observance. Such interference with subject-matter is a pronounced example of neo-classic despotism, but luckily these extreme measures were not common. Racine's tragedies of passion aroused no such crass opposition.

Under cover of the customary interpretations of Horace's remarks on the mixing of the useful and pleasant, and of Aristotle's on the subject of Probability, the Academy delivers a fierce attack on the 'immoral' conclusion of the play. It maintains that propriety is outraged by a virtuous lady marrying the slayer of her father, and that probability is violated by Don Fernand's unjust order that the marriage shall take place. Unconsciously damning the 'Rules', it admits that Chimène's passion for Rodrigue is the principal theme of the play, and that its presentation is admirably and convincingly wrought, but asserts that this ought not to please, and that it pleases only those who are ignorant of the rules (of probability). It admires the poet's choice in depicting a conflict between love and honour, but insists that a greater beauty as well as more probability would have been secured had Chimène's honour triumphed over her love, and the lovers remained for ever apart. But if honour yielding to love had to be portrayed, it suggests that it would have been better to have depicted Rodrigue's refusal to avenge his insulted father, than Chimène's eventual consent to marry Rodrigue. It is curious that the

Academy should be chiefly impressed with the unnatural conduct of Chimène, for what strikes the unbiased reader is just the opposite; she seems over-solicitous of her honour, and persists in regarding Rodrigue as her foe even though her father had been the aggressor in the quarrel scene, though Rodrigue had saved the state by his victory over the Moors, though chivalry required her to marry the victor of the duel which was fought to satisfy her vengeance, and though the king had commanded the marriage. 'The dramatist', the Academy decided, 'should have regard to propriety rather than to historical truth';[1] it would have been better had he made changes in the story—had he let it be discovered, for instance, that the Comte was not the true father of Chimène, or that he did not die of his wound, &c. But (it added) it would have been best not to have made a dramatic poem out of the story at all, since the latter was too well known to be altered in so essential a particular.[2]

As has been said, Corneille was cautious and over-respectful in his reply[3] and occupied himself chiefly with details. In it he points out that it is unjust to blame Chimène, as the Academy had done, for uttering this or that 'unnatural sentiment', for she is at the mercy of conflicting emotions, and soon contradicts any of her remarks that might have given offence. Thus, though in an interview with her lover[4] she lets escape from her 'Sors vain-

---

[1] '. . . que s'il est obligé de traiter une matière historique de cette nature, c'est alors qu'il la doit réduire aux termes de la bienséance, sans avoir égard à la vérité, et qu'il la doit plutôt changer toute entière que de lui laisser rien qui soit incompatible avec les règles de son art.'

[2] Tasso was in favour of both epic and tragedy using historical material in the interests of verisimilitude, but he allowed writers a full liberty to distort history in the service of art. The French neo-classicists may well have been influenced by his judgement, cf. Pendlebury, *Dryden's Heroic Plays*, pp. 17, 18.

[3] The *Examen du Cid*, 1660.   [4] V. i.

queur d'un combat dont Chimène est le prix', soon after,
when alone with Elvire and no longer influenced by her
lover's presence, she utters a wish which expresses her
virtue as well as her love, viz. 'Sans faire aucun des deux
ni vaincu ni vainqueur.'[1]

When he deals with the much-reviled dénouement of
the play, Corneille's excuses, besides being obsequious,
ring false. He pleads that Chimène protests against being
made the prize of the duel at the cost of her honour;
and that she is silent only when the king postpones the
marriage for a year, silence being 'the only means of
respectfully contradicting the commands of a king'—
meanwhile she hopes that in the interval some obstacle
will occur to prevent her marriage. Actually, of course,
the last scene of the play conveys a different impression,
and Chimène's silence is eloquent of joyous acceptance
combined with modesty. Furthermore, he alleges that he
wrote the happy ending solely so as not to contradict
history, but that by the postponement and other devices
he made the best compromise he could between historical
truth and propriety: thus implying that he did not realize
at the time of writing the play what the Academy had since
made him realize, that it was legitimate to tamper with
history in the interests of dramatic art. With his Romantic
proclivities it is unlikely that he would have demurred at
such alteration if it had suited him, and one cannot help
feeling that he preferred the happy ending—as who does
not?

2. TRAGICOMEDY

That the Academy was not antagonistic to happy endings
in general is shown by the fact of its considering that
the author in composing his morally exceptionable

[1] V. iv.

dénouement had 'sacrificed everything to the "Rules" of Tragicomedy'. This is one of the earliest instances in French criticism of the use of the term Tragicomedy to denote a serious play with a fortunate conclusion. The Academy's acceptance of the species is important in that it indicates that the temper of the age was already prepared (maybe by the gradually-forming Cartesian outlook, and by the vogue of the Renaissance Epic in its various forms) to regard 'heroic' admiration rather than tragic awe as the proper appeal of the serious play,[1] and so was ready to welcome the many plays with happy endings which Corneille was about to compose.

'Tragicomedy', however, was not a precise term, either in France or in England, though French critics laboured to make it so. It might either indicate what Fletcher understood it to mean, viz.

'It is not so called in respect of mirth and killing; but in respect it wants deaths, which is enough to make it no tragedy, yet brings some near it, which is enough to make it no comedy'

or else signify a serious play (ending happily or unhappily) with a comic element in it. In France, once the classical drama had been established, comic admixture was banned as being undignified,[2] hence, when French dramatists used the term, they did so in the former sense. In Restoration England, where there was no such prohibition, we

---

[1] As instances of the prevalence of this mood in England, we may again mention Tate's alteration of the ending of *King Lear* and Otway's of *Bérénice*. In the early 18th century we get such absurdities as the resuscitation of Hippolyte in Phèdre (Edward Smith's *Phaedra and Hippolytus*) and of the Comte in *Le Cid* (Colley Cibber's *The Heroick Daughter, or Ximena*). Some of the adaptations, however, preserved the original tragic conclusions, as Dryden's *All for Love* and *Troilus and Cressida*. The age could tolerate these, but could not accept the cataclysm of *Lear* and the blow to true love in *Romeo and Juliet*.

[2] Partly due, perhaps, to a misinterpretation of Aristotle's σπουδαῖος.

find that while critics usually interpret it in the latter sense, there is the wildest inconsistency as to its use (and of the terms Tragedy and Comedy) among the dramatists themselves. Thus Killigrew's *Ormasdes* (1665), which is of the type defined by Fletcher, is duly styled a tragicomedy; but Orrery's *Black Prince* (1669), which has the same characteristics, is designated a tragedy. Dryden's *Rival Ladies* (1663) and *Marriage à la Mode* (1672) resemble each other in combining a serious action with farcical incidents and dialogue, yet Dryden described the former as a tragicomedy and the latter as a comedy. French neo-classic criticism invariably banishes comic admixture from the serious drama. Scudéry, for example, had complained that the braggart Comte in *Le Cid* was no better than a comic type, a captain of farce. The Academy is more moderate; it admits that his arrogance is unduly exaggerated, but points out that Don Diègue himself had called the Comte one of the most valiant men in Spain, and that the latter's boastings were pardonable vanities rather than comical blusterings to conceal a lack of courage. But there is no doubt of its aversion to the idea of a blending of comedy and tragedy.

We find that Sarasin deals with the subject of tragicomedy in his *Discours de la Tragédie* (1639). This essay is an adroit combination of theoretical and applied criticism: the main portion of the work (a narrow yet not wholly unintelligent commentary on Aristotle's *Poetics*) being supported by illustrations from de Scudéry's *L'Amour Tyrannique*, which was in Sarasin's estimation the only play—since Mairet's *Sophonisbe* had shown the way—to have achieved a wholly correct beauty. Some of his interpretations of the *Poetics* (notably the remarks on recognition and reversal) are suggestive and show insight, but he was deficient in any sense of depth or significance in tragedy, and we may cite his curiously matter-of-fact interpretation of *catharsis*: he holds that just as doctors by their practice cultivate an efficient insensitiveness to the physical sufferings of their patients, and just as veteran troops are the bravest in the field, so the cultivated spectator of tragedy will gradually acquire 'une mediocrité des passions, lorsqu'on s'accoutume à voir souvent les objets qui les excitent dans nos esprits'.[1]

In *L'Amour Tyrannique*, Tyridate is the tyrant, Tygrane and Polyxéne are the lovers in his power. He is about to destroy them when Polyxéne's brother Ormène appears on the scene and requites Tyridate's injustice with good, which so smites the latter's conscience that he repents and makes amends to the lovers, and the play ends happily. The author called the play a tragicomedy, but Sarasin asserts that this designation is unnecessary. 'Most of the Tragic Poems of our theatre end happily. This has persuaded some of our poets—who are averse from the term "tragedy" unless their conclusions depict bloodshed—to term their works tragicomedies, as having more in common with the endings of comedies than of tragedies.' But that the practice is legitimate (in tragedy) ancient example in the shape of the Alcestis and the two Iphigeneias shows, while 'Aristotle has included the happy issue among the possible endings of tragedy'. Yet Sarasin—who had lavished praise on the play *because* of its rigid adherence to Aristotle's 'Rules'—carefully avoids mentioning that Aristotle specifically condemns the happy ending in tragedy; thus:

'The change of fortune should be not from bad to good, but reversely, from good to bad. . . . Hence they are in error who

---

[1] In England, however much it may have simulated a classical chill at first, the general purpose of the heroic play was to shock and astound the audience to the utmost out of its cynicism and ennui.

censure Euripides because he follows this principle in his plays, many of which end unhappily. It is, as we have said, the right ending. . . . In the second rank comes the kind of tragedy which some place first. Like the Odyssey, it has a double thread of plot, and also an opposite catastrophe for the good and for the bad. It is accounted the best because of the weakness of the spectators; for the poet is guided in what he writes by the wishes of his audience. The pleasure, however, thence derived is not the true tragic pleasure. It is proper rather to comedy, where those who, in the piece, are the deadliest enemies—like Orestes and Aegisthus—quit the stage as friends at the close, and no one slays or is slain.' [1]

The quotation from the *Poetics* may also afford us the clue to the origin of this use of the word tragicomedy in France; for the neo-classic playwrights may have sought to escape Aristotle's censure of their favourite type of play by using the hybrid term in the sense indicated, in deference to his remark 'it is proper rather to comedy'.[2]

While Sarasin was eagerly in favour of the happy ending —so much so as to risk compromising his position as a disciple of Aristotle—he was strongly averse to an intrusion of the comic element. 'Quoique la plupart des Tragédies versent du sang sur la scène, et s'achèvent par quelque mort, il ne faut pas pour cela conclure, que la fin de tous ces Poèmes doive être funeste; mais surtout il faut bien s'empêcher d'y mêler rien de Comique.' Laughter and tears, dignity and scurrility are mutually exclusive. The *Cyclops* of Euripides and the *Amphitruo* of Plautus, by endeavouring to mix these incompatible elements, sink below the true level of tragedy.[3]

[1] *Poetics*, xiii.

[2] There are, of course, numerous earlier instances of the word in the sense of comic admixture, ranging from Plautus to Sidney.

[3] Did he conveniently ignore, or had he no misgivings about the applicability of his remarks to plays such as the *Antigone* and the *Alcestis*?

His colleague, La Mesnardière, in his *Poétique* (1639),[1] also condones the practice of the happy ending and, like Sarasin, appeals to ancient example. He points out that though the word tragicomedy—first used by Plautus—was not current among the Greeks, yet they had the *thing*: 'Leur Tragédie comprit ce que nous mettons à présent dans la Tragicomédie . . . qui signifie fort bien "Une Avânture de Théâtre, où les malheurs sont effacés par quelque bon événement".' He has nothing to say concerning comic admixture, but refusal to consider the topic, in a critic of La Mesnardière's voluminous orthodoxy, almost amounts to a condemnation of the practice.

Our next critic, Hédelin, Abbé d'Aubignac, author of *La Pratique du Théâtre*,[2] is, perhaps, most widely known through the anecdote which Saint-Evremond tells of him:

'On n'a jamais vu tant de règles pour faire des belles tragédies; et on en fait si peu, qu'on est obligé de représenter les vieilles. Il me souvient que l'abbé d'Aubignac en composa une,[3] selon toutes les lois qu'il avait impérieusement données pour le théâtre. Elle ne réussit point; et comme il se vantait partout d'être le seul de nos auteurs qui eût bien suivi les préceptes d'Aristote: "Je sais bon gré a M. d'Aubignac," dit M. le Prince, "d'avoir si bien suivi les règles d'Aristote, mais je ne pardonne point aux règles d'Aristote d'avoir fait faire une si méchante tragédie à M. d'Aubignac." '

Harsh and arbitrary though he is in surrounding the dramatist with a network of prohibitions, he yet had a

---

[1] It was published later in the year than Sarasin's *Discours*, but was composed earlier than it. Sarasin explains that he has not considered the various sub-divisions of tragedy such as 'mœurs', 'sentiments', 'diction', &c., because 'M. de la Mesnardière has divinely treated of all these in his *Poétique* which is shortly to appear'.

[2] Published in 1657, but begun in 1640 at Richelieu's request. It was translated into English in 1684, and was entitled *The Whole Art of the Stage*. The quotations are drawn from this translation.

[3] *Zénobie*.

considerable enthusiasm for things of the theatre, and no
doubt believed sincerely that the irregularities of the popular drama were as injurious to art as the disorders which
frequently occurred during performances.[1] He comes to
almost the same conclusions as Sarasin concerning tragicomedy, though he treats of it in greater detail. Ignoring
the passage in the *Poetics*, he asserts that while in the
ancient drama there were plays with both happy and
unhappy endings, those of the latter kind must have been
composed solely 'out of complaisance to the Athenians,
who loved spectacles of horror'; thus revealing his own
insensibility to the true appeal of tragedy. He considers
that owing to the fact that the plays of the ancients frequently end unhappily, 'many people have thought that
the word Tragical never signified anything but some sad,
bloody event; but they are mistaken, that word in its true
signification meaning nothing else but a magnificent,
serious, grave Poem, conformable to the Agitations and
sudden turns of the fortune of great people'. The correct
use of the word tragicomedy, on the other hand, is that
which signifies a mixture of dignity and scurrility—as
Plautus applied it to his *Amphytruo*, in which 'Jupiter and
Amphytrio go to Fisty-cuffs'. He disapproves, however,
of this type of play, and is gratified to find that the French
stage is becoming rid of the species. The incorrect use of
the word may even

'destroy all the beauty of a Play, which consisting particularly
in the Peripeteia, it may discover that too soon; since the most
agreeable thing in a Drama is, that out of many sad and Tragick
appearances, the event should at last be happy, against the
expectation of the whole audience; but when once the word
Tragicomedy is prefix'd, the Catastrophe is presently known,
and the audience the less concern'd . . . so that all their Pathetick

[1] See p. 61, footnote.

complaints do but weakly move the spectator, who is pre-
possessed with an opinion that all will end well; whereas if we
were ignorant of the event, we should tremble for them.'

This is a damaging admission and clearly shows how he
overrated the story interest and the mere involutions of
the plot.

To turn to Corneille's *Trois Discours* (1660): we have
previously noted that Corneille appears more of a heretic
in them than he had been in his plays. Yet towards tragicomedy, or, more properly, 'Poetic Justice' (he does not
discuss the possibility of comic admixture), his attitude is
fairly orthodox, though he seems chiefly bent on adjudicat-
ing between the relative merits of the two sorts of endings
according to which type of conclusion he had happened
to favour the most in his plays. Aristotle had disapproved
of the downfall of the completely virtuous man as a subject
for tragedy, but Corneille, with the success of *Polyeucte* in
mind, pleads the legitimacy of both the happy and the
unhappy ending. 'The success of virtue in spite of perils,
excites us to embrace it; while the fatal triumph of injustice and crime increases our natural horror of them.'
'Poetic Justice is not a precept of art, but a usage which
we have adopted, from which, however, any dramatist is
at his own risk at liberty to depart.' [1] He deplores, however, the scantiness of poetic justice in ancient tragedy, and
maintains that the 'solid usefulness' which it gives to the
French drama enables the latter to ignore Aristotle's objection to depicting the downfall of the utterly wicked man.
He says he can find no meaning in Aristotle's *catharsis*,
and suspects that it was a mere expedient employed in the
attempt to justify poetry against Plato, but suggests that
the practice of the French stage might render the term
more precise and valuable, as indicating a kind of moral

[1] *Du Poème dramatique.*

object-lesson: thus the witnessing of the death of the Comte in *Le Cid* is likely to *purge* us of the proud envy of the glory of others which the Comte possessed.[1]

It is worthy of observation that just as the 'heroic' mood vitally altered the conception of tragedy, and in so doing encouraged the practice of the happy ending, it also penetrated the realm of comedy and gave rise to plays such as Corneille's *Don Sanche* (1650). In his *Discours du Poème dramatique* Corneille says that we have now many plays which (like *Don Sanche*), though not concerned with tragic issues and whose heroes fall into no peril, are yet thoroughly dignified, and deal with kings, court intrigues, and the like; and since this type is not to be found among the Ancients, he suggests naming them *comédies héroïques* to distinguish them from the ordinary sort. 'We need not so servilely imitate the ancients that we dare not invent something of our own, so long as we do not infringe the rules of art.'

With Saint-Evremond[2] the partiality for the happy ending becomes more pronounced; indeed, he would seem to favour the total abolition of the tragic conclusion. Corneille's more comprehensive outlook enabled him to manipulate the current cant concerning the didactic purpose of the serious play so as to legitimize both types of ending, but Saint-Evremond's moral preoccupation (whether real or assumed) is so violent as to lead him into a wild attack on the 'barbarous' Greek drama in its continual efforts to evoke pity and terror. Saint-Evremond considers that so far from these latter having the beneficent chastening effect so often claimed for them,[3] the over-stimulus of 'terror' in the Greek drama may even have caused the pusillanimity of the Athenian armies, while the Spartans and

[1] *De la Tragédie.*   [2] *De la Tragédie ancienne et moderne*, 1672.
[3] Cf. Sarasin's 'une médiocrité des passions'.

Romans, who did not witness such plays, were more re-
doubtable in the field. On the other hand (he continues)
our 'terror' is a saner affair—an agreeable inquietude
caused by suspense, while our 'pity' is less feeble than
theirs, and is largely mingled with *admiration* for the hero
in his adversity. The ancient dramatists refrained from
endowing their heroes with the indomitable qualities which
ours possess, lest the *admiration* aroused by them should
detract from the (as they thought) more worthy sentiments
of pity and terror. As regards 'Purgation', Aristotle invented the word in order to guard the over-pitiful, over-
terrible Attic drama from attacks on its weakest side. No
one has understood what he meant by it, least of all himself. In any case, what is more ludicrous than to invent
a malady in order to establish a cure? After more of such
specious argumentation, Saint-Evremond concludes and
summarizes his whole essay with (as one might have
expected) a declaration of allegiance to Horace:

'Avec les bons exemples que nous donnons au public, sur
le théâtre; avec ces agréables sentiments d'amour et d'admiration, discrètement ajoutés à une crainte et à une pitié rectifiées,
on arrivera chez nous à la perfection que désire Horace;—
omne tulit punctum qui miscuit utile dulci—ce qui ne pouvait
jamais être, selon les règles de l'ancienne Tragédie.'

We have seen that all the French critics from whom we
have quoted are unanimous in accepting the serious play
with a fortunate issue, while many of them prefer this type
to that with an unhappy ending; we have also noted that
they forbid the intrusion of the comic element whenever
they discuss this topic, which is not frequently. On turning to English criticism, although we find in general a far
more tolerant attitude concerning the last-mentioned
point, yet there are one or two upholders of the play of
sustained decorum.

Thus, though Milton's aloofness from controversies of this nature and his incapacity to influence the fashionable drama one way or the other might appear to disqualify a reference here to his opinion—

'This is mention'd to vindicate Tragedy from the small esteem, or rather infamy, which in the account of many it undergoes at this day with other common Interludes; hap'ning through the Poet's error of intermixing Comic stuff with Tragic sadness and gravity; or introducing trivial and vulgar persons, which by all judicious hath bin counted absurd; and brought in without discretion, corruptly to gratifie the people' [1]—

yet the Puritanical antagonism of the passage is not so acute as wholly to obscure a genuine critical preference in the matter. Milton's nephew, Edward Phillips, echoes him, but not unintelligently, in the preface to *Theatrum Poetarum* (1674). '[There is] one [indecorum] incident to Tragedy alone, as namely that Linsie-woolsie intermixture of Comic mirth with Tragic seriousness, which being so frequently in use, no wonder if the name of Play be apply'd without distinction as well to Tragedy as Comedy.'

Apart from Milton and his nephew, and unless Lisideius's objections against English tragicomedy in the *Essay of Dramatic Poesy* represent the actual opinion of Sir Charles Sedley, I am aware of only one other contemporary condemnation of 'mongrel tragicomedy', and that is on the part of Sir Robert Howard, who in his *Address to the Reader*, prefixed to the 1665 Folio edition of his *Four New Plays*, argues thus:

'I confess I am now convinc'd in my own judgment, that it is most proper to keep the audience in one entire disposition both of concern and attention; for when scenes of so different natures immediately succeed one another, 'tis probable the audience may not so suddenly recollect themselves, as to start

[1] Preface to *Samson Agonistes*, 1671.

into an enjoyment of the Mirth, or into a concern for the sadness: yet I dispute not but the variety of this world may afford pursuing accidents of such different natures: but yet though possible in themselves to be, they may not be so proper to be presented.'[1]

He also pleads—somewhat insincerely, like many another fashionable writer of the time—for the removal of obscenity from comedy. It is probable that the early date of this essay (1665) is largely responsible for Howard's strict adherence here to the neo-classic formula. For it was the first group of heroic plays, as has been previously noted, that was most closely modelled on the French drama, and least interspersed with comic relief.

The Hon. Edward Howard (in the preface to his tragicomedy *The Woman's Conquest*, 1670) is one of those who defy the prohibition of comic admixture. *The Women's Conquest* has a pseudo-romantic setting, but the two husbands, Foscaris and Andrages, supply the mildly entertaining comedy of the piece. The author, in the preface, refreshingly contends that successes in this *genre* in the previous age of English drama provide good and sufficient reason for resisting hard and fast rules on the subject:

'The word Tragicomedy was doubtless created by former Poets, who finding that mixt Plays were very suitable to the English stage, and that it was somewhat below the denomination of their Heroicks to call them simply Comedies (which as they are corruptly understood, imply, little more than scurrility and laughter, though of far greater dignity, if rightly apply'd).[2]

---

[1] The fact that Dryden, when writing the *Essay of Dramatic Poesy* three years later, made Lisideius and not Crites deliver the main attack on comic admixture, provides an additional reason for supposing that Crites was not intended to represent Sir Robt. Howard. *Vide infra*, pp. 102–3.

[2] Edward Howard, later in the preface, speaks extremely disparagingly of the comedy of the Restoration, and says it falls far below that of Ben

they allow'd them the names of Tragi-Comedies, and I do not find but the highest of our English Tragedies (as *Catiline*, *The Maids Tragedy*, *Rollo*,[1] *The Cardinall and Traytor*) considerable enough to be rank'd with the best of these, are at all undervalued by their authors, in being sweetened with mirth, . . . nor do I believe that it is less natural (as some have thought) to form a Play, that shall have this variety of genius than I do to find of mankind some grave, reserv'd, fierce, cruel, others of more airy and pleasant converse, to mingle humours and affairs together.'

In a later passage the author shows perception when he insists that the grafting on of the humorous element must only be undertaken in the service of a completer synthesis.

'. . . Nor do I conceive any kind of Plays more difficult to be truly form'd, than such as have this Heroick mixture, because it is not easy *to give humour and mirth a natural rise and generous correspondency with the grandeur of the other*, which if suitable in point of character, cannot render it less grateful to the audience, it being as it were two Plays in one.'

Unfortunately there are but few signs, in the practice of contemporary drama, of this ideal having been striven for; much less attained. Dryden, as we know, admitted on one occasion that his 'chief endeavours' were directed towards the fulfilment not of dramatic theory but of the caprices of his audience. But—happily for us—he was not one to let such an admission deter him from composing prefaces of a brilliant speciousness, arguing the legitimacy of this or that licence with which he had sought to popularize

Jonson, who more rightly understood comedy as 'an instrument for exposing vice and correcting folly'.

[1] Thomas Rymer (*Tragedies of the Last Age*, 1678) inverting the usual distinction, considers the 'drolls' permissible in *Rollo* and *A King and No King* because in these plays 'they keep some distance, and make a sort of interlude', but considers them inexcusable in *The Maid's Tragedy*, where 'they thrust into the principal places, when we should give our full attention to what is Tragedy'.

his play. The variations of his opinions concerning comic admixture (a practice which he never disallows) are due partly to the type of play momentarily in demand (or to the type which he had newly fashioned in the hopes of catching the popular fancy) and partly to the kind of dramatic criticism he had been recently hearing or reading.

Thus, in the *Essay of Dramatic Poesy*, Neander's advocacy of a somewhat indiscriminate use of comic relief in tragedy [1] was to a large extent provoked by Sir Robert Howard's undiscriminating attack on the practice.[2] Again, we have previously drawn attention to the probability of the comic element in Dryden's *Marriage à la Mode* having been hastily foisted on to the play in deference to the stinging satire of *The Rehearsal*; though we may add that the mingling of mirth and heroics itself did not escape some ridicule in Buckingham's burlesque.[3] In the essay entitled *The Grounds of Criticism in Tragedy*,[4] however, there is a change of attitude; and Dryden, who had

[1] 'Does not the eye pass from an unpleasant object to a pleasant in a much shorter time than is required to this? and does not the unpleasantness of the first commend the beauty of the latter? The old rule of logic might have convinced him, that contraries, when placed near, set off each other. A continued gravity keeps the spirit too much bent; we must refresh it sometimes, as we bait in a journey that we may go on with greater ease. A scene of mirth, mixed with tragedy, has the same effect upon us which our music has betwixt the acts.'

[2] See pp. 79 sq.

[3] In IV. i, Bayes says 'Gentlemen, because I would not have any two things alike in this play, the last act beginning with a witty scene of mirth, I make this to begin with a Funeral'. Cf. also Fielding's preface to *Tom Thumb* (1730): 'And here I congratulate my Contemporary Writers, for their having enlarged the Sphere of Tragedy: The ancient Tragedy seems to have had only two Effects on an Audience, viz. it either awakened Terror and Compassion, or composed those and all other uneasy sensations, by lulling the Audience in an agreeable Slumber. But to provoke the Mirth and Laughter of the Spectators, to join the Sock to the Buskin, is a Praise only due to Modern Tragedy.'

[4] Included in the preface to *Troilus and Cressida*, 1679.

formerly shown the utmost tolerance, and had even seemed to relish the type of drama in which the comic played an inorganic part, now only allows the comic element so long as it is subservient to and yet connected with the main design,[1] while at the same time he singles out his own *Marriage à la Mode* for blame in this respect. The altered viewpoint is due to the restraining influence of the more recent critical authorities,[2] Rapin, Bossu, and 'my friend Mr. Rymer', and this influence is perceptible throughout the essay, though not for the better as perhaps here. But he soon grew tired of this exacting standard, and in the following year (1680) wrote his next play, *The Spanish Friar*, in which the serious and comic portions are as discordant as ever. The preface[3] (in which he is quite unabashed in bringing up the point) makes it clear that the taste of the audience was the determining factor in the issue.

'There are evidently two actions in it; but it will be clear to any judicious man, that with half the pains I could have raised a play from either of them; for this time I satisfied my own humour, which was to tack two plays together; and to break a rule for the pleasure of variety. The truth is, the audience are grown weary of continued melancholy scenes.'

This flourish, however, was not Dryden's final word on the subject, for in his *Parallel betwixt Painting and Poetry* (1695) he reverts to the more sober viewpoint, probably

---

[1] 'If the poet's business be to move terror and pity, and one of his actions be comical, the other tragical, the former will divert the people, and utterly make void his greater purpose. Therefore, as in perspective, so in Tragedy, there must be a point of sight in which all the lines terminate; otherwise the eye wanders, and the work is false.'

[2] It can hardly be due to the fact that Dryden was employed on Shakespeare's play. Pandarus in Dryden's version is assigned a much coarser part than in the original.

[3] 1681.

encouraged thereto by Du Fresnoy's censure of 'Gothic' extravagances:

'Neither can I defend my *Spanish Friar*, as fond as otherwise I am of it, from this imputation: for though the comical parts are diverting, and the serious moving, yet they are of a unnatural mingle: for mirth and gravity destroy each other, and are no more to be allowed for decent than a gay widow laughing in a mourning habit.'

As regards poetic justice, Dryden is the only English critic in our period who bestows much attention on it. The comparative dearth of discussion of the matter in England in itself indicates a state of liberty. Writers were free to compose plays of both sorts of endings, like Orrery, or consistently to terminate their plays tragically, like Lee. But the general tendency was to depict the triumph of love and valour, as is shown in the practice of Dryden and Settle, and in the work of the translators and adapters. Dryden's periodic disquisitions on the subject may have been due to his having thought it necessary to justify his almost invariable habit of writing plays with happy endings, but they are equally likely to have been aroused by his close interest in all matters which were fully treated by contemporary French criticism.

His earliest reference to the topic appears to be in the *Epistle* to the Earl of Orrery, prefixed to *The Rival Ladies* (1664).[1] In admiring the tragic fatalism of 'his lordship's poems', Dryden seems for once to approve of an avoidance of poetic justice; but it may be that his chief aim was to flatter, and in any case he had not at that time written any of his own characteristic pieces.

[1] 'All your heroes are more than your subjects, they are your creatures; and though they seem to move freely in all the sallies of their passions, yet you make destinies for them which they cannot shun. . . . Instead of an absolute power over their actions, they have only a wretched desire of doing that which they cannot choose but do.'

He had, however, scored one or two successes in this kind, and was also fresh from an acquaintance with French criticism when he came to write the *Essay of Dramatic Poesy*, so we are not surprised to find in it Eugenius taking exception to the ancient drama on the following grounds:

'So in the instructive part they have erred worse: instead of punishing vice and rewarding virtue, they have often shown a prosperous wickedness, and an unhappy piety: they have set before us a bloody image of revenge in Medea, and given her dragons to convey her safe from punishment; a Priam and Astyanax murdered, and Cassandra ravished, and the lust and murder ending in the victory of him who acted them: in short, there is no indecorum in any of our modern plays, which if I would excuse, I could not shadow with some authority from the ancients.'

He reiterates these time-worn arguments in the preface to *An Evening's Love; or, the Mock Astrologer* (1671), but here it is interesting to observe a feeling of guilt at having dashingly proclaimed delight to be 'the chief, if not the only end of poetry', in the recent *Defence of the Essay*. Delight, he holds, is the end of comedy more than of tragedy. 'In Tragedy, where the actions and persons are great, and the crimes horrid, the laws of justice are more strictly observed; and examples of punishment to be made, to deter mankind from the pursuit of vice.'

The essay entitled *The Grounds of Criticism in Tragedy*[1] reflects the most recent French criticism. In it, he embroiders on Le Bossu's sterile maxims as to the moral aims which every serious heroic poet should have in mind, complains that Shakespeare leaves Cressida false and unpunished, and includes an interpretation of *catharsis*—'to purge the passions by *example*'—reminiscent of Corneille's explanation of the word.

[1] Preface to *Troilus and Cressida*, 1679.

Finally, in the *Epistle Dedicatory* to *The Spanish Friar*, 1681 (the play is a tragicomedy, in both senses of the word), Dryden's comment:

'Neither is it so trivial an undertaking to make a tragedy end happily; for 'tis more difficult to save than 'tis to kill. The dagger and the cup of poison are always in a readiness; but to bring the action to the last extremity, and then by probable means to recover all, will require the art and judgment of a writer, and cost him many a pang in the performance'

shows that he regarded play-making largely as an exercise in virtuosity.

M. Lanson has shrewdly remarked that a greater amount of incident is a natural consequence of the happy ending; and Dryden's heroic plays illustrate this only too well, while few things are so prominent in his criticism as his endeavours to slacken the unity of action so as still to preserve the intricately plotted play within the law. He shared, too, in the widespread preference for the invincible type of hero, and this combined with his craving for variety of action to prompt his eulogies of the abstract 'poetic justice'.

CHAPTER THREE

THE UNITIES

1. *THE UNITIES OF TIME AND ACTION*

IT will not be our business to account for the importance which was attached to the Unities from the Renaissance onwards, nor to point out their theoretical weakness or merits, these questions having been exhaustively dealt with by others. Had not Scaliger introduced the fatal principle of verisimilitude, and Castelvetro hardened Aristotle's observations into dogma, we might have heard but little of the Unities in the seventeenth century, and the critical ingenuity of Corneille and Dryden would then have doubtless found out more vital problems to deal with. Here, as before, we shall be concerned with the immediate critical background of the rhymed heroic play, one which hardly extends further afield than the France of the early years of the Academy. I propose to reserve the unity of place for separate treatment later, since, being closely connected with the types of stage settings then in use, it demands a more detailed consideration than the other Unities.

The twenty-four-hour rule had been established in France some years before the appearance of *Le Cid*; the first authoritative recognition of its claims is usually assigned to Chapelain, who in a letter written to Godeau, Bishop of Grasse, in November 1630 pointed out that it was sustained by both the practice of the Ancients and the theory of the Italians, but that it chiefly deserved acceptance on the score of *vraisemblance*, since it involved a close approximation of the time of performance and the time represented. Corneille probably first became acquainted with the rule through Mairet's preface to

Silvanire (1631), and he took pains to conform to it in *Le Cid*(1636), even going so far as to draw attention in the dialogue itself to the number of hours which had elapsed between events. His conscientiousness, however, only served to provide the Academy with further grounds of objection to the play. Both the Observateur and the author of *Les Sentiments* blame Corneille for having crowded so many remarkable actions into the space of twenty-four hours—one night separates Rodrigue's slaying of the Comte and his victory over the invading Moors, while he no sooner returns from the latter exploit but he must engage in a duel with Chimène's suitor, Don Sanche. The violation of decorum, however, as we have seen, was what chiefly perturbed the Academy, in whose eyes the crowning fault was to represent Chimène consenting to be betrothed to Rodrigue within twenty-four hours of his having killed her father. 'The author,' it said, 'in avoiding one fault, has fallen into another, and for fear of transgressing the rules of Art has preferred to transgress those of Nature.' In his reply, the *Examen* of *Le Cid* (1660), Corneille admits the unnatural crowding of the incidents, but pleads that the severity of the rule obliged him to compress events which were more widely separated in the original story: while in his *Discours de la Tragédie* he suggests that when a dramatist is confronted with the opposite evils of indecorum and infringement of the rule he should be permitted to escape the difficulty by slightly altering his historical material 'provided the story is not so universally known as to make the alteration a matter of hostile comment'.

The unity of action, if intelligently applied, is likely to be the least cramping in its effects of the three, and may prove salutary in ruling out a purposeless diffuseness, such as was characteristic of the Romantic drama in its decadence. At its worst, the enforcement of the rule induces monotony by banishing those interesting side-issues which often throw unexpected gleams of light on to the main action. Though there is nothing to suggest that the Academy would have sanctioned a play which was disciplined only to 'unity of impression', there is little doubt that, as far as *Le Cid* was concerned, it was right in declaring that the affair of the Infanta and everything connected with her is episodic and unnecessary. Her real function is suggested by a remark of Corneille in the *Discours du Poème Dramatique*: 'Though we have progressed since the Greeks, we must not throw over their rules; and though our suppression of the Chorus has obliged us to include more episodes in our plays than they did, this does not invalidate their general principles.' The Infanta is an unsuccessful attempt to embody in one of the personages of the story the requisite additional viewpoint which is usually provided by the Chorus. In his subsequent plays and, as we shall see, in his *Discours des Trois Unités* Corneille strove for a more natural association of subplot and main story. Moreover, in the *Discours du Poème Dramatique* he decides that episodes—'whether the minor concerns of the chief characters or the chief concerns of the minor characters'—are only admissible if they have been adumbrated in the Exposition, and recognizes that the Infanta scenes of *Le Cid* are blameworthy, as constituting the kind of detached episode which Aristotle deprecated. The Academy is somewhat more lenient than the Observateur in the matter of unity of action. The latter had complained that Don Sanche was a superfluous character, and that he was introduced only to be beaten by Rodrigue in the duel, but the Academy points out that he is an essential part of the plot, and that his real function is to purge Rodrigue of his guilt in having slain the Comte.

La Mesnardière and Sarasin,[1] though both in favour of the unities of time and action, are inclined to prefer the play of variety and fullness of plot to the play of chastened simplicity of design, which is usually engendered by a strict observance of the 'Rules'. Sarasin suggests that Aristotle prescribed the twenty-four-hour rule in order to aid the *memory* of the spectators who, he declares, find it more difficult to retain in their minds actions distributed over several days than those confined to one. 'Moreover, as soon as the Unity of Time is relaxed, the Unity of Place [2] is liable to disappear too.' Many of our modern playwrights, he continues, have violated the unity of time, and we have been astonished to see those who were lovers in Act I become decrepit with age in Act V. Their reason for thus breaking the rule, he adds, has doubtless been the inclusion of a greater amount of incident in their plays: this desire is praiseworthy enough in itself; yet had they attentively considered the work of the best dramatists they would have found that multiplicity of incident is not always incompatible with unity of time. The final phase of an action, the last day of the Siege of Troy, should be chosen. He points out that M. de Scudéry has well observed the rule (in his *L'Amour Tyrannique*) and has even a few hours in hand; this, too, without improbability, in spite of the fact that the tyrant Tyridate captures a town during the course of the play. La Mesnardière recognizes that, in general, the nearer the time of performance approaches the time represented the better, but he stipulates that the action must not be rendered obscure by compression. He would permit the poet slightly to exceed the twenty-four-hour allowance so as to include a fine incident which would otherwise have to be sacrificed. As regards

[1] Op. cit.
[2] Which is, of course, not mentioned by Aristotle.

the unity of action, Sarasin curiously argues that a complex plot is more likely to evoke the emotions of pity and terror than a simple one, since the latter usually lacks the element of surprise. He maintains that the plot should comprise the actions of many men, but that these actions should be disposed so as to converge on one end, and points out that everything that happens in *L'Amour Tyrannique* bears on the violent love of Tyridate, and that none of its incidents could be removed without seriously impairing the argument.

Hédelin, Abbé d'Aubignac, in his *Pratique du Théâtre*[1] states that he had urged the enforcement of the Unities in Cardinal Richelieu's time, but that his efforts were then received with ridicule. Within a few years, however, the Unities had come to be respected by all serious playwrights, and his gratification at this fact may account for the extreme arbitrariness with which he propounds the laws of time and action anew. Hypnotized by the notion of *vraisemblance*, he would reduce the time limit to twelve hours, and he contends that Aristotle, in spite of saying 'one revolution of the sun' really meant the artificial day of twelve hours, 'for it is unusual for the activities of men to be prolonged through the night'.[2] In his opinion the ideal is, of course, that the time represented should coincide with the two or three hours required for performance, 'but that being hard and almost impossible, in certain occasions the Poet has the liberty to suppose a longer time by some hours, in which the Musick that marks the intervals of the Acts, and the Relations of the Actors upon the stage while the others are busy off it . . . do help to deceive the audience and make them think there has passed time enough for the performance of the things

[1] Published 1657.
[2] He probably derived this view from Castelvetro.

represented'. He says that the skilful use of the rule may be observed to advantage in *Horace*, *Cinna*, and *Polyeucte*, in which plays there is no sense of restraint or undue crowding of incidents, and he urges that the best and most natural way of complying with the rule is (*a*) to take the most notable incident of the whole story, and represent only the day on which it occurred, and (*b*) to take up the action as nearly as possible to the catastrophe 'that you may employ less time in the negotiation part, and have more liberty in extending the passions and discourses which please'. In considering the unity of action, Hédelin is strongly averse to the inclusion in a play of any incidents which are not strictly relevant to the main issue, and joins in denouncing the Infanta episode of *Le Cid*; 'such episodes slacken the motion of the Incidents which tend to a Conclusion'.

It is worthy of note that as the neo-classic creed progressed in France, so preoccupation with the Unities came to extend beyond those who concerned themselves only with the drama. Thus Saint-Amant in his preface to *Moÿse Sauvé* (1653) delightedly advertises his having compressed the time covered by his heroic poem (a year being the usual allowance for epic) into little more than twelve hours: '. . . par une manière toute nouvelle, je renferme mon sujet non seulement dans les vingt et quatre heures, comme le poème dramatique est obligé de faire, mais presqu'en la moitié de ce temps-là. C'est plus qu'Aristote mesme, qu'Horace, que Scaliger, que Castelvetre, que Picolomini et tous les autres modernes n'en auroyent demandé.' It is necessary to add, however, that he has achieved this by making liberal use of dreams, prophecies, and the like wherewith to provide narratives within the narrative.

Corneille's *Trois Discours* (1660) constitute a brilliant

attempt to reconcile the 'Rules' with a drama which was planned to succeed on the stage.[1] It was undoubtedly this conviction of the need for a measure of conformity, coupled with a full realization of the practical difficulties involved—on the part of a man who was no barren theorist, but the foremost dramatist of France—which caused Corneille's criticism to be read and appreciated in England. His skill in critical compromise is particularly apparent when he is dealing with the Unities. He accepts the 'Rules' in principle, but justifies his suggested modifications of them by showing how the rigorous application of the rules is apt to impair the very *vraisemblance* which they set out to create. Thus, he welcomes the unity of time,[2] and considers that the theory that a greater illusion of reality is produced when the time represented coincides with the time of performance is a sound one. But he recognizes that, in practice, the choice of 'a day famous and long expected' (while serving for a great ornament in a play) necessitates the inclusion of much retrospective narrative in the dialogue, and that, since this both offends probability and unfairly taxes the spectators' memory, it cannot often be done effectively. [3]

The chief improbability caused by the demands of the time rule, however, is the undue compression of incidents. Corneille contends that the fifth act alone is likely to be exempt from this disadvantage since during it the audience will probably be unaware of any crowding owing to its eagerness for the denouement: thus in *Le Cid*, though

[1] In a letter to the Abbé de Pure (25 Aug. 1660) Corneille said 'J'avoue que ces trois préfaces m'ont plus coûté que n'auraient fait trois pièces de théâtre'.

[2] *Discours des Trois Unités.*

[3] Corneille considers that he has done it well in one or two of his plays, viz. *Horace, Rodogune, Don Sanche.* Cf. Sarasin's view on the effect of unity of time on the memory of the audience.

insufficient time has been allowed for the duel of Rodrigue and the Comte to take place, this is excusable owing to the fact that the encounter occurs in the last act.

To turn to Corneille's proposed emendation of the rule: he admits that there has been a dispute as to whether twelve hours or twenty-four are intended, but for his part considers it so difficult to fit in all the actions within a limited time, that he takes it to be twenty-four, and then makes use of Aristotle's licence 'slightly to extend this limit', thus increasing the allowance 'without scruple' to thirty hours. This privilege, however, is only allowed to tragedy, since the latter frequently deals not only with private but also with public events, such as battles, the taking of towns, and revolutions; whereas in comedy, which is chiefly concerned with intrigues and the like, the rule should be more strictly applied. While he advises the dramatist to confine his action to two hours if it can be done naturally, he acknowledges that it is difficult to find either in history or in human imagination many illustrious actions suitable for tragedy which can take place within twenty-four hours and in one spot without doing violence to common probability. But he points out that there are many fine themes which, though subject to this disadvantage, may yet be dramatized; and, to meet the difficulty, he advises the playwright not to refer in the play to the course of time, nor to set the action in a specific place, but to idealize both. Here Corneille has ingeniously hit on something calculated both to placate the theorists and to befit the special nature of neo-classic tragedy, which, with its tendency to the abstract and grandiose, was apt to be impeded rather than helped by precise associations with time and place. Some of Corneille's plays had, indeed, been adversely criticized on account of their vague settings, but the practice received greater respect and grew

in popularity after the appearance of the *Trois Discours*.
We shall have more to say on the subject when discussing
the unity of place: meanwhile we must consider Corneille's views on the unity of action.

This consists, he holds, in comedy of the unity of
intrigue or of obstacle to the designs of the principal
characters; and in tragedy of the unity of peril to which
the hero is subjected. He encourages the inclusion of sub-
plots: 'There should be only one complete action, but it
can only become so by means of several contributory
actions'—a remark which Crites quotes in the *Essay of
Dramatic Poesy*—but he stipulates that they must be
closely connected with the main theme. That he does not
favour the play of bareness of plot and uniformity of
situation which a punctilious following of the unity of
action is apt to produce, is indicated in several ways, as,
for instance, when discussing the treatment of the catastrophe, he urges that the latter should not be too clearly
foreseen, and that it should be postponed for as long as
possible, in order to promote the suspense of the audience.[1]
Corneille also advocates the employment of the practice
known as *Liaison des scènes*—a device for promoting the
illusion of continuity—which provides that at least one
actor shall remain on the stage from one scene to the next,
and that whatever time-gaps there are shall take place in
the intervals between the acts; thus also helping to secure
the unities of place and time. But Corneille does not
always observe *Liaison des scènes* in his plays, and in the
Discours he states that however powerful an aid to continuity the practice may be, it is only an ornament and
not a rule.

We may conveniently conclude our survey of French
criticism on the unities of time and action with a glance

[1] *Discours du Poème Dramatique.*

at Saint-Evremond's essay *De la Comédie anglaise* (1677). Saint-Evremond's criticism, as we have seen, shows surprising alternations of open-mindedness and intolerance, but it has the unusual merit in French writing of the period of occupying itself occasionally (and in no unsympathetic spirit) with the English drama. He has especial admiration for Ben Jonson's comedy, which he ranks equal to that of Molière, and holds that the comedy of each nation possesses what the other lacks—the quality of the English is weightiness, and of the French, grace: 'Les plus honnêtes gens du monde, ce sont les Français qui pensent et les Anglais qui parlent.' Saint-Evremond had been in England, and so had the opportunity of forming an opinion of the English stage at first hand. Dryden, however, in his *Character of M. Saint-Evremond*,[1] alleges that he misused this opportunity:

'His examination of the *Grand Alexandre*[2] in my opinion is an admirable piece of criticism; and I doubt not, but that his observations on the English Theatre had been as absolute in their kind, had he seen with his own eyes, and not with those of other men. But conversing in a manner wholly with the court, which is not always the truest judge, he has been unavoidably led into mistakes, and given to some of our coarsest poets a reputation abroad, which they never had at home.'

But Dryden's long-standing hostility to Shadwell—the 'coarsest poet' whose work Saint-Evremond had praised— must be taken into account here. Saint-Evremond maintains that the English, in comedy, nearly always ignore the unity of action, and that they often neglect the chief characters in order to depict what happens to the less

[1] Prefixed to the 1692 collection of *Miscellaneous essays by M. St. Evremont, translated out of French.*
[2] By Racine.

important ones. But he considers this irregularity excusable and recognizes that in order to produce variety the English authors justly prefer these licences to the sterile and exact rules whereby an inferior writer guards himself against cavil and complaint of boredom. Whereas 'un événement principal doit être le but et la fin de la représentation dans la Tragédie, où l'esprit sentiroit quelque violence dans les diversions qui détourneroient sa pensée', this is not so important in comedy, where 'il faut ôter à la règle toute contrainte qui gêne' in order to secure the necessary vivacity and ease.

The foregoing evidence will have made it sufficiently clear that the unities of time and action were highly respected by the French critics of our period, most of whom regarded them as restraints which but served to evoke greater felicities from the practising playwright. Some, indeed, like Corneille and Saint-Evremond, perceiving that the exact observance of the Unities involved more sacrifice than gain, reinterpret and readjust them in an original manner, but none of the critics from whom we have quoted is so revolutionary as to denounce them altogether, a course which was occasionally adopted in Restoration England. The authority conferred on the Unities by the Academy helps to account for the fact that there was more uniformity in complying with them, and less diversity in the way in which criticism received them, in France than in England.

Taking them in chronological order as we do, we may observe that on the whole the earlier pieces of English criticism of our period show a desire on the part of their authors to conform to the Unities, while the later ones adopt a more independent attitude. This is, perhaps, what we should expect, but it must be remembered that critical opinions were determined more often in England than in France by controversial motives or by concern for personal reputation. Particularly is this the case with playwrights who content themselves with a passing mention of the 'Rules' in preface or prologue, and who do not attempt, like Dryden or Rymer, to formulate their own critical theory.

One of the earliest declarations of belief in the time rule occurs in Sir Samuel Tuke's prologue to his *The Adventures of Five Hours* (1662/3), a serio-comic 'intrigue' play:

> The possible Adventures of Five Hours!
> A copious design! Why in some of ours [1]
> Many of the adventures are impossible,
> Or, if it be achiev'd, no man can tell
> Within what time; this shows a rare invention,
> When the design's above your comprehension.

Priority in dealing with the unity of action must be given to Richard Flecknoe,[2] who, in his *Discourse of the English Stage* (1663), upholds it thus:

'There are few of our English Plays (excepting only some few of Jonson's) without some faults or other; and if the French have fewer than our English, 'tis because they confine themselves to narrower limits, and consequently have less liberty to err. The chief faults of ours are our huddling too much matter together, and making them too long and intricate; we imagining we never have intrigue enough, till we lose ourselves and Auditors, who shu'd be led in a Maze, but not in a Mist; and through turning and winding ways, but so, still, as they may find their way at last.'

---

[1] i.e. some of our English plays.

[2] D'Avenant had set himself to follow 'the meanders of the English stage' in his *Gondibert* (1650) and had found the French plays unpleasing owing to 'the contracted walks of their Designs' in his *Playhouse to be Lett* (1662)—see p. 21, note 2—but these cursory remarks hardly constitute a discussion of the unity of action.

As we have previously seen, however, Flecknoe's remarks must be taken as applying chiefly to the pre-Restoration drama, on account of the early date of the essay.

Apart from these two examples there is no (published) treatment of the 'Rules' in England of any importance before we come to Dryden's *Essay of Dramatic Poesy* (1668), so there is justification for Dryden's subsequent plea that his 'sceptical discourse' was written when he was 'sailing in a vast ocean, without other help than the pole-star of the Ancients, and the rules of the French stage, among the moderns'.[1] The gusto and skilful intellectual manœuvre of his four disputants have rendered their views so well known that a short summary of them will serve our purpose. Thus, on the subject of time, Crites commends the Ancients' practice of 'setting the audience at the post where the race is to be concluded' by means of retrospective narrative, and goes so far as to maintain that the few hours which are represented should be distributed equally among the five acts. Eugenius follows Corneille in demonstrating by means of the instance in the *Supplices* of Euripides, that the Ancients themselves have been careless about time. Lisideius blames Shakespeare for destroying verisimilitude by cramping the affairs of thirty or forty years into two and a half hours in his Histories, and extols the regularity of the French dramatists in this respect, pointing out (perhaps with D'Aubignac's views in mind) that the French are so scrupulous that it yet

---

[1] *Discourse concerning Satire*, 1693. The 'sceptical' method, Dryden points out, is that employed in 'the modest inquisitions of the Royal Society'. The reference may be directed specially to the work of those of its members who, while occupied with promoting the growth of the new science, at the same time subjected the philosophical deductions which were drawn from it to rigorous criticism. In the *Essay of Dramatic Poesy* Dryden did not set out, of course, to imitate a Royal Society treatise, but his sympathy with the spirit of free inquiry, as here additionally illustrated, deserves comment.

remains a dispute among them as to whether Aristotle meant twenty-four hours or twelve. And Neander (Dryden) contends that by their servile observance of the Unities the French playwrights have brought on themselves a dearth of plot and narrowness of imagination; he shows, moreover (by quoting the concluding remarks of Corneille's third *Discours*), that the French themselves have chafed against the 'Rules', and refreshingly asks, 'How many beautiful accidents might naturally happen in two or three days, which cannot arrive with any probability in the compass of twenty-four hours?' From this it might appear that Dryden at the time of writing the essay was in favour of rejecting the time rule (he offered no definite emendation of the rule until he composed the *Defence of the Essay*) were it not for the fact that in his *Examen* of *The Silent Woman* he finds that Jonson's adherence to the Unities is one of the many merits of the play; pointing out that the time represented is three and a half hours, that the place is confined to two houses in London, and that the whole action centres in the settling of Morose's estate on Dauphine, while liaison of scenes 'is not broken above twice or thrice at most in the whole comedy'.

The last-mentioned point is given a separate treatment in the dialogue, the general conclusion amounting to Corneille's, to the effect that liaison is only an ornament and not a rule. Crites urges that, "Tis a good mark of a well-contrived play, when all the persons are known to each other, and every one of them has some affairs with all the rest'; Lisideius supports him, as usual, with a quotation from the *Trois Discours*; Eugenius points out that though it was much easier for the Ancients to preserve *liaison des scènes*—'one of their acts was written in less compass than one of our well-wrought scenes'—yet they frequently neglected it; while Neander is concerned to

show that if all the persons of a play must have some
business or other to enter the room in which an act happens to begin, the poet is often 'forced upon absurdities'.

To turn to the unity of action; it is significant that
Dryden, in his eagerness to justify the prolixity of his
tragic plots, does not hesitate to make Crites, the most
rigidly correct of his four critics, speak in favour of sub-
plots. Crites insists, however, that these should be properly
subordinated to the main theme: 'For two actions, equally
laboured and driven on by the writer, would destroy the
unity of the poem; it would be no longer one play, but
two.'[1] Lisideius considers that the majority of English
plays are cumbered with intricate adventures 'not linked
by cause to effect, but barely following' and maintains
that 'one half of our actors are not known to the other;
they seldom begin an acquaintance till the last scene of the
fifth act, when they are all to meet upon the stage'. He
considers that the possible disadvantage of the otherwise commendable French practice of closely pursuing
one argument, namely the undue conspicuousness of the
principal character, only arises if the rest of the characterization is neglected, which is not the case with the
best dramatists, like Corneille. Neander's spirited defence
of the unrestricted plot follows. He remarks that Lisideius
had said that a play ought to be a lively imitation of Nature,
whereas these regularities of the French stage are artificial,
not natural beauties. He condemns the barrenness of
the French plots[2] and disapproves of the French notion

[1] Cf. Dryden's *Epistle Dedicatory* to *The Spanish Friar* (1681),
'There are evidently two actions in it; but it will be clear to any
judicious man, that with half the pains I could have raised a play
from either of them; for this time I satisfied my own humour, which
was to tack two plays together; and to break a rule for the pleasure of
variety'.

[2] Here Dryden ignores the fact that many of Corneille's later plays

of having only one outstanding character in their plays. Neander maintains that there should be many persons approaching the hero in importance, so that greatness may be opposed to greatness. He concludes, 'Provided that the variety become not a perplexed and confused mass of accidents, you will find it infinitely pleasing to be led in a labyrinth of design, where you see some of your way before you, yet discern not the end till you arrive at it', and says that *The Maid's Tragedy*, *The Alchemist*, and *The Silent Women* show that this is practicable.[1]

It will be seen from the foregoing that however much interested in the 'Rules' Dryden was, he was far more disposed towards laxity than Corneille. Yet Sir Robert Howard, in his *Address to the Reader* prefixed to *The Duke of Lerma* (1668) accused Dryden of magisterially imposing certain rules on the drama. 'I rather blame the unnecessary understanding of some that have laboured to give strict rules to things that are not Mathematical . . . such argumentative Poets will grow as strict as Sancho Panza's Doctor was to our very appetites.' Dryden had previously been in controversy with Howard about the suitability of rhyme as a medium for the serious drama, and it has been generally assumed that the *Duke of Lerma* preface is Howard's retaliation for having been represented as Crites in the *Essay of Dramatic Poesy*. It is, however, highly doubtful whether Dryden ever intended Crites for Howard; for the former is the most reactionary and con-

(e.g. *Rodogune*, produced in 1644, which Corneille regarded as his best play) have complicated plots.

[1] It should be noted that in the preface to *Troilus and Cressida* (1679), a play in which he takes care to observe the unities of place and action, Dryden recognizes that characterization is liable to suffer when 'the surprises of fortune take up all the business of the stage', and he blames Fletcher for neglecting the consistency of his characters in the interests of the scene.

ventional minded of Dryden's four critics, while the
latter showed an impatience of formal restraints, both in
theory and practice. It is true that Crites makes use, often
verbatim, of the anti-rhyme arguments of Howard which
appeared in his preface to the Folio edition (1665) of his
Four New Plays, but the fact that Neander recognizes that
Crites' arguments are borrowed ones [1] is generally over-
looked, or taken for a roundabout compliment. Nor is it
likely that Howard affected to suppose that he had been
portrayed as Crites; there is ample incentive in Dryden's
Epistle Dedicatory to the *Essay of Dramatic Poesy* [2] for his
heated rejoinder. But while controversial acrimony serves
to account for his wilfully depicting Dryden as a critical
tyrant, there is little doubt that his own repudiation of the
'Rules' was sincere, if superficially considered, as is evidenced

---

[1] In the *Essay of Dramatic Poesy*, when Crites has finished, Neander
at once takes up the subject (rhyme) and says, 'Yet since you are
pleased I should undertake this province, I will do it, though with all
imaginable respect and deference, both to that person from whom
you have borrowed your strongest arguments, and to whose judgment,
when I have said all, I finally submit'.

[2] e.g. 'But I am no way altered from my opinion of it [rhyme], at
least with any reasons which have opposed it. For your lordship may
easily observe, that none are very violent against it, but those who
either have not attempted it, or who have succeeded ill in their attempt.'
After this there would be slender chance of further collaboration in
a rhymed play, as previously in *The Indian Queen*. Dryden precedes
this remark by saying, 'For the way of writing plays in verse [i.e.
rhyme], which I have seemed to favour, I have, since that time, laid
the practice of it aside, till I have more leisure, because I find it
troublesome and slow'. 'That time' refers to when he was engaged in
writing the essay. He wrote no rhymed plays between *Secret Love*
(March 1666/7) and *Tyrannick Love* (1669). Scott erroneously
supposed that the *Epistle Dedicatory* did not accompany the first
edition of the *Essay of Dramatic Poesy*. He assumed, therefore, that
Dryden made this statement in 1684 (the date of the second edition)
and that he was referring to the relinquishment of rhyme after the
appearance of *All for Love*. Saintsbury overlooks Scott's error, in his
revised edition.

by his neglect of them in practice, particularly in *The Duke of Lerma*, which he had just written. Dryden was obviously fonder of the 'Rules' than Howard was, and the latter imagined that in attacking the 'Rules' he was also discomfiting his adversary.[1] His method is to ridicule the Unities (of time and place) by means of a spurious chop-logic:

'To show therefore upon what ill grounds they dictate Laws for Dramatic Poesie, I shall endeavour to make it evident that there's no such thing as what they all pretend; for, if strictly and duly weighed, 'tis as impossible for one Stage to present two Houses, or two Rooms, truly, as two Countries or kingdoms; and as impossible that five hours or four and twenty hours should be two hours and a half, as that a thousand hours or years should be less than what they are; or the greatest part of time to be comprehended in the less; for all being impossible, they are none of them nearest the truth, or nature, of what they present, for Impossibilities are all equal, and admit no degrees. ... I would have all attempts of this nature be submitted to the fancy of others, and bear the name of Propositions, not of Confident Laws ... and then I shall not discommend any Poet that dresses his play in such a fashion as his fancy best approves; and fairly leave it for others to follow, if it appears to them most convenient, and fullest of Ornament.'

In his reply, the *Defence of an Essay of Dramatic Poesy* (1668), Dryden had no difficulty in showing the absurdity of the charge that he had set himself up as a dictator; and in demonstrating the tentative nature of his essay. He demolished Howard's arguments against the Unities brilliantly, though at unnecessary length, but while doing so he gave his rulings on the questions of time and place, the discussion of which he had purposely left inconclusive

---

[1] It should be noted that the *only* reason for the assumption that Crites represents Howard is the former's employment of the latter's views on rhyme; yet these, as I have shown, are recognized in the essay as having been borrowed.

in the *Essay of Dramatic Poesy*. We must reserve his decision on the unity of place till later; as regards the others, after pointing out that 'the author of *The Duke of Lerma* is to be excused for his declaring against the unity of time; for, if I be not much mistaken, he is an interested person; the time of that play taking up so many years as the favour of the Duke of Lerma continued', he concludes:

'In few words, my own opinion is this, ... that the imaginary time of every play ought to be contrived into as narrow a compass as the nature of the plot, the quality of the persons, and variety of accidents will allow. In comedy I would not exceed twenty-four or thirty hours: for the plot, accidents, and persons of comedy are small, and may be naturally turned in a little compass: But in tragedy the design is weighty, and the persons great; therefore there will naturally be required a greater space of time in which to move them.'

Dryden changed his mind several times on the subject of the Unities after the *Defence*,[1] and his criticism must be considered to have failed if judged as an attempt to formulate durable artistic principles. But it would not be unfair to take the *Defence of an Essay of Dramatic Poesy* as most nearly representing the resultant of his many attitudes to the 'Rules'.

In the same passage, during his discussion of the compression of incidents which is apt to follow an exact observance of the time rule, there is an indication of his partiality for a liberal interpretation of the unity of action:

'But as it is an error on the one side, to make too great a disproportion betwixt the imaginary time of the play, and the real time of its representations; so on the other side, it is an oversight to compress the accidents of a play into a narrower

---

[1] Cf. the Dedication of the Translation of Ovid's *Metamorphoses* (1693), the preface to *Don Sebastian* (1690), and the Dedication of *Love Triumphant* (1694).

compass than that in which they could naturally be produced. Of this last error the French are seldom guilty, because the thinness of their plots prevents them from it; but few Englishmen, except Ben Jonson, have ever made a plot with variety of design in it, included in twenty-four hours, which was altogether natural. . . . Yet of the two, I think that error the most pardonable, which in too straight a compass crowds together many accidents; since it produces more variety, and consequently more pleasure to the audience; and because the nearness of proportion betwixt the imaginary and real time does speciously cover the compression of the accidents.'

Thus he strives, characteristically, to reconcile the opposites of baroque exuberance and neo-classic 'verisimilitude'.

Thomas Shadwell, in his preface to *The Sullen Lovers* (1668), is strongly in favour of conformity to the 'Rules'.

'I have in this play, as neer as I could, observed the three Unities of Time, Place, and Action. The time of the Drama does not exceed six hours; the place is in a very narrow compass; and the main-action of the Play, upon which all the rest depend, is the Sullen-Love betwixt Stanford and Emilia, which kind of love is only proper to their characters.' [1]

He also advocates the observance of *liaison des scènes*:

'I have here, as often as I could naturally, kept the scenes unbroken, which, though it be not so much practised or so well understood by the English, yet among the French Poets is accompted a great beauty.'

Prolixity of plot he considers an essential element of the heroic play:

'The want of design in the play has been objected against me; which fault, though I may endeavour a little to extenuate, I dare not absolutely deny. I conceive, with all submission to

---

[1] The strong difference in the opinions of Shadwell and Sir Robert Howard concerning the Unities may help to account for the former's caricature of the latter in the above-mentioned play as Sir Positive Atall.

better judgments, that no man ought to expect such intrigues in the little actions of Comedy as are required in Plays of a higher nature.'

Though he is more 'correct' than Dryden, their views would not seem to be strikingly dissimilar; yet Shadwell shows considerable animosity towards him in various ways, as in his censure of 'Positive men, that justify all their faults . . . always endeavouring magisterially to impose upon our understandings against the freedom of mankind'; in his indignant defence of the quality of Ben Jonson's wit, which Dryden had belittled in the *Essay of Dramatic Poesy*, and in advertising his own slight borrowing from Molière's *Les Fâcheux* for his play—unlike some playwrights 'who by their continual thieving reckon their stolen goods their own'. Dryden was frequently subjected to these petty charges of plagiarism from other authors, and he answered them conclusively in his preface to *An Evening's Love; or, The Mock Astrologer* (1671), pointing out how Shakespeare borrowed nearly all his plots from prose romances or earlier plays, and remarking 'But these little critics do not well consider what is the work of a poet and what the graces of a poem; the story is the least part; I mean the foundation of it. . . . On this foundation the characters are raised; and, since no story can afford characters enough for the variety of the English stage' it follows that the work of adaptation almost amounts to a complete renovation.[1]

[1] Shadwell retorted in his preface to *The Humorists* (1671). He wisely dropped the subject of plagiarism; but managed to confute Dryden's remarks on 'Observation' (or 'Realism', as we should term it), and continued to champion Ben Jonson as a dramatist. Langbaine in his *Account of the English Dramatick Poets* 1691, industriously presents the sources of nearly every play which he mentions, with the alleged motive of 'exposing our Modern Plagiaries, by detecting part of their thefts'. Dryden is the object of his most extensive attack, Langbaine being no doubt irritated, like many smaller men, by Dryden's high-

Dryden's fondness for the involved plot is satirized in *The Rehearsal* (1672), and the dissipation of interest and confusion which the welter of incident produces in the minds of the spectators is amusingly portrayed. In IV. i, there enters 'a Funeral, with two Usurpers, and Attendants'. After they have been lamenting the deceased for a while, Bayes interposes

You must know they were both in love with her.

Smith. With her? with whom?

Bayes. Why, this is Lardella's Funeral.

Smith. Lardella! I, who is she?

Bayes. Why, Sir, the sister of Drawcansir. A lady that was drown'd at sea, and had a wave for her winding sheet.

King Usher. Lardella, O Lardella, from above,

Behold the Tragic issues of our love,

Pity us, sinking under grief and pain

For thy being cast away upon the Main.

Bayes. Look you now, you see, I told you true.

Smith. I, sir, and thank you for it, very kindly.

Bayes. Ay, Igad, but you will not have patience;

honest Mr.—You will not have patience.

handed manner. In the course of presenting a formidable array of the latter's 'thefts', Langbaine remarks, 'But tho' the Poet be allow'd to borrow his Foundation from other Writers, I presume the Language ought to be his own; and when at any time we find a Poet translating whole Scenes from other Writings, I hope we may without offence call him a Plagiary'. Langbaine was a personal friend of Shadwell's, but he was committed to his method, so when he comes to discuss the latter's plays he observes, 'I like his Comedies better than Mr. Dryden's; as having more Variety of Characters, and those drawn from the Life; I mean Men's Converse and Manners, and not from other Mens Ideas, copied out of their publick Writings: tho' indeed I cannot wholly acquit our Present Laureat [i.e. Shadwell] from borrowing; his Plagiaries being in some places too bold and open to be disguised, of which I shall take Notice as I go along; tho' with this Remark, that several of them are observed to my Hand, and in a great measure excused by himself, in the publick Acknowledgment he makes in his several Prefaces, to the Persons to whom he was obliged for what he borrowed.'

And in the preface to *The Tragedy of Tragedies* (1731), Fielding ridicules the frequent pretensions of heroic dramatists, in their prefaces, of having contrived to keep the wildest diversity of sensational events within the limits of the unity of action. He ironically commends a 'Fable' which is:

'One, regular, and uniform, not charged with a multiplicity of incidents, and yet affording several revolutions of Fortune; by which the Passions may be excited, varied, and driven to their full Tumult of Emotion. . . . Nor is the Action of this Tragedy less great than uniform. The Spring of all, is the love of Tom Thumb for Huncamunca; which causeth the quarrel between their Majesties in the first Act; the Passion of Lord Grizzle in the second; the Rebellion, Fall of Lord Grizzle, and Glumdalca, Devouring of Tom Thumb by the Cow, and that bloody Catastrophe, in the Third.'

Milton and his nephew, Edward Phillips, may be briefly mentioned here on account of their both advocating the observance of the unity of time; though their influence on the theatre, as has been said, was slight. Milton, in his preface to *Samson Agonistes* (publ. 1671) mentions 'verisimilitude and decorum', but does not explain his use of these terms; and we are left to infer from the general tone of the poem (in which the unities of time and place are carefully kept) that no aim has been made at 'Illusion'. On the unity of time he is explicit: 'The circumscription of time wherein the whole Drama begins and ends, is according to antient rule, and best example, within the space of twenty-four hours.' Edward Phillips, in the preface to his *Theatrum Poetarum* (1674) also mentions and commends only the unity of time; and the source of the following passage is sufficiently clear: 'I shall only leave it to consideration whether the use of the Chorus, and the observation of the ancient law of Tragedy, particularly as to limitation of Time, would not rather by reviving the pristine glory of the Tragicall, advance than diminish the present.' That his personal opinion concerning the 'Rules' was tolerant enough, however, is indicated by his declaring that 'Though all the Laws of Heroic Poem, all the Laws of Tragedy were exactly observed, yet still this *tour entrejeant*, this Poetic Energie, if I may so call it, would be required to give life to all the rest, which shines through the roughest, most unpolish't and antiquated Language,[1] and may haply be wanting in the most polite and reform'd'.

To turn to a work which for a short while undoubtedly influenced both contemporary theory and the heroic play just at the period of the latter's transition to blank verse, *The Tragedies of the Last Age* (1678), of Thomas Rymer (who may be justly considered the D'Aubignac of English criticism). This essay is an unsparing disparagement of Elizabethan laxity. Rymer sees a certain rude power in the Elizabethan drama, and feels that English writers have a natural ability for tragedy, but he deprecates their indifference to the canons of Aristotle and Horace. The Elizabethan dramatists, he maintains, should have paid more heed to ancient example: 'And, certainly, had our Authors began with Tragedy as Sophocles and Euripides left it, had they either built on the same foundation or after their model, we might e're this day have seen Poetry in greater perfection, and boasted such Monuments of wit as Greece or Rome never knew in all their glory.' It was these chilly pronouncements which called forth Samuel Butler's doggerel lines *Upon Critics who judge of Modern Plays precisely by the Rules of the Antients* (1678), in which the author scoffs at the testing of plays by arbitrary

---

[1] He speaks elsewhere of Spenser's 'rustic words' and Shakespeare's 'rambling and indigested Fancies'.

standards, particularly when the latter are imported from abroad and applied by 'a witless plagiary':

> An English Poet should be try'd b'his Peres
> And not by Pedants and Philosophers,
> Incompetent to Judge Poetique Fury,
> As Butchers are forbid to b'of a Jury;
> Beside the most Intollerable wrong,
> To try their matters in a Forrain Tongue,
> By Forrain Jury men, like Sophocles,
> Or Tales [sic] falser than Euripides;
> When not an English Native dares appear,
> To be a Witness for the Prisoner;
> When all the Laws they use t'Arraigne and try
> The Innocent and wrong'd Delinquent by,
> Were made b'a Forrain Lawyer and his Pupils
> To put an end to all Poetique scruples;
> And by th'advice of virtuosi-Tuscans
> Determin'd al the Doubts of Socks and Buskins.

Rymer, it is true, observes (like Dryden) that the Unities are mere 'mechanic beauties of the plot' and not in themselves tests of a play's merit, but his main attack is, nevertheless, directed against the diversity of action and looseness of structure of those plays of Beaumont and Fletcher which he selects for detailed examination. He censures *The Maid's Tragedy* on account of its diffuseness: 'We may suspect that the Action of the Tragedy is double; where there seem two centres, neither can be right, and the lines leading towards them must all be false and confus'd; the preparation, I mean, and conduct must be all at random, since not directed to any one certain end.'

There is no doubt that when writing *All for Love* (1678) Dryden had Rymer's strictures in mind. 'I have endeavoured in this play,' he remarks in the preface, 'to follow the practice of the Ancients, who, as Mr. Rymer has

judiciously observed, are and ought to be our masters.'
And on the subject of the Unities he says:

'The fabric of the play is regular enough, as to the inferior
parts of it; and the Unities of Time, Place, and Action, more
exactly observed than perhaps the English theatre requires.
Particularly, the action is so much one that it is the only one
of the kind without episode, or underplot; every scene in the
tragedy conducing to the main design and every act concluding
with a turn of it.'

That these assertions are true, the play clearly shows. The
action, extending in *Antony and Cleopatra* over ten years,
is limited here to one day, the story being taken up just
before the final conflict with Caesar. The scene is throughout confined to Alexandria, though there are occasional
changes of locality within the town. The number of
dramatis personae is greatly reduced, all those members
of it who do not further the main design being rejected;
but to compensate for this and also to provide a parallel
conflict of love and honour, two new characters, Octavia
and Dolabella, are introduced.[1] *All for Love* is certainly
the most interesting of the many Restoration attempts to
regularize Shakespeare, presenting, as it does, the business-
like transformation of a vast panorama of decadence,
glory, and passion into a display of rhetorical crises and
striking, but somewhat mechanically contrived, situations.
It was unfortunate that Restoration playwrights, who
considered themselves entitled to violate the 'Rules' when
seized with 'Poetique Fury', should have denied this
licence to Shakespeare. In D'Avenant's hands *Macbeth* is
made to conform to the unity of place, and we lose the
sense of relief and contrast provided in the original by the
temporary transition from lawless Scotland to England;

---

[1] That is to say; in *All for Love*, Dolabella's passion for Cleopatra
conflicts with his loyalty to Antony.

and in Cibber's *Richard III* the episodes concerning
Clarence and Queen Margaret are cut away in deference
to an imaginary unity of action. One can understand,
however, that to make a play of Shakespeare resemble a
heroic play at all, so much alteration was required that
the Unities may have seemed a convenient means of
making the preliminary adjustments.

To cite a final critic on the unity of action, it is interesting to find that Nathaniel Lee, in the preface to *Oedipus*
(1679), in which play he collaborated with Dryden,
censures the licence of which Dryden himself was so fond,
in these terms: 'Perhaps, after all, if we cou'd think so,
the antient method, as't is the easiest, is also the most
natural, and the best: For Variety, as 'tis manag'd, is too
often subject to breed Distraction; and while we would
please too many ways, for want of Art in the conduct, we
please in none.' It is probable that he too was deferring
to Rymer's recent pronouncement on the subject.

The foregoing instances are enough to show that there
was a lively interest in the 'Rules' in England; indeed, there
is a preponderance in favour of them among the critics from
whom we have quoted. Nor were they regarded chiefly as
theoretical entities in this country, though they were
certainly more so beheld than in France, where, on the
whole, to accept them in theory was to incorporate them
in practice. Occasionally the gap between profession and
performance is derisively remarked on, as by John Sheffield,
Earl of Mulgrave, who, in his *Essay on Poetry* (1682), says:

> The Unities of Action, Time and Place,
> Which, if observed, give Plays so great a grace,
> Are, tho' but little practis'd, too well known
> To be taught here; where we pretend alone
> From *nicer* Faults to purge the present Age,
> Less obvious Errors of the English Stage.

I

For all this, however, Sheffield broke the Unities himself in a subsequent play.

Antipathy towards the 'Rules' became more marked towards the close of the seventeenth century, and this hostility, which culminated in Farquhar's *Discourse upon Comedy* (1702)—a vigorous exposure of the fallacy of verisimilitude—is already apparent in our period in the satire of Butler and that of the author of *The Rehearsal*.

2. THE UNITY OF PLACE

While investigating the various discussions of unity of place in the period under review, one is forcibly struck by the far greater importance attached to the rule by French than by English critics. The preponderance of French writing on this subject is remarkable, even when allowance has been made for the natural reluctance of English critics to submit to the restrictions of a foreign code. Once the fallacious principle of verisimilitude became established, the unity of place had to come in with the other rules, and the fact that the Ancient writers did not prescribe any limitation of place in the drama was conveniently ignored. But even Corneille, who admits that there is no precept about place in either Aristotle or Horace, bestows as much care in treating of the rule and in suggesting ways in which the drama of his time should adjust itself thereto as he does for the other unities. The explanation of these phenomena is that the French dramatists, anxious to conform, had a traditional stage setting which rendered exact conformity exceptionally difficult.

The only theatre which was open to the public, the Hôtel de Bourgogne, was originally the property of the Confrérie de la Passion, who in 1548, being forbidden to present any but secular plays, secured a hall in the building and converted it into a theatre, retaining, however, the *décor simultané* of the Mystery plays, or as much of it as could be put on to the smaller stage. Whereas the religious drama had been enacted in a series of *mansions* (usually eight or ten in number) which were placed side by side on a stage fifty yards wide, the secular drama had to confine itself to at most six *mansions*, which was all the new stage could accommodate. Partly because it was the most natural means of doing so, partly, no doubt, under the influence of Italian scenic innovations,[1] these were grouped two at each side, with one or two at the background, leaving the centre of the stage and the proscenium free for the actors to move about in. Though incongruous, these scenes were popular on account of their spectacular nature,[2] and this ensured their continuance down to a comparatively late date. We know that when the confrères leased their theatre to Hardy, he had to concede to the audience by preserving the simultaneous settings to which they had been accustomed.

The chief contemporary source of information on the subject, the *Mémoire* begun by Mahelot and continued by

[1] Particularly those of Serlio. His *Architettura*, which appeared in 1551, shows how the attempt to reconstruct a Roman stage was carried out in the light of contemporary knowledge. The knowledge was chiefly derived from a treatise of the architect Vitruvius (fl. *c.* 15 B.C.), according to whom there were three types of stage setting: tragic, comic, and satyric. These Serlio attempts to reproduce by means of a painted backcloth and two-sided painted canvas 'houses' facing each other on each side of the stage, the whole being set severely in perspective. The action took place *in front of* a semi-solid background, for, unlike those of the medieval drama (or those of the Hôtel de Bourgogne, which the Mahelot-Laurent *Mémoire* shows to have been occasionally so used) the Serlian *case* were not 'practicable'. The *mise-en-scène* presents an odd mixture of medieval motifs and classical imitation.

[2] D'Aubignac, speaking of changing scenes as applied to the multiple settings, advises that all permanent scenes to be represented should be placed in position on the stage at the beginning of the play, in order that the applause may be over before the actors begin to speak.

Laurent, stage carpenters of the Hôtel de Bourgogne (1633–78), shows that *décor simultané* (though it was gradually modified as the neo-classic drama progressed) was up to 1600 the usual setting for the play. The theatrical incongruity displayed in the earlier designs shows what an awkward task the exponents of the Unities were confronted with. Thus, in the sketch of the setting for Durval's tragicomedy *Agarite*, the background is taken up with a bedstead, while the lateral decoration includes the sea, a painter's shop, a castle, and a wood. By means of their polemics against the 'horrible derèglement qui mettait Paris, Rome et Constantinople sur le même théâtre', the critics managed to reduce the simultaneous settings to some degree of probability, but they could not entirely abolish them. The ultimate disappearance of this type of scenery was chiefly caused by Corneille's proposals in the *Trois Discours* (1660), but it is also attributed to a chance occurrence, when, at a certain performance of *Le Cid* the audience was so large that some members of it were given seats on the stage, so obstructing the view of the lateral decoration from the rest of the spectators. Thereafter, these conspicuous seats were eagerly sought for by the young gallants,[1] as in the Elizabethan theatre, and the lateral scenes, being no longer visible, were discarded. The type of setting which they gave way to (and for which the plays of Racine were written) was the vague *Palais à volonté*, an architectural scene which remained unchanged throughout the play. The *Palais à volonté* has affinities with, and (though much later in date) was probably derived from the Palladian Teatro Olimpico at

---

[1] Cf. Perrault, *Les dix Livres d'Architecture de Vitruve*, 1684, Bk. V, cap. vi, note: '. . . nos comédies, dans lesquelles les gens de grande qualité se placent quelquefois sur le Théâtre, et occupent une partie de la place qui est destinée aux Acteurs.'

Vicenza.[1] Even the *Palais à volonté*, however, sometimes retained characteristics of the old mutiple settings; thus the scene for *Andromaque* is described, in the second part of the Mahelot-Laurent *Mémoire*, as 'A palace with columns and a sea with ships'. The latter corresponds to some extent to the illustrative scenery which prevailed in England during the early years of the Restoration, which will be discussed later. The scenic arrangements for the French regular drama were conservative, for not till the middle of the eighteenth century did successive scenes become an established practice, whereas in England they were fairly common from 1635 onwards.

To examine in their proper order our selected French critics on the subjects of unity of place is to become aware of the gradual transformation (often, it is true, by the most singular and ungainly contrivances) of an inherently improbable system of scenery into one which it was hoped would satisfy the demands of 'Illusion'. The amount of ingenuity spent in trying to convert improbable simultaneous settings into probable ones may well rank among the curiosities of literature.

Scudéry's observations on *Le Cid* show that the play was originally produced with an indistinct multiple setting, in the attempt to avoid infringement of the place rule. He complains that 'un même lieu représentant l'appartement du roi, celui de l'Infante, la maison de Chimène et la rue, *presque sans changer de face*, le spectateur ne sait le plus souvent où sont les acteurs'.[2] On the

---

[1] The Teatro Olimpico was completed in 1584. With its wide, shallow stage, and its proscenium consisting of an elaborate architectural façade containing three archways, it is a much nearer approach to the Roman theatre than was the Serlian scheme.

[2] No setting of *Le Cid* earlier than 1678 is recorded in the Mahelot-Laurent *Mémoire*, but the sketch and notes for the production of Rotrou s *Les Ménechmes* (1631) give a purely formal street setting

other hand, the Academy (i.e. Chapelain), ignoring the production of the play, objects that the above localities should be found in the text at all: 'A fault which is to be found, it is true, in most of our dramatic poems.' It maintains that the author, who had been so strict in complying with the unity of time, should have observed unity of place as well. Both critics are captious in their straining after correctness, but so prevalent is the uncertainty as to how to reconcile the unity of place with existing stage conditions, that neither know how to suggest a remedy.

In his reply, the *Examen* of *Le Cid* (1660), Corneille points out how even a measure of adherence to the unity of place may result in improbabilities as noticeable as those which the rule strives to efface. He says he had to lay the scene in Seville, so as to enable the Moors to invade then and there; that whereas in the romance Rodrigue goes to fight them on the frontier, in the play they seem to descend on Seville for the express purpose of being beaten. Again, though everything takes place in the one town, it was impossible to represent everything as taking place in the same spot in that town. The scene of Don Diègue's lyrical monologue (I. iv), which follows the insult which he received in the quarrel, must either take place in the open street, or else abruptly shift to his own house—either of which involves artificialities. The vague setting was

which may well have been of the type used for the original production of *Le Cid*. See p. 89 of H. C. Lancaster's edition of the *Mémoire* (Paris, 1920). In case the phrase 'presque sans changer de face' may seem ambiguous, we may point out that Scudéry can hardly have been advocating scene-changes in the ordinary sense, since, as the *Mémoire* shows, it was very seldom that the individual façades of a multiple setting were changed during the course of a play. Instances of the latter appear in Hardy's *Le Cintre*, and in Mairet's *Criseïde et Arimant* (1626)—'Le dit tombeau et l'autel ne paroissent qu'au cinquiesme acte'.

designed as an escape from these difficulties, and Corneille
contends that when the play is acted, the interest of the
audience is sufficiently engaged by the pathos of the scenes
and the conflicting emotions of the characters not to
require representational scenery. The vague setting was,
of course, eminently suited to Corneille's intellectual
drama, but the pedantry of the critics and the preference
of a spectacle-loving audience combined to delay for many
years its regular appearance.

La Mesnardière, who discusses *décor simultané* more
fully than any other of our critics, probably had Corneille's
recent inexact settings in mind (though he does not
directly refer to them) when he censures the practice in
his *Poétique* (1639). It is somewhat surprising to find a
critic who in other respects is such a typical exponent of
the neo-classic creed adhering so doggedly to the old
system of scenery. On account of the insight into actual
conditions which they provide, his injunctions concerning
the disposition of the scenery may be quoted at length:

'La scène . . . désignant pour l'ordinaire une ville tout
entière, souvent un petit pays, et quelquefois une maison, il
faut de nécessité qu'elle change d'autant de faces qu'elle
marque d'endroits divers, qu'elle ne découvre pas un
jardin, ni une forêt, pour la scène d'une action qui s'est
passée dans le palais, et que, même en ce palais, elle ne
fasse pas voir dans l'appartement du roi ce qui doit avoir
été fait dans le cabinet de la reine. Si la chose a été
faite à la côte de la mer, il faut nécessairement que la scène
soit maritime en quelqu'une de ses façades, de peur que, s'il ne
paraissait pas quelque trace manifeste du voisinage de la mer,
le spectateur ne conçût, au désavantage du poète et contre son
intention, que la mer est fort loin de là, puisqu'on n'en voit
point le rivage. Si l'Avanture s'est passée moitié dans le
Palais d'un Roi en plusieurs appartements, et moitié hors de
sa maison en beaucoup d'endroits différents; il faut que le

grand du Théatre, le προσκήνιον des Grecs, je veux dire cette largeur qui limite le parterre serve pour tous les dehors où ces choses ont été faites; et que les Renfondrements soient divisés en plusieurs chambres, par les divers Frontispices, Portaux, Colonnes, ou Arcades.'

The whole space occupying the centre of the stage and the proscenium, in other words, should be taken to represent the immediate foreground of the particular piece of scenery temporarily brought into play. He continues, showing his aversion to vague settings:

'Car il faut que les spectateurs distinguent, par ces différences, que la diversité des endroits ou les particularités que le Poëte aura démeslées, seront exactement depeintes, et que les Distinctions de Scène empeschent que l'on ne trouve de la confusion en ces Lieux, qui embarrasse l'Auditeur, et qui seule soit capable de gaster le plus bel Ouvrage, et de le rendre ridicule.'

The object of the strict place rule, with its limitation to a single scene, was to create in the minds of the audience an illusion of being present at a chosen spot in order to watch all that might befall there. La Mesnardière, we may suppose, conceiving this to be impracticable owing to the scenic conventions of his time, argues as above in order to extract the largest possible amount of *vraisemblance* from the scenery with which he has to deal. He felt obliged, however, to pay some deference to the plain prohibition contained in the rule, so he limits the extent of his *mise-en-scène* thus far:

'Le Poëte ne doit jamais transporter sa scène à des climats différents; il faut la borner, pour sa plus grande étendue, par celle d'un petit pays, de qui les divers endroits communiquent en peu de temps.'

Sarasin, we know, had read La Mesnardière's treatise before he wrote his own *Discours de la Tragédie* (1639).

He does not directly criticize his friend's views on the unity of place, but it is clear that he disagrees with them. In tracing the rise of the regular drama, he points out that Hardy, though he 'raised Tragedy from the streets and from the scaffoldings of the cross-roads', was yet notoriously negligent of the unity of place in his plays, in many of which places as far apart as Naples and Cracow are represented on the stage together. He considers that the poets of the present day have improved in this respect, but are not not yet quite correct. They confine their scene, it is true, to one town, but not to one spot in that town. He disapproves of the ambulatory stage which a blind adherence to the *décor simultané* results in; the scene, he says, becomes like a 'common-room', and one does not know whether the actors are supposed to be in their houses or in the streets. But there is a method, he says, whereby the requirements of the place rule may be fulfilled without materially altering the existing stage convention. It is that which is employed in de Scudéry's *L'Amour Tyrannique*. This play, though it contains many adventurous incidents, has its scene laid in one composite spot; for Tyridate 'plante ses pavillons au pied de ces rampars'. One side of the stage is taken up with a bastion of the town of Amasie, on the other side are the tents of Tyridate. Imitation of this play is, as we have seen, Sarasin's panacea for dramatic irregularities, but it is doubtful whether the happy combination in its setting of propinquity and mutual seclusion would be afforded by more than a few plots.

D'Aubignac, as we should expect, is stricter and more dogmatic on this subject than any of the foregoing critics. It may be that he is referring to *L'Amour Tyrannique* when he points out that even when a 'probable spot' has been chosen and preserved unchanged, the poet must not shirk the consequences which the choice of that spot involves: 'One of our Modern Poets fell into a great error of this kind, having placed a Bastion upon the stage, and having afterwards caused the town to be taken by that Bastion, which was never seen to be either attacked or defended.' He vigorously exposes other common errors; 'the mistake of those who suppose in one side of the stage one part of the town, as for example, the Louvre, and on the other side another part, as the Place Royale; thinking by this fine invention to preserve the Unity of Place',[1] whereas this device, perhaps pardonable if there were no houses intervening, is monstrous if there are; and 'I desire the Reader to consider, that if the Poet did represent by his stage all the places and rooms of a palace, or all the streets of a town, he should make the spectators see not only all that happened in his story, but all that was done besides in that palace, or in the town; for there is no reason to hinder the Spectators from seeing all that, nor why they should see one thing sooner than another, . . . to which it cannot be answered that to mark the different apartments there may be *Curtains* shut and drawn; for these curtains are fit for nothing, but to toss their Inventors in, like dogs in a blanket'.[2]

D'Aubignac is successful in reconciling the existing settings with *vraisemblance* and the extremity of the rule. As to the latter, he is precise: 'The Place where the first actor, who opens the play, is supposed to be, ought to be the same to the end of the play.' He maintains that when

---

[1] Probably a tilt at Corneille's *Le Menteur* (1643). For the indication in the play of these localities cf. I. iv, v, II. v, xii, and V. vii, x, S.D.

[2] This indicates that during a play, curtains were drawn over those sections of the *décor simultané* which were not in use. To get as near as this to successive scenes and yet not to adopt them, shows how strongly established was the traditional setting.

we see it written that the scene is at Aulis or Argos, it
does not mean that where the actors appear represents the
whole town, but merely that the whole action, including
that which takes place behind the scenes, is confined to
Aulis or Argos. The proscenium can only represent some
open place of ordinary extent; 'as far as a man can see
another walk, and yet not know perfectly that 'tis he'. He
advises, accordingly, that the poet will do well to determine
beforehand where his best scene is to be enacted; having
done so, he will have to accommodate the rest of his play
to that one spot of ground, and whatever cannot be represented there that is necessary must be circumvented by
reported action; this, moreover, must be done in a likely
enough time for the actor to have been there and back
again. All this would result, on the stage, in a setting akin
to that of the Serlio scene, with the important exception
that D'Aubignac's façades were both 'practicable' and
capable of being varied in a most spectacular manner
without change of place. Thus, the poet 'might feign a
Palace upon the sea side, forsaken, and left to be inhabited
by poor Fishermen; a Prince landing, or being cast away
there, might adorn it with rich furniture; after this it
might by some accident be set on fire; and then behind
it the sea might appear, upon which one might represent
a sea fight; so that in all the five changes of the stage, the
Unity of Place would still be ingeniously preserved'. All
this ingenuity was nominally in the service of 'Illusion',
yet we cannot but believe that in effect D'Aubignac's
transformation scenes were both unwieldy and rococo.
M. Rigal[1] sums up the matter by saying: 'C'est que toute
cette génération avait été formée à l'école de Hardy, et
qu'elle avait beau y faire effort, elle ne pouvait se défaire
des habitudes d'esprit qu'elle y avait contractées.'

[1] *Le Théâtre français avant la période classique*, 1901.

It was Corneille who first advocated a break with the old settings, and the changes which he wished to introduce are indicated, as we have seen, in his *Examen* of *Le Cid*. In the *Discours des Trois Unités* he elaborates these proposals. They are to some extent conditioned by the fact that pseudo-realistic scenes, however many were allowed to a play, distracted attention from the 'drama of the mind', which was his own mode of composition. But, like his views on the unity of time, his proposals are chiefly the outcome of a desire to attain a more satisfactory compromise between expediency and 'Illusion' than had hitherto been reached. He is still pledged to 'Illusion' (his remedies if considered by themselves might indicate otherwise), for, while admitting that the rule is not discoverable in either Aristotle or Horace, he approves of it for the reason that 'since the theatre is stationary, it is less improbable if the scene should be so too'.

Accordingly he decides that the action of a play should be confined to one town, but that two or three separate spots within that town may be represented. In order to atone for this latitude, there are two conditions. The scene must never be changed within the act, and there must be no change of scenery, though there is of scene; the individual scenes, moreover, should never be named, but merely the general place, such as 'Paris' or 'Rome'. On the stage this results in what he terms a *lieu théâtral*, a general theatrical place—'no single apartment, but a place on to which the apartments of the various characters open, and where each character may be presumed to speak with the same secrecy as in his own room'. Thus no longer could such an anomaly as Don Diègue's street soliloquy occur. It is almost certain that the setting for *Le Cid* recorded by Laurent in 1678 as *une chambre à quatre portes* is the stage representation of Corneille's *lieu théâtral*. By means of some such stationary setting the unity of place was in appearance strictly maintained, though in fact each Act could take place in a different part of a city. As Corneille puts it: 'Cela aiderait à tromper l'auditeur, qui, ne voyant rien qui lui marquât la diversité des lieux, ne s'en apercevroit pas, a moins d'une réflexion malicieuse et critique.'

It may be wondered that Corneille's idealization of place did not provoke the 'malicious' censure of some critic of D'Aubignac's severity, for his scheme is but an ingenious makeshift, and evades the difficulties which playwrights and critics had so long encumbered themselves with. We may surmise, however, that by 1660 (the date of the *Trois Discours*) it had become recognized that there was no clear way out of these difficulties, and, therefore, a plan which combined an outward and visible conformity with freedom from precise considerations of place was readily acquiesced in, especially when it was suggested by a critic of Corneille's conscientiousness and eminence, and when it was found so suited to the intellectual drama which he had popularized. Moreover, the *chambre à quatre portes* still retained some of the *décor simultané* convention (the four doors being the survivals of the separate *mansions*) and so was a less drastic innovation than, for instance, successive scenes would have been. The Mahelot-Laurent *Mémoire* shows, it is true, that multiple settings were still in use during the latter half of the seventeenth century. But they did not appear frequently, and their continuance must be attributed not to the conservatism of critics but to the existence of serviceable or easily adaptable 'sets' of the old scenery. The acceptance of Corneille's scheme prepared the way for the *Palais à volonté*, which was the setting used for Racine's plays, and which prevailed until the middle of the eighteenth century.

In order to make clear the different conception of the unity of place which prevailed in England, it is necessary to give some account of the system or systems of staging employed during the Restoration. As has been previously mentioned, English critics discussed the unity of place far less, and gave the playwright a correspondingly greater freedom in the matter than did the French. Broadly speaking, the reason for this is that the Restoration playwrights continued to use the scheme of changing settings which on the eve of the closing of the theatres was being speedily perfected by Inigo Jones, and which was then used both in masques and the private theatres. It was so manifestly superior to the other types of scenery that there was little inclination to revert to the single stationary setting out of respect for the opinions of foreign critics. It is true that occasional experiments with the French ideas were made; with *décor simultané*, as in Flecknoe's *Demoiselles à la Mode*, with Sarasin's composite scene, as in Thomas Stapylton's *Hero and Leander* (1668), and, later, with Corneille's *lieu théâtral*, as in Congreve's *Double-Dealer* (1694). But, for the most part, plays were presented with successive scenes, and we have evidence, moreover, of the admiration which they aroused in French visitors, who had seen nothing of the kind in their own theatre. Thus Samuel de Sorbière, in his *Relation d'une voyage en Angleterre* (1669), writing of his visit to the King's Theatre [1] in 1663, says, 'Le théâtre est fort beau, couvert d'un tapis verd, et la scène y est toute libre, avec beaucoup de changemens et des perspectives'. Similarly, M. de Monconys, in the same year, records of this playhouse that 'Les changemens de Théâtre et les machines sont fort ingénieusement inventées et exécutées'.

---

[1] The Theatre Royal, Bridges Street, Covent Garden. It was burnt in 1672, and was replaced by the Theatre Royal, in Drury Lane, which was built by Wren, and opened in 1674.

The early years of the Restoration witnessed the transition in the theatre from illustrative to realistic scenery. Both types were employed by Inigo Jones (the latter, however, only at the end of his career), and both were derived by him from Italian example, such as prevailed at the Teatro Farnese at Parma. The earlier type is exemplified in his designs for the masque of *Florimène* (1635). In this, the stage was provided with a series of two-sided 'flats', or side-wings, which remained unaltered in spite of frequent changes of backcloth. A similar scheme appears in Webb's designs for the original production of *The Siege of Rhodes* (Part I) at Rutland House, in 1656. The wings, which remained unchanged throughout the play, represent a series of rocky prominences, behind which is a varying background intended to illustrate the action rather than to provide a definite setting for it.[1] Thus the scenery for the 'Second Entry' consists of 'A prospect of Rhodes beleaguer'd at Sea and Land', yet the action of this part of the play takes place within the city. Groups of figures, armies, and the like were sometimes painted on the backcloths of such scenery regardless of the strange contrast they made with the actors on the stage. Webb's plans and sketches for the production at Whitehall of Orrery's *Mustapha* (1666) show that the play was performed with the same type of setting. The foreground, made up of side-wings which were arched to meet on top, was permanent, and represented a pillared arcade with a vaulted roof, while in the background were four movable shutters, which probably depicted, as the text requires, various spots in the town of Buda and in the Turkish lines outside.

[1] Prof. E. J. Dent, *Foundations of English Opera* (1928), cap. iii, suggests that Webb would possibly have employed changing side-wings, sliding in grooves, had it not been for the smallness of the Rutland House stage, of which D'Avenant complains in his preface to the play.

Antiquated and unsatisfactory as such a system may appear to be now, it had at least one advantage over the stage arrangements of the Elizabethan public theatre. By causing dramatists to think more carefully than they had done about place, it compelled them to tighten up the structure of their plays; a reform which was urgently needed during the decadence of the Elizabethan drama. The moving of the scene to an impossibly distant clime would be more noticeable than formerly, and a succession of short scenes involving continual change of place would look awkward if accompanied with changes of scenery, and would be incongruous without them. All this called for a closer co-ordination of material. It is true that during the first few years of the Restoration dramatists continued to provide their plays with swift changes of scene, in the Elizabethan manner. Thus Tuke does so in *The Adventures of Five Hours* (1663), in spite of his respect for the unity of place; for though the general scene of the play is 'Seville', there are abrupt changes between 'Don Henrique's house', 'a garden', and 'the city' in the third act.

Gradually, however, playwrights came to adapt their plays to the new conditions, with the result that in practice a loose unity of place became the rule rather than the exception. The change was further facilitated by the adoption, about 1664, of a more realistic kind of scenery. This type was modelled, no doubt, on the later productions of Inigo Jones, as appears from the close resemblance between Wren's designs for the stage of the Theatre Royal, Drury Lane, and Inigo Jones's for the masque of *Salmacida Spolia* (1640). In both, the side-wings are flat, not two-sided, and run in grooves, so that when they are drawn off the stage other side-wings behind them are revealed, corresponding to the changes of backcloth. It was by this method that the elaborate transformation scenes of Dryden and Howard's *The Indian Queen* (first acted January 1663/4) were effected, such as from the prison of the fourth act to the spectacular setting of the fifth, where 'The Scene opens, and discovers the Temple of the Sun, all of Gold, and four Priests in habits of white and red Feathers, attending by a bloody Altar, as ready for Sacrifice'.[1] Though the adoption of this type of scenery did not necessarily imply fewer changes of scene, it facilitated the observance of the unity of place by furthering the principle of illusion.

One feature of the stage, however, for long prevented the attainment of complete verisimilitude. This was the semicircular 'apron', which extended some seventeen feet beyond the proscenium into the midst of the pit. It was a survival of the Elizabethan platform stage, and was retained because, like the latter, it gave the actors the opportunity of intimacy with the audience. Here the leading characters of the heroic play could strut and vociferate with more dominating effect, and the nuances and asides of the comedy of manners could be more delicately (or indelicately) observed than on the stage proper. In front of the proscenium arch on either side were doors which opened directly on to the apron. Entrances and exits were made through these as frequently as through the doors and archways of the scenery, and hence, however realistic it might be, the scenery frequently tended to become a mere illustrative background. Moreover, the curtain was only

---

[1] The novelty of the scenic method is indicated in the prologue, e.g.

> Shows may be found that never yet were seen;
> 'Tis hard to find such Wit as ne'er has been.

Cf. also Evelyn, 5 Feb. 1664; 'I saw *The Indian Queene* acted, a tragedie well written, so beautified with rich scenes as the like had never ben seene here, or haply (except rarely) elsewhere on a mercenary [i.e. public] theater.'

lowered at the end of a play, so that scene changes took place in full view of the audience.[1] Sometimes the scenes were changed while the actors remained on the apron, so that without moving they were supposed to be transported to another spot.

In view of these considerations, it is not surprising that the prevailing French interpretation of the unity of place should have met with so little favour in England. The extreme reverence for illusion which restricted the action of a play to one spot of ground was scoffed at by most English critics. But while they were justified, no doubt, in rejecting French theory as being incompatible with English stage conditions, they were slow to make allowance for the fact that it had been evolved to suit the stage requirements of the Hôtel de Bourgogne. It is possible, of course, that they were not aware of the peculiarities of the French stage.[2] But even Dryden (Neander), whose words on the subject indicate a knowledge of French

[1] On the French stage portions of the *décor simultané* were sometimes changed during the course of the action, but the curtain was not lowered to conceal these changes. It is noteworthy that this was due not so much to lack of inventiveness as to the fact that the use of a curtain was looked on as a confession of failure on the part of the machinists. This attitude is shown clearly in a note of Perrault, in his translation of Vitruvius (*Les dix livres D'Architecture de Vitruve*, 1684, Bk. V, cap. vii). After describing the various methods of scene-changing employed by the Ancients, he remarks 'Il est néanmoins difficile de croire que ces changemens fussent aussi prompts que ceux de nos Théâtres, qui se font presque en un moment et sans qu'on s'en apperçoive: car nous lisons que lorsque les Anciens vouloient changer les ornemens de leur scene; ils tiroient un rideau qui estoit appellé *Siparium*, derrière lequel ils faisoient à loisir ce qui estoit necessaire au changement'.

[2] *Décor simultané* was not uncommon in England in the early seventeenth century; it was used occasionally at court and at the universities, and, more often, by the boy companies. But a Restoration critic who bore this in mind might well not realize that in the country of its origin this setting was prescribed by tradition rather than adopted for the sake of convenience.

theatrical conditions, is too much prejudiced against French theory to allow that the latter was inevitably affected by the former.

The rule, as might be expected, was almost invariably interpreted by English writers as a general unity of place incorporating a variety of scenes within it. Thus any number of places within the bounds of a city could be represented.

Occasionally we find a critic disapproving, like Corneille, of the practice of changing the scene within the act,[1] but in general the dramatist was given freedom within the above limits. Sir Samuel Tuke in his play *The Adventures of Five Hours* (Jan. 1662/3) employed, as we have seen, many changes of place within the act, but in his prologue he takes pride in showing how he has observed the unity of place.

> Here's a fine play indeed, to lay the scene
> In three houses of the same town, O mean!
> Why, we have several plays,[2] where I defy
> The devil to tell where the scene does lie:
> Sometimes in Greece, and then they make a step
> To Transylvania, thence at one leap
> To Greece again; this shows a ranging brain,
> Which scorns to be confined t'a town in Spain.

A respect for the same sort of loose unity of place is to be seen in Shadwell's preface to *The Sullen Lovers* (1668), though in his play, unlike Tuke's, the scenes are preserved unbroken.

[1] e.g. Dryden, in the preface to *Troilus and Cressida* (1679), who maintains that he has adjusted the scenes of the play so that 'there is a coherence of them with one another, and a dependence on the main design; no leaping from Troy to the Grecian tents, and thence back again, in the same act, but a due proportion of time allowed for every motion'.

[2] The early date of Tuke's play renders it probable that his reference is chiefly to pre-Restoration plays.

Dryden's reflections on the subject, as is generally the case, far excel those of his contemporaries in range and perspicacity. In the *Essay of Dramatic Poesy*, though the discourse is 'sceptical', and though Neander is non-committal, the author's attitude emerges clearly enough to enable us to summarize it as follows: The rule if slavishly followed is likely to become an intolerable evil, and it is apt to place an arbitrary restriction on the poet's choice of subject-matter. It is far better that a dramatist should infringe the unity of place in his play than that he should spoil a fine theme by cramping the movements of his characters or by forcing them into an unlikely proximity. On the other hand the rule, if intelligently applied, may prove an additional refinement to a play (as in Ben Jonson's *Silent Woman*, in which the scene 'lies all within the compass of two houses in London'), for on the whole its principle is sound. It is true that it was not a written law in ancient times, and did not become one 'till in our age the French Poets first made it a precept of the stage'.[1] But the Ancients certainly observed it in practice, and in these matters they are infallible guides.

In addition to the foregoing, which briefly represents the issue of the discussion concerning the theory of the rule, we may refer to two speeches in the *Essay* which bear on the staging question. One of these is Neander's well-known taunt at the absurdities which he considers the French dramatists are forced to commit owing to their servile adherence to the letter of the law, particularly the practice of changing the scene without altering the scenery: 'In this ridiculous manner the play goes forward, the stage

---

[1] D'Aubignac (op. cit.) maintains that he is the first to treat of the subject at all thoroughly, so perhaps Dryden took him at his word. Actually both La Mesnardière and Sarasin had preceded him, not to reckon the Italian critics.

being never empty all the while; so that the street, the window, the houses, and the closet are made to walk about, and the persons to stand still.' He sarcastically inquires whether it is not more easy to write a regular French play in this manner than to write an irregular English one, but does not pause to reflect (or probably finds it inconvenient to do so) that the device which he ridicules was patiently evolved by Corneille as a means of evading an unusually troublesome stage dilemma. Dryden's words also seem unfortunate in that they serve to remind us that the stationary actors and moving scenes might sometimes be seen in actuality on the English apron stage, though from another passage in the same speech it may be gathered that he was averse to this slovenly practice.[1]

The second speech is that of Crites, and, coming from the most correct of Dryden's four critics, it enables us to see the more clearly how Dryden preferred a reasonably controlled system of changing scenes to the barren unchanged setting prescribed by the over-punctilious interpreters of *vraisemblance*. Crites points out that since the stage on which a play is represented 'is but one and the same place, it is unnatural to conceive it many,—and those far distant from one another', but adds, 'I will not deny but, by the variation of painted scenes, the fancy, which in these cases will contribute to its own deceit, may sometimes imagine it several places, with some appearance of probability; yet it still carries the greater likelihood of truth if those places be supposed so near each other as in the same town or city; which may all be comprehended under the larger denomination of one place.'

[1] i.e. 'By tying themselves strictly to the Unity of Place, and unbroken scenes, they [the French] are forced many times to omit some beauties which cannot be shown where the act began; but might, if the scene were interrupted, *and the stage cleared for the persons to enter in another place*.'

With such half-measures Sir Robert Howard, in his animosity towards Dryden and the 'Rules', would have nothing to do, and he contends (to requote his words in the preface to *The Duke of Lerma*) that "tis as impossible for one Stage to present two houses, or two Rooms truly, as two countries or kingdoms; and as impossible that five hours or four and twenty hours should be two hours and a half, as that a thousand hours or years should be less than what they are; or the greatest part of time to be comprehended in the less; for being all impossible, they are none of them nearest the truth, or nature, of what they present, for Impossibilities are all equal, and admit no degrees'. Undismayed by this parade of logicality, Dryden in his reply, *The Defence of an Essay of Dramatic Poesy*, took the opportunity of giving his precise opinion as to how the rule should be followed: 'there is a latitude to be allowed to it—as several places in the same town or city, or places adjacent to each other in the same country, which may all be comprehended under the larger denomination of one place; yet with this restriction, that the nearer and fewer those imaginary places are, the greater resemblance they will have to truth'.

When Dryden comes to grips with Howard over the question of 'Illusion', he cannot, for all the persuasiveness of his eloquence, help betraying the fallacy which was inherent in the unity of place; the fallacy concerning the behaviour of the imagination—which he asserts 'will be less *shocked* with the appearance of two rooms in the same house, or two houses in the same city, than with two distant cities in the same country, or two remote countries in the same universe'—the precarious assumption that a shift, for instance, from the council chamber of one palace to the council chamber of another is more incredible than one from the council chamber to the kitchen of the same palace. Had the supporters of the unity of place but contented themselves with advocating it as a means of regularizing the construction of plays (which consideration no doubt unconsciously impelled Dryden to accept it) rather than as a means of securing a dubious illusion, much needless stress and effort would have been spared to critics and playwrights both in France and England; though in England, owing to an independent temper and favouring stage conditions, it resolved itself in practice, as we shall see, into the admission of any sort of spectacular display [1] within the bounds of one vague city.

[1] Especially in plays which were produced at the Dorset Garden Theatre, which was renowned for the ostentation of its settings.

CHAPTER FOUR

VIOLENT ACTION. BOMBAST

1. VIOLENT ACTION

WE have touched on this subject in the Introduction, but we must now pursue it further in order to exhibit the trend of critical opinion in the matter. In dealing with the question of violent action on the stage, neo-classic criticism was confronted with two facts which called for some reconciliation. First there was the fact (sometimes questioned, but in the main unchallenged) that in the Greek drama murders and all scenes of violence were relegated to behind the scenes. Secondly, there was the statement of the arch-authority, Horace, which though it prohibited the exhibition on the stage of the unduly horrible or of the ordinarily incredible, yet encouraged the representation of action rather than the relation of it. To quote the passage in the *Ars Poetica*:

'The theatre proceeds either by action, or by narration of action. Things heard affect the soul less vividly than what is put before the faithful eyes, and what the spectator administers to himself. But you will not bring on the stage what ought to be done behind the scenes, and you will keep out of sight much which can be presently narrated. Let not Medea slaughter her sons in public, nor wicked Atreus cook the human joint, nor Procne be turned into a bird, Cadmus into a snake. If you show me anything of this kind, I disbelieve it, and feel disgust.'[1]

As was natural, there was considerable diversity of opinion among critics, not only as to whether the theory of Horace outweighed in importance the practice of the Greeks, but also as regards the amount of action that might be shown, under Horace's ruling. The English heroic dramatists'

[1] Trans. Saintsbury.

profited by this uncertainty among the critics to the extent
of continuing fearlessly the Elizabethan practice of introducing scenes of violence in their plays, which scenes were
almost as much favoured by Restoration as by Elizabethan
audiences.

While Italian critics, such as Castelvetro, were generally
content to favour the adoption of the Greek practice
merely in order to preserve stage decorum, the French
usually inquired more closely into the matter. Thus Corneille (though he made no attempt to evolve a rule) points
out in his *Examen* of *Le Cid* how he has complied with
the first part of Horace's precept. The blow which the
Comte gives Don Diègue in the quarrel scene (I. iv) is, he
contends, permissible,[1] since the witnessing of such an
affront given to a venerable old man enlists the sympathy
of the audience on the latter's behalf. On the other hand,
the duel in which Rodrigue kills le Comte is enacted off
the stage, for fear of detracting sympathy from the hero.
Corneille does not venture to say, however, whether death-
scenes which are likely to have the right effect on the
audience are admissible on the stage. Nor does Sarasin
attempt to define how much may be exhibited; he contents
himself with pointing out that though pity and terror are
the true ends of tragedy, there must be no violent means
employed to arouse these; 'the scene should not be
drenched in blood'.

La Mesnardière, on the other hand, is explicit on all
these points, and, though he endeavours to legislate for
the drama in the matter, he imposes as few restrictions on
it as he thinks compatible with *les bienséances*. He maintains that Castelvetro was mistaken in wishing to banish
all dramatic murders from the scene, and says that of all
ideas which strike the mind through the medium of the

[1] Voltaire thought it indefensible.

senses, those which enter through the eyes are the most effective. Nevertheless, he considers some spectacles inadmissible. He divides spectacles into three kinds, which he terms *spectacles généreux*, *spectacles horribles*, and *spectacles pleins de hasard*. The last kind, involving incidents such as the dismemberment of Hippolytus, cannot be represented on the stage without endangering the actors. The second type includes scenes of torture and execution, which are too detestable to witness; moreover, they are banned by Horace—*ne pueros coram populo Medea trucidet*. La Mesnardière holds that both these kinds of events should be narrated on the stage by a witness, and he provides a model example of a 'Narration d'une avanture horrible, faite par une Personne bien née'. *Spectacles généreux*, however, are legitimate, and should on no account be hid from view. Typical examples are: the virtuous repentance of the tragic character, who, having committed a crime in the heat of passion which momentarily blinded him, cannot survive the grief of remorse, and dies in expiation; or the courageous despair of an heroic person who, having lost the object of his ambition or affection, puts an end to his life. 'Et certes ces beaux Homicides ont toutes les qualités qui produisent les deux passions que demandent la Tragédie.' Two conditions, however, are attached to *spectacles généreux*: there must not be scenes of general carnage on the stage, nor must violent deaths, however noble, be too frequent on it.

D'Aubignac, as we have seen, was partial to spectacular scenes; and his fondness for them is the cause of his inconsistency on the subject of violent action. A passing allusion which he makes to the latter in the early part of his treatise (Book I) shows him approving of the principle of an actor 'making recitals of things that ought to be known and yet ought not to appear', while he takes care to point out that

in the Greek drama, contrary to what was sometimes supposed, incidents like the killing of Clytemnestra were
executed just off the stage. When, however, he comes to
catalogue the various types of stage spectacles which may
be shown (Book III), he mentions two kinds which seem
to admit a wide diversity of sensational happening; one is
'Of Actions; when the spectacle depends principally upon
some extraordinary fact, as that one should throw himself
headlong from a tower, or from a rock in the sea', and the
other is 'Of mingled Things and Actions; as a Sea-Fight,
where at the same time is the sea and ships, and men
acting upon it'.

When Saint-Evremond discusses the matter, we are
conscious of an entirely different background, resulting
from the fact that in the interval between D'Aubignac's
Pratique and Saint-Evremond's essay *Sur les Tragédies*
(1677), plays, and particularly the settings of plays, had
become more classicized. It was less likely that scenes of
violence would be condoned within a fixed formal setting
than on a stage which had the irregular *décor simultané*.
Saint-Evremond, discussing the English drama, looks on
its exhibition of scenes of violence as a curiosity. English
tragedies, he says, ignore *la bienséance*; the eyes of the
spectators are eager for spectacles of cruelty, of murders,
and bleeding bodies. To make use of narrative for these
incidents, as we do, would be to deprive the people of what
affects them most keenly. But, he continues, while we justly
reproach their drama for appealing too much to the senses,
we must not ignore their complaint that our tragedies go
to the opposite extreme, and are not strong enough;[1] 'il
manque à nos sentiments quelque chose d'assez profond'.

[1] The essay was written in London, and it is not unlikely that he
was influenced by Dryden's analogous remarks on the subject in the
Essay of Dramatic Poesy.

On turning to English criticism we find that, while the licence of the drama in the matter of violent action was usually condemned, there was but little attempt to formulate rules on the subject, since it was recognized that it was not likely that they would be adhered to. Sir Robert Howard, however, was averse to the prohibition of violent action,[1] chiefly out of fear lest the English drama should adopt the chilly decorum of the French classical stage. He shows how Horace emphasized the importance of the appeal to the eye, and contends that the convention of the Ancients in concealing deaths and the like was mainly determined by the traditional subject-matter which their drama employed; 'it was impossible to show Medea throwing old mangled Aeson into her Age-renewing cauldron, or to present the scattered limbs of Hippolytus upon the stage, or to show Hercules burning upon his own Funeral Pile'. He maintains that 'whoever chuses a subject that inforces him to Relations, is to blame', for at that rate 'a whole Play might be as well related as acted'.

Nevertheless, scenes of death and tumult on the English stage, however necessary to the plot, generally succeeded in evoking the derision of a section of the audience. Samuel Chappuzeau (*Le Théâtre françois*, 1674), describing his visit to the English theatres, says:

'Estant à Londres il y a six ans, j'y vis deux fort belles troupes des comédiens, l'une du Roy, et l'autre du Duc D'York, et je fus à deux représentations, à la mort de Montezume Roy de Mexique,[2] et à celle de Mustapha, qui se défendoit vigoureusement sur le Théâtre contre les muets qui le

---

[1] *Address to the Reader*, prefixed to the 1665 folio ed. of his *Four New Plays*.

[2] i.e. Dryden's *The Indian Emperor* (1665), in which Montezuma, the heroic emperor, stabs himself on the stage in the fifth act. The whole play, however, is full of stage deaths and fights.

vouloient étrangler;[1] ce qui faisoit rire, et ce que les François n'auraient representé que dans un recit.'

Lisideius, in the *Essay of Dramatic Poesy*, bears witness to the same effect: 'I have observed that in all our tragedies, the audience cannot forbear laughing when the actors are to die; it is the most comic part of the whole play.' He points out the absurdity of representing an army by a drum with five men behind it, and commends the French for their avoidance of these crude displays; though he disagrees with the idea that the French produce no action on the stage—'every alteration or crossing of a design, every new-sprung passion, and turn of it, is a part of the action, and much the noblest, except we conceive nothing to be action till the players come to blows'. The types of scenes of violence which should be avoided, he concludes, are those involving horror, tumult, and theatrical improbability; apart from these the dramatist may have freedom to represent what he pleases, and to provide for the appeal to the eye which Horace considered so important.

Dryden's reply is interesting, since it shows his respect for the reasonableness of the theory conflicting with allegiance to his own successful type of heroic play, which flagrantly abused the rule. Thus he approves of the French custom of resorting to narration for what would be either 'incredible or undecent' on the stage, and admits that Ben Jonson set a worthy example in causing the deaths of Sejanus and Catiline to be 'related'. But he alleges that the demands of the English audience are too insistent to be neglected—'whether custom has so insinuated itself into our countrymen, or nature has so formed them to fierceness, I know not; but they will scarcely suffer

[1] The incident takes place in the fifth act of Orrery's play of that name. We shall have more to say on the subject when examining the play in detail.

combats and other objects of horror to be taken from them'
—and to some extent he inclines to their point of view himself: 'For my part I can with as great ease persuade myself
that the blows are given in good earnest, as I can that they
who strike them are kings or princes'; and he concludes,
somewhat evasively, 'if we are to be blamed for showing
too much of the action, the French are as faulty for discovering too little of it'.

It may be said that, for the most part, Restoration
theorists were commendably open-minded on this topic,
and were prepared to see the appropriateness both of
Desdemona being smothered on the stage and of Cordelia
being killed off it. Nevertheless, many an Elizabethan play
had been spoilt by scenes of 'horror' and 'tumult', and the
critics were right in desiring to impose some restriction on
the contemporary drama, which was rapidly approaching
the state of affairs depicted in the last scene of Fielding's
Tragedy of Tragedies.[1] Fielding's footnote to this scene is
as follows:

'No scene, I believe, ever received greater Honours than
this. It was applauded by several encores, a word very unusual
in Tragedy—and it was very difficult for the actors to escape
without a second slaughter. This I take to be a lively assurance

---

[1] III. x. Noodle comes to deliver the fatal news that Tom Thumb
has been swallowed up by a cow. Having done so, he says:

Her Majesty the Queen is in a swoon.

Queen. Not so much in a swoon, but I have still strength to reward the
Messenger of ill News.   [*Kills Noodle.*
Noodle. Oh! I am slain.
Cleora. My Lover's kill'd, I will revenge him so.   [*Kills the Queen.*
Huncamunca. My Mamma kill'd! vile Murthress, beware.
                                                        [*Kills Cleora.*
Doodle. This for an old grudge, to thy heart.   [*Kills Huncamunca.*
Mustacha. And this I drive to thine, Oh Doodle! for a new one.
                                                        [*Kills Doodle.*
King. Ha! Murthress vile, take that.   [*Kills Mustacha.*
    And take thou this.   [*Kills himself, and falls.*

of that fierce Spirit of Liberty which remains among us, and which Mr. Dryden in his *Essay of Dramatic Poesy* hath observed—"Whether custom (says he) hath so insinuated itself into our countrymen, or Nature hath so formed them to fierceness, I know not; but they will scarcely suffer combats and other objects of horror to be taken from them".—And indeed I am for having them encouraged in this Martial Disposition: Nor do I believe our victories over the French have been owing to anything more than to those bloody spectacles daily exhibited in our Tragedies, of which the French stage is so entirely clear.'

It obviously misrepresents Dryden's standpoint in the *Essay of Dramatic Poesy*, but Fielding probably read the essay in the light of Dryden's subsequent excesses. The latter were indulged in to win popularity, and Dryden became so accustomed to making a virtue of necessity in the matter, that for a time he convinced himself that violent action of the kind introduced in *The Conquest of Granada* was an essential feature of the heroic play. The scenes of violence in that play were, of course, abundantly satirized in *The Rehearsal*,[1] but by this time Dryden was confident enough to be able to defend them in the following manner:

'Shakespeare used them frequently; and though Jonson shows no battle in his *Catiline*, yet you hear from behind the scenes the sounding of trumpets, and the shouts of fighting armies. But I add farther, that these warlike instruments, and even their presentations of fighting on the stage, are no more than necessary to produce the effects of an heroic play; that is, to raise the imagination of the audience, and to persuade them,

---

[1] e.g. In IV. i, where Bayes says: 'Why, I have design'd a Conquest, that cannot possibly, Igad, be acted in less than a whole week: and I'll speak a bold word, it shall Drum, Trumpet, Shout and Battle, Igad, with any the most warlike Tragedy we have, either ancient or modern.' Cf. also V. i, where Drawcansir intervenes in a stage battle, and in the heat of his ardour kills friend and foe alike.

for the time, that what they behold on the theatre is really performed. The poet is then to endeavour an absolute dominion over the minds of the spectators.

This kind of dominion, however, could not but be transitory, and Dryden perceived that as soon as these scenes lost their power to astonish, the heroic play would be in danger of becoming an outworn form, unless by some means it could be made truer to life. This he eventually decided could best be achieved by submitting reservedly to some form of neo-classic convention, and accordingly he occupied himself with the tenets of the latest school of French criticism, which was led by Rapin and Le Bossu, and heralded in England by Rymer. Their theories did not, it is true, differ strikingly from those of the Mesnardière-D'Aubignac school which Dryden had in earlier days repudiated, and it is certain that he would not have bestowed so much attention on them had the heroic play not urgently needed a new sense of direction.

This it acquired, and was helped to do so by a closer following of the rules, by an avoidance of bombast, and, somewhat later, by the return to blank verse. Of these we are here only concerned with the rule as to violent action. Rapin had singled out this excess as characteristic of the English drama, and had attributed it to the national temperament. Rymer, as we should expect in so ardent an advocate of imitation of the Ancients, wholeheartedly agreed with Rapin's condemnation of the practice, and in his preface to his translation of Rapin (1674) remarked:

'And perhaps it may be true that on our stage are more murders than on all the Theatres in Europe. And they who have not time to learn our language, or be acquainted with our conversation, may there in three hours time behold so much bloodshed as may affright them from the inhospitable shore, as from the Cyclops den. Let our Tragedy-makers consider this, and examine whether it be the People, or their own Caprice that brings this censure on the best natur'd Nation under the sun.'

The above-mentioned work undoubtedly influenced Dryden in his composition of *Aureng-Zebe* (1675); just as Rymer's remarks on the Unities in his *Tragedies of the Last Age* had their effect on *All for Love*. In the present connexion, two things are to be noticed of *Aureng-Zebe*. It is the first of Dryden's heroic plays in which he abstains from the exhibition of violence; the nearest approach to the latter being when at a certain point the empress Nourmahal 'offers to stab' Indamora. We may also instance the sound of clattering weapons which is heard behind the scenes in the fifth act: a device for securing vividness without incurring theatrical improbability, which Dryden commended in Ben Jonson, as we have seen. Secondly, the Epilogue reproduces the drift of Rymer's argument, though in a much more spirited fashion, as the following quotation will show:

> True English hate your Monsieur's paltry arts,
> For you are all silk-weavers in your hearts.
> Bold Britons, at a brave Bear-Garden fray,
> Are roused: and, clattering sticks, cry—Play, play, play!
> Meantime your filthy foreigner will stare,
> And mutters to himself, Ha! gent barbare!
> And, gad, 'tis well he mutters; well for him;
> Our butchers else would tear him limb from limb.
> 'Tis true, the time may come, your sons may be
> Infected with this French civility:
> But this, in after ages will be done:
> Our poet writes a hundred years too soon.
> This age comes on too slow, or he too fast:
> And early springs are subject to a blast!

Dryden, however, was not the only, nor yet the first, heroic dramatist to refrain from the cruder forms of stage violence. From 1672 onwards we find increasing use being made of the device known as 'Discoveries', that is to say, the revealing of dead bodies and the like by drawing aside a 'scene'; the deaths taking place off the stage. By this means the audience were still indulged in their taste for spectacle and sensation, while the requirements of classical decorum were held to be satisfied. It is possible, though not likely, that the playwrights who employed discoveries considered that the ἐξώστρα of the Greek stage supplied the classical precedent for their practice. There were various kinds of discoveries. In ordinary death-scenes, the prostrate bodies of the actors were usually revealed, but scenes of torture and carnage (such as that depicted in one of the 'Sculptures' of Settle's *Empress of Morocco*, 1673), were represented by painted backcloths or shutters. Sometimes the discovery was used, not to conceal action, but to indicate a happening which in any case it would have been impossible to present on the stage. Thus in Banks's *The Destruction of Troy* (1678), Achilles kills Troilus on the stage, but in Act IV 'The scene draws, and discovers Polyxana weeping over the *dragg'd* Body of Troilus'.[1] In general, however, as time went on, violent action grew less frequent on the stage, and this must be attributed partly to the audience's growing sense of fitness, partly to the increasing hostility towards the custom on the part of both French and English critics, which we have attempted briefly to trace.

BOMBAST

Violent Action was an adjunct to the Bombast of the heroic play; the two reached their height together, as in *The Conquest of Granada*, and declined together soon after-

---

[1] Quoted by Lily Campbell, *Scenes and Machines on the English stage*, Cambridge, 1923.

wards. Overstrained rhetoric is usually accounted to be the most characteristic feature of the heroic play, but it must be remembered that the most formidable rants were confined to a short period: that which elapsed between, roughly speaking, the production of *Tyrannic Love* (1669) and of *Aureng-Zebe* (1675). Before this period the language of the heroic play in its scenes of animation resembled that of the French heroic romances, besides being indebted to some extent to the drama of Corneille. Yet even in the early years of the Restoration, when French influence was at its strongest, the English *tirade* had a distinct quality of its own; it was more impetuous, less carefully built up than the French equivalent, it addressed the ear more than the mind. The change-over from moderate to extreme bombast was due to an altered notion of what constituted epic grandeur. In the Romances (which, as we have seen, were considered to be prose epics) exalted standards of honour prevailed, and the chief characters indulged in lengthy discussions of abstract points of conduct. These high-flown discussions, somewhat vitalized to suit the needs of the English stage, were common in the heroic play for a time. Between 1650 and 1660, however, there was a vogue in France for the heroic poem, as the result of which a more indomitable type of heroism became fashionable. The latter was furthered by the emerging Cartesian doctrine of the supremacy of the will, which, as we have seen, was to a large extent responsible in Corneille's drama for the evolution of 'le caractère brillant et élevé d'une habitude vertueuse ou criminelle'.

Dryden welcomed with ardour the dismissal of the 'faultless monster'. His preferences resembled Boileau's in *L'Art Poétique*:

Voulez-vous longtemps plaire et jamais ne lasser?
Faites choix d'un héros propre à m'intéresser,

En valeur éclatant, en vertus magnifique;
Qu'en lui, jusqu'aux défauts, tout se montre héroïque;
Que ses faits surprenants soient dignes d'être ouïs;
Qu'il soit tel que César, Alexandre, ou Louis.

He perceived that once the artificial love and honour code of the Romances was supplanted in the popular esteem by something more vigorous and stirring, the opportunity arose for conferring an individuality on the English heroic drama which it had hitherto largely lacked. Profiting by the new freedom, the heroic play could be endowed with such virility that there would no longer be grounds for the allegation that it was merely an outgrowth of the French classical drama; while at the same time, by becoming more English, it would not cease to share in the European movement for the exaltation of the epic. Actually, Dryden continued to draw on the Romances for his plots and his dramatis personae (especially in *The Conquest of Granada*, as Langbaine was not slow to point out), but little else of the romance element survived, and in the new type of heroic play the place of the valorous personage of high breeding who was excessively bound by scruples of honour was taken by the formidable unscrupulous character, while the protracted casuistical debates gave way to tirades of arrogance and invective. It was, of course, a field for the latter that Dryden chiefly desired; he knew that his strength lay in his ability to elevate a theme, however commonplace, by sheer magnificence of diction, in his command of

The varying verse, the full resounding line,
The long majestic march, and energy divine.

The rodomontades which held sway in the plays of so many playwrights after production of *Tyrannick Love* are a tribute to Dryden's instinct for perceiving the kind of stimulus which would best invigorate the national drama, such as it was.[1]

We may now inquire to what extent contemporary criticism was prepared to admit bombast into the serious drama. French critics, naturally, hardly concerned themselves with the affairs of the English drama; consequently we get few explicit statements from them as to the admissibility or otherwise of the extreme type of bombast. But though the background which they provide is for our purpose mainly relevant to the earlier heroic play, their

[1] As a specimen of the earlier kind of heroics, embodying most, if not all of the above-mentioned characteristics, we may quote a passage in Act II of Orrery's *Mustapha* (acted 1665), where the Queen of Hungary, having sent her infant son to Solyman's camp in order to move Solyman's clemency towards the besieged town of Buda, comes to thank Roxolana (Solyman's queen) for befriending her cause:

Queen. Buda for your acceptance, Madam, waits;

> Your virtue by a charm unlocks her gates.
> *Buda* will bow to you, though it the power
> Proudly withstood of every conqueror.

Rox. Your virtue has a greater wonder wrought;

> It conquers where it but protection sought.
> Above this height, Honour can never get;
> For it does conquer, while it does submit.
> Madam, 'tis only Solyman and you
> Can boast they Roxolana did subdue.

Almost any of Maximin's outbursts in *Tyrannick Love* will serve to illustrate the more flamboyant style; e.g. when (in Act II) Placidius urges Maximin to reflect on the impiety of loving a Christian (St. Catherine):

> Could you forgive it, yet the Gods above
> Would never pardon me a Christian love,

and Maximin replies

> Thou ly'st—there's not a God inhabits there
> But for this Christian would all Heav'n forswear.
> Ev'n Jove would try more shapes her love to win—
> At least, if Jove could love like Maximin.

A passage in *The Rehearsal* (IV.ii) is reminiscent of Maximin's rant, viz.:

Prince Volscius. Were all Gods join'd, they could not hope to mend

> My better choice: for fair Parthenope,
> Gods would, themselves, un-god themselves to see.

remarks also enable us to estimate how far the later heroic play defied accepted views about the kind of diction appropriate for tragedy.

The Academy, in *Les Sentiments*, supplies us with an instance of the pervading influence of the code of etiquette of the Romances, in its aversion to the employment of brusque language in a delicate situation. It blames the 'rudeness' of Rodrigue, in saying to Chimène after he had killed her father,

Je le ferais encore si j'avais à le faire.

and considers that he ought rather to have 'excused himself with humility'; thus showing itself insensible to Rodrigue's passionate sincerity, which is the essence of the scene. In the same way La Mesnardière insists that the dramatist should never let his characters depart from the courtesy of speech which their rank demands. Blasphemy in particular is 'odious to all right-thinking persons'. As to the Deity, so must tragic heroes pay respect to sovereign power: 'il faut révérer dans les Princes cette puissance indépendante dont ils ne sont que la figure: et bien qu'ils soient imparfaits aussi bien que les autres hommes, on doit cacher leurs défauts, parce qu'ils président aux hommes comme Lieutenants de Dieu.' He considers that Homer set a bad example in making Achilles insolent to Agamemnon, he points to the frequent scenes of angry and insulting dialogue in the Greek drama, and deprecates the effronteries which are sometimes witnessed on the modern stage:

'Le Poète ne doit pas douter que tous les honnêtes gens qui fréquentent le Théâtre, ne soient étrangement choquées, lorsqu'ils voyent des sujets outrager leurs Souverains, des Héros faire des rudesses à des Reines et à des Dames, dont les plus simples villageois seraient à peine capables.' [1]

---

[1] It is not improbable that La Mesnardière had Hardy's plays in mind, in making the above statement.

D'Aubignac, actuated by admiration for Corneille's *héros raisonneurs*, maintains that passionate speeches should be logically constructed and of a sufficient length and eloquence to elevate the minds of the audience. 'The Figures,' however, 'ought to be very various, and not stayed too long upon, because a mind that is in agitation cannot talk long the same way; the Figures of tenderness and grief ought to be mingled with those of fury and rage.' He holds that declamatory language is seldom justifiable: 'A man is to complain and sigh, and not to roar and scold, and he is seldom to break out into the highest violence, but when there is enough to make him rave.' Contrary to D'Aubignac, Saint-Evremond (*Sur les Caractères des Tragédies*, 1672) considers that passionate speeches, to carry conviction, must be short. It is not unlikely that he was influenced by Dryden's arguments to the same effect in the *Essay of Dramatic Poesy*. He discusses the appropriate language to be used in love-scenes and scenes of grief. In the latter he considers that eloquent and prolonged recitations are a matter for ridicule; grief seeks expression in order to alleviate pain, not to embellish periods: 'Je suis aussi peu persuadé de la violence d'une passion qui est ingénieuse à s'exprimer par la diversité des pensées. Une âme touchée sensiblement ne laisse pas à l'esprit la liberté de penser beaucoup.' Similarly, he holds that in love-scenes, unduly protracted dialogues often convey a different impression to that which the author intended. Sometimes the lover becomes a philosopher and reasons about his passion or analyses it at length. The external signs of the commonest phase of love, *languir* (as opposed to *brûler*, which connotes violent transports and despairing torments), are no more than a sigh or a tear which involuntarily escapes us. But the long love-debates and extravagant protestations with which a dramatist too

often burdens us express no more than the weakness of
the lover.

The first critical passage of importance in which Dryden
discusses tragic diction occurs in the *Essay of Dramatic
Poesy*. The latter was written in the year preceding the
production of *Tyrannick Love*, the first of Dryden's plays
in which blustering rants appear, and in it we may already
discern an impatience with the orthodox set speeches
which had hitherto prevailed, and a desire for a more
striking mode of utterance. Corneille had required that
in tragedy 'the versification should be easy and elevated
above prose diction, but not so heightened as that of Epic
poetry, since those who speak are not poets'. Dryden,
however, showed no reluctance to make his characters
speak like poets, even in his early dramatic period. In the
essay, Neander animadverts upon the formal *tirades* of the
French drama:

'. . . their verses are to me the coldest I have ever read.
Neither, indeed, is it possible for them, in the way they take,
so to express passion, as that the effects of it should appear in
the concernment of an audience, their speeches being so many
declamations, which tire us with the length. . . . When the
French stage came to be reformed by Cardinal Richelieu,
those long harangues were introduced to comply with the
gravity of a churchman. Look upon *Cinna* and *Pompey*; they
are not so properly to be called plays, as long discourses of
reason of state; and *Polyeucte* in matters of religion is as solemn
as the long stops upon our organs. Since that time it is grown
into a custom, and their actors speak by the hour-glass, like
our parsons.'

He feels that passionate speeches should contain the element of surprise:

'But to speak generally; it cannot be denied that short
speeches and replies are more apt to move the passions and

beget concernment in us, than the other; for it is unnatural
for any one in a gust of passion to speak long together, or for
another in the same condition to suffer him, without inter-
ruption. Grief and passion are like floods raised in little brooks
by a sudden rain; they are quickly up; and if the concernment
be poured unexpectedly in upon us, it overflows us; but a long
sober shower gives them leisure to run out as they came in,
without troubling the ordinary current.'

Soon afterwards came *Tyrannick Love* and *The Conquest of
Granada*, which, while astonishing the town by the audacity of their bombast, presented an easy target to the
satirist and the lampoonist, and an irresistible one to the
mountebank lord who at all costs had to have his jest. In
The Rehearsal extravagant rants form the staple of the
burlesque, but it was impossible to outdo Dryden in flights
of arrogant rhetoric, and all that Buckingham could do
was to make them appear more ludicrous, in the person
of Drawcansir:

> Others may boast a single man to kill:
> But I the blood of thousands daily spill.
> Let petty Kings the names of Parties know:
> Where e'er I come, I slay both friend and foe.
> The swiftest Horsemen my swift rage controls,
> And from their bodies drives their trembling souls.
> If they had wings, and to the Gods could fly
> I would pursue and beat 'em through the sky:
> And make proud Jove, with all his thunder, see
> This single arm more dreadful is, than he.

In IV. i Johnson inquires, 'Pray, Mr. Bayes, who is that
Drawcansir?' and Bayes replies, 'Why, Sir, a fierce Hero,
that frights his Mistress, snubs up Kings, baffles Armies,
and does what he will, without regard to numbers, good
manners, or justice.' It was the preoccupation with good
manners which Dryden considered irrelevant to tragedy,

and his ranting plays constitute a wholesome if excessive reaction against the parlour standards of politeness which had prevailed.

The *Essay of Heroic Plays* (1672) is partly a manifesto, partly a defence. Facing the opposition represented by *The Rehearsal*, Dryden with great élan vindicates Almanzor's fiery temper and insolent language by citing illustrious precedents for the inexorable type of character in the epics of Homer and Tasso. He describes the object of the English heroic play as the 'imitation, in little, of an heroic poem', thereby giving definite shape to what had hitherto been but a vague aspiration on the part of heroic dramatists. At the same time he holds up the Romances to scorn, but reluctant to appear a borrower from contemporary French literature, he omits to acknowledge his debt to the writers of French heroic poems. After providing examples of the fiery language of the heroes of Homer and Tasso, he declares:

'You see how little these great authors did esteem the *point of honour*, so much magnified by the French, and so ridiculously aped by us. They made their heroes men of honour; but so as not to divest them quite of human passions and frailties: they contented themselves to show you what men of great spirits would certainly do when they were provoked, not what they were obliged to do by the strict rules of moral virtue. For my own part, I declare myself for Homer and Tasso, and am more in love with Achilles and Rinaldo, than with Cyrus and Oroondates. I shall never subject my characters to the French standard, where love and honour are to be weighed by drachms and scruples.'

It has been observed that in Corneille's drama duty usually wins in the love and honour conflict, in Dryden's emotion. Whereas Corneille portrays unflinching adherence to duty in Pauline,[1] stoical resignation in Polyeucte and Félix, Dryden frequently gives us characters whom overmastering passion or jealousy drives to ruin, such as Zempoalla, Maximin, and Nourmahal. Nevertheless, Dryden was not averse to the ethical background of Corneille's drama, since it encouraged the display of an heroic will withstanding the forces of fate; it was the over-refined, chivalrous sentiment of the Romances which Dryden rightly singled out as being unfit for the living drama.

In 1677, that is to say in the interval between *Aureng-Zebe* and *All for Love*, Dryden published his unacted 'opera' *The State of Innocence*. This was based on *Paradise Lost*, with the object *inter alia* of maintaining the affinity between the epic and the heroic play. In its preface, entitled *An Apology for Heroic Poetry and Poetic Licence* (which has perhaps not much direct bearing on the play), Dryden again takes up the subject of exalted diction, and persuasively defends the latter in the hope of securing a continuance of favour for the bombastic type of play, which had by now almost run its course. He does not conceal his impatience with those who would sacrifice vigour to correctness.

'Are all the flights of Heroic Poetry to be concluded bombast, unnatural, and mere madness, because they are not affected with their excellencies? . . . Ought they not rather, in modesty, to doubt of their own judgments, when they think this or that expression in Homer, Virgil, Tasso, or Milton's *Paradise* to be too far strained, than positively to conclude that 'tis all fustian, and mere nonsense? . . . But I will presume for once to tell them, that the boldest strokes of poetry, when

---

[1] Cf. *Polyeucte* IV. v :

Pauline. Je sais que c'est beaucoup que ce que je demande;
   Mais plus l'effort est grand, plus la gloire en est grande.
   Conserver un rival dont vous êtes jaloux,
   C'est un trait de vertu qui n'appartient qu'à vous.

they are managed artfully, are those which most delight the reader.'

Hyperboles, he contends, are especially permissible in scenes of emotional vehemence 'when we speak more warmly and with more precipitation than at other times: for then . . . the poet must put on the passion he endeavours to represent: a man in such an occasion is not cool enough, either to reason rightly, or to talk calmly. Aggravations are then in their proper places; interrogations, exclamations, hyperbata,' &c.

The popularity of bombast, however, could not but be transitory, and once the heroic play had asserted its right of independence, it was ready to return to a measure of sobriety if public taste should declare itself in favour of the latter. Among critics the turn of the tide was heralded by Edward Phillips, who in the preface to his *Theatrum Poetarum* (1674) points out that Tragedy presents 'the unbridled passions of Love, Rage, and Ambition, the violent ends or downfalls of great Princes, the subversion of Kingdoms and Estates, . . . all of which require a style not ramping, but passionately sedate and moving'; while in his list of modern poets he reflects on Elkanah Settle that 'his soaring up to too much affected and immoderate heights, which I take to be his chief failing, may possibly be allayed by the more mature judgment of riper years, he being yet but a young man'.[1] Rymer, in his *Tragedies of the Last Age* (1678), shows himself to be averse (like La Mesnardière) to the portrayal in tragedy of disrespectful subjects and tyrannical kings. He deprecates the disloyalty shown to the king in *The Maid's Tragedy*: 'If it be said that the King was accessary to the falsehood, I question whether in Poetry a King can be accessary to a crime',

---

[1] At this date his two chief productions were *Cambyses* and *The Empress of Morocco*.

and in another passage he maintains that 'Poetry will allow no provocation or injury where it allows no revenge. And what pleasure can there be in seeing a King threaten and hector without cause, when none may be suffer'd to make return? Poetry will not permit an affront where there can be no reparation'.

Dryden's change of attitude, which is betokened in the Preface to *All for Love*,[1] is complete in his essay on *The Grounds of Criticism in Tragedy* (1679). Here he maintains that 'bombast is commonly the delight of that audience which loves poetry but understands it not', and contends that 'the roar of passion, indeed, may please an audience, three parts of which are ignorant enough to think all is moving which is noise, and it may stretch the lungs of an ambitious actor who will die upon the spot for a thundering clap; but it will move no other passion than indignation and contempt from judicious men'. Yet it was not the use but the abuse of bombast which Dryden deprecated, and there is an implied slight on his imitators (who for the most part had made their plays consist of little but turgidity) when he points out that if an inflated style is sustained too long 'it follows of necessity that no man can be distinguished from another by his discourse when every man is ranting, swaggering, and exclaiming with the same

---

[1] After some taunts, less virulent than usual, at the French poets, and how they would have contrived that the meeting of Cleopatra and Octavia should have been a polite one, he says, referring to his rejection of rhyme and the modelling of his style on Shakespeare's, 'Not that I condemn my former way, but that this is more proper to my present purpose'. *Aureng-Zebe* and *All for Love* were experiments in a more restrained medium, but Dryden had not yet completely severed himself from rant, for in January 1679 he produced, in collaboration with Lee, *Oedipus*, which has rhetorical outbursts akin to those in *The Conquest of Granada*. The essay on *The Grounds of Criticism in Tragedy* was written later than *Oedipus*, and for ten years after the essay Dryden's plays are comparatively free from bombast.

excess'. He was not unmindful of his own errors, however, for while insisting that 'no man is at leisure to make sentences and similes when his soul is in agony',[1] he cites one of his own lapses in this direction:

'Montezuma, pursued by his enemies and seeking sanctuary, stands parleying without the fort and describing his danger to Cydaria in a simile of six lines—

As on the sands the frighted traveller
Sees the high seas come rolling from afar, etc.[2]

My Indian potentate was well skilled in the sea for an inland prince, and well improved since the first act, when he sent his son to discover it. The image had not been amiss from another man at another time.'

The Epistle Dedicatory to *The Spanish Friar* (1681) is a sort of pendent to the above, and proclaims the final break with rant. Dryden shows his regret that bombast should have ever been exploited for the purpose of catching applause, the more so since he himself had occasionally been guilty of the offence: 'I remember some verses of my own, *Maximin* and *Almanzor*, which cry vengeance upon me for their extravagance. . . . All I can say for those passages, which are, I hope, not many, is, that I knew they were bad enough to please, even when I writ them.' He saw that the meretricious splendour of this kind of diction had resulted in debasing the standard of appreciation. The real worth of a play, he contends, is seldom apparent in a stage performance, and he says his own ambition is to survive the test of being read.

---

[1] Perhaps remembering D'Aubignac's disapproval of elaborate 'images' in scenes of emotional stress. Cf. also *The Rehearsal*, II. iii (cited by Prof. J. E. Spingarn in *Seventeenth Century Critical Essays*), where Bayes enunciates the 'general Rule; you must ever make similes when you are surpris'd: 'tis the new way of writing'.

[2] *The Indian Emperor*.

'The most discerning critic can judge no more of these silent graces in the action than he who rides post through an unknown country can distinguish the situation of places, and the nature of the soil. The purity of phrase, the clearness of conception and expression, the boldness maintained to majesty, the significancy and sound of words, not strained into bombast, but justly elevated;[1] in short, those very words and thoughts, which cannot be changed, but for the worse, must of necessity escape our transient view upon the theatre; and yet without all these a play may take.'

Just as the success of Dryden's *Tyrannick Love* (1669) had prompted several dramatists (including Settle, Pordage, Banks, and Lee) to swell out their plays with fustian, so Dryden's abandonment of the practice induced his followers (with the exception of Banks) to adopt a calmer tone, and to turn the heroic play into other channels. *All for Love* fostered the imitation of Elizabethan models, while Otway, in *The Orphan* (1680) and *Venice Preserv'd* (1681–2), established the school of pathos, which persisted into the eighteenth century. Shadwell, in the Prologue to his *Squire of Alsatia* (1688), alludes to bombast as a thing of the past:

> Soon after this[2] came ranting Fustian in,
> And none but plays upon the fret were seen:
> Such Roaring Bombast stuff, which Fops would praise,
> Tore our best Actors' lungs, cut short their days.
> Some in small time did this distemper kill;
> And had the savage Authors gone on still,
> Fustian had been a new Disease i'th Bill.

But the following year saw the close of this peaceful inter-

---

[1] 'Neither do I discommend the lofty style in Tragedy, which is naturally pompous and magnificent; but nothing is truly sublime that is not just and proper.' Ib.

[2] i.e. after the first period of rhymed heroic plays, when French influence was strong.

regnum, and flights of bombast began to appear in blank verse plays almost as frequently as they had done in the period of rhyme. Dryden participated in this revival, as *Don Sebastian* (1689) shows. In this later period, however, the rants were less extravagant than formerly, and did not take control of the plays as they had done, and it is possible that Dryden's pleas for a more discriminating use of the licence had had their effect.

CHAPTER FIVE

THE CONFLICT BETWEEN RHYME AND BLANK VERSE

THE rhyme of the heroic play started by being a modish importation from France, but the vigour and momentum which it acquired under Dryden's direction soon established it in its own right, and for some time it was felt to be the ideal vehicle for English heroic dialogue. It may be contended that since the closed couplet had been perfected and popularized in non-dramatic verse by Waller, and was not infrequently used in late pre-Restoration drama in declamatory and sententious passages,[1] the heroic play would in time have resorted to rhyme whatever the example of foreign drama; particularly as (dramatic) blank verse was in an overworked and exhausted condition. But this consideration, though it may be true, does not detract from the boldness and initiative of D'Avenant in introducing the fashion and adapting it to English uses, in the first serious play of the new régime. As Dryden says: 'If we owe the invention of it to Mr. Waller, we are acknowledging for the noblest use of it to Sir William D'Avenant, who at once brought it upon the stage, and made it perfect, in the *Siege of Rhodes*.'[2] It may also be urged that the element of rhyme in *The Siege of Rhodes* was hardly an important innovation, since the play being first performed as an opera, its rhyme was due merely to the exigencies of the music. Dryden, moreover, though

---

[1] e.g. In the plays of Goffe (*c*. 1631) and Quarles (*c*. 1649), as Professor. Saintsbury has pointed out.

[2] We have seen that in this essay—The Epistle Dedicatory of *The Rival Ladies* (1664)—Dryden refused to admit that the rhyme of the heroic play was borrowed from France, but that he did so later on.

he gives D'Avenant the credit of first employing the couplet successfully in the contemporary drama, suggests that the idea of turning *The Siege of Rhodes* into a 'just drama' only occurred to D'Avenant after the Restoration, when the ban on play-acting was removed. New light, however, has been recently thrown on the subject by Professor Dent, in his *Foundations of English Opera* (1928), and the following suggestion appears to be very probable in view of the supporting evidence, though the latter cannot be summarized here:

'The plain fact was that D'Avenant was not really attempting to start English opera as a primary object of his efforts. His first desire was to get the theatres reopened and plays (naturally, his own) performed. It is fairly clear, if we compare the different versions of *The Siege of Rhodes*, that it was originally written not as an opera but as a play. The scenes for the Sultan's wife Roxolana and other persons, which are found in the later versions, were cut out of the first, partly to save time, and mainly for want of people to act the parts. But the chorus of the Sultan's wives at the end of the fourth entry—

1 *Woman*. This cursed jealousie, what is't?
2 *Woman*. 'Tis love that has lost itself in a mist. etc.—

sung in the version of 1656 has no reason for its existence unless preceded by the scene in which Roxolana explains to the women her jealousy of Ianthe, a scene not restored to the opera until 1661. Although no positive proof can be adduced, it seems highly probable that D'Avenant originally wrote the work as a drama in rhymed heroic couplets, and that it was only when he found it impossible to produce it as a play, that he decided to turn it into an opera by cutting it down, altering the lengths of the lines here and there, inserting songs and choruses, and finally getting the whole set to music.[1]

D'Avenant, indeed, in his *Address to the Reader* (prefixed to Part I, 1656), considers it necessary to apologize for

---

[1] Ch. iv.

these short lyrical measures:[1] 'You may enquire, being a reader, why in an heroick argument my numbers are so often diversify'd and fall into short fractions; considering that a continuation of the usual length of English verse would appear more heroical in reading. But when you are an auditor you will find that in this I rather deserve approbation than need excuse; for frequent alternations of measure are necessary to recitative music for variation of ayres.' He evidently regarded them as unnecessary in a play; yet they had been successfully handled by Corneille in *Le Cid* for lyrical monologues and soliloquies of an emotional nature. La Mesnardière, writing three years after the production of *Le Cid*, holds that, though varied measures are not essential to the drama, they are admissible provided they 'express convincingly the conflicting emotions of a violently agitated mind'. La Mesnardière's remarks on rhyme illustrate the difference between the contemporary English and French points of view. 'Rhyme', he says, 'is the least considerable part of versification; it is no more than a species of paint, or artifice, which languages inferior to Greek and Latin have invented at their need, in order to approach by some means to the beauty of these languages which they cannot equal.' And, in fact, French spoken verse requires the enrichment of rhyme, for without it it is not sufficiently distinguishable from prose; while in English dramatic verse, which is not subject to this limitation, the employment of rhyme seems to modify the whole expression and tone of thought. In both languages, however, the couplet, with its capacity for antithesis and sententiousness, tends to the production of long, formally built-up arguments. La Mesnardière considers that these should be used sparingly, and avoided altogether

---

[1] They appear in both parts of the play, though in Part II there is no chorus.

in passionate scenes: 'Rien n'est plus opposé aux expressions passionnées que les Sentences morales, les Comparaisons ajustées, et les Conclusions que l'on tire par des espèces d'Arguments'—they are suitable only to a mind which is master of itself. Corneille, of course, excelled in portraying a mind endeavouring to gain a mastery of itself by means of these rhetorical arguments, in which, and in the corresponding debates in the English heroic drama, we are constantly reminded of Descartes' prescription.[1] It was doubtless admiration for Corneille's plays which prompted D'Aubignac to differ from La Mesnardière and declare in favour of length and logic in passionate speeches. He maintains that however disordered passionate speech may be naturally, in dramatic poetry 'the mind is not to be hurried from one Motion to another, without connexion or dependence upon what has been said; nor is it to leap from one consideration to another, and then back again to the first; the subject of which the actor is to speak, ought to be carefully considered; the place, time, and other particulars, which may contribute to the passion, and then of all that make up the most judicious and moving discourse that may be.'

Since in France there was virtually no alternative to rhyme for serious plays, French criticism was not occupied with the position of rhyme in drama to anything like the same extent as English criticism. Before turning to the latter, however, it will be convenient to glance at the early history of rhymed plays subsequent to *The Siege of Rhodes*. The foremost writer who took up rhyme after D'Avenant was the Earl of Orrery; and we have seen that before January 1661/2 (the date of his letter containing the information) he 'presumed to lay at his majesty's feet a tragi-

---

[1] 'Une excitation volontaire des passions contraires à celle qu'on veut ôter, par la représentation des choses qui y sont jointes.' Cf. pp. 28–9.

comedy, all in ten feet verse and rhyme ... because I found
his majesty relished rather the French fashion of writing
plays than the English'. The following passage in Mor-
rice's memoir of Orrery shows that there prevailed a
general curiosity concerning the expressiveness of the new
medium, and a willingness to continue the experiment
which D'Avenant had begun:

'King Charles was the first who put my lord upon writing
plays, which his majesty did upon occasion of a dispute that
arose in his royal presence about writing plays in rhyme: some
affirmed it was not to be done; others said it would spoil
the fancy to be so confin'd, but Lord Orrery was of another
opinion; and his majesty being willing a trial should be made
commanded his lordship to employ some of his leisure that
way, which my lord readily did and upon that occasion composed *The Black Prince*.'

Though none of Orrery's plays were performed before
1664, it is probable that most persons who were interested
in the drama (including Dryden, Howard, and Katharine
Phillips) were familiar with them at an earlier date; and
certainly their influence was considerable, as may be partly
estimated by the many flattering references to the earl's
'poems' which appear in contemporary prefaces. The
acclimatization of rhyme was furthered by the translations
of the plays of Corneille and Quinault. Mrs. Katharine
Phillips's rendering (1663) of Corneille's *Pompée* was the
first of these rhymed translations, and it met with much
success, partly owing to its own merits, and partly to the
warm patronage of Orrery, who declared, in the com-
mendatory verse prefixed to the play, that

> The French to learn our language now will seek
> To hear their greatest wit more nobly speak.

The same play was also translated, some months later, by
'certain persons of honour', one of whom was the poet

Waller, whose proficiency in rhyme was of long standing. Another translation of this period was Carlell's *Heraclius* (printed 1664), in which the use of the closed couplet is uniform and somewhat monotonous.

The first play in which Dryden used rhyme was probably his tragicomedy *The Rival Ladies* (1663?). Authorities differ as between the priority of this play and that of *The Indian Queen*, but in the absence of conclusive evidence it seems safest to assume that the former play, in which the use of rhyme is tentative,[1] is earlier in date than the latter, which is rhymed throughout. As the staple medium of *The Rival Ladies* is a somewhat ramshackle blank verse, it is of interest to inquire what situations in the play Dryden considered specially appropriate for rhyme. There are two principal rhymed passages. The first is a lyrical monologue consisting chiefly of descriptive poetry. It is spoken by the disguised Angellina, who is wandering apprehensively in a deserted street at twilight:

> Silence and solitude dwell everywhere
> Dogs cease to bark, the Waves more faintly roar,
> And roll themselves asleep upon the shore:
> No noise but what my footsteps make, and they
> Sound dreadfully, and louder than by day.

The other is one of the long amatory debates typical of the heroic play, and is evidently intended to be a 'set piece', analogous to an operatic duet. Julia, who is unresponsive to the advances of Gonsalvo, the magnanimous lover, finds herself temporarily in his power, but knows her surest defence is to appeal to his honour:

> *Julia.* Can you pretend to Love, and see my grief
> Caus'd by yourself, yet give me no relief?

---

[1] The few rhymed passages which occur are generally printed in italics in the quarto and folio editions.

Gonsalvo. Where's my Reward?
Julia.   The Honour of the Flame.
Gonsalvo. I lose the substance then, to gain the Name.[1]

The bandying to and fro of scruples and honourable abnegations is long continued in this manner until Gonsalvo not only gives her her freedom but undertakes to promote the cause of his rival. The dexterous use of rhyme confers a precision on the passage which somewhat atones for its artificiality. In the rhymed heroic plays of D'Avenant and Orrery there are many examples of these amorous disputes, which doubtless served as models for the foregoing. Thus in the *Siege of Rhodes* we may instance the protracted altercation between the headstrong Solyman and his jealous consort which occurs in Pt. II, IV. iii:

Solyman. You make my frowns, yet seem to think them
    strange.
Roxolana. You seek a stranger, and abandon me.
Solyman. Strange coasts are welcome after storms **at sea.**
    Monarchs, who onward still with conquest move,
    Can only for their short diversion love . . .
    Whilst they, to save a sullen mistress, stay,
    The world's dominion may be cast away.
Roxolana. Why is dominion prized above
    Wise nature's great concernment, love?

The conflicting claims of love and honour are often argued out in soliloquy. The following example, in Orrery's *Henry the Fifth*, shows the same casuistry of 'losing and meriting the lover' as is employed in the passage from *The Rival Ladies*:

Tudor. I must unworthy or else wretched prove,
    Be false to Honour, or else false to Love. . . .
    If I her right above my Love prefer,
    In that, by losing, I shall merit her.

[1] IV. i.

And to obtain, not merit her, will prove
Less than to lose her and deserve her Love.
'Tis worthy of my flame and of her eyes
To make Love be to Love a sacrifice.[1]

It is noteworthy that in Etheredge's first play, *The Comical Revenge* (1664), rhymed passages, which are often mixed with prose in the same scene, are used, as in *The Rival Ladies*, to express heroic sentiment. The serious portions of the two plays resemble each other in several ways,[2] and it is not unlikely that Etheredge modelled his play on Dryden's first experiment in tragicomedy.

Such, in outline, was the record of the contemporary rhymed drama when the first important piece of Restoration criticism on the subject appeared—the Epistle Dedicatory of *The Rival Ladies* (addressed to the Earl of Orrery) which Dryden prefixed to the play in 1664. In English criticism there was an unfortunate tendency to argue that if rhyme was legitimate, blank verse was illegitimate, and vice versa. It had shown itself conspicuously in the Campion-Daniel controversy, where the issue was confined to non-dramatic verse;[3] Campion showing a Renaissance aversion to rhyme as a 'barbarous' product, and Daniel, in spite of his praiseworthy defence of 'Custom that is before all law', disparaging blank-verse measures in the following terms:

'Nor will the general sort for whom we write (the wise being above books) taste these laboured measures but as an orderly

---

[1] II. i.

[2] e.g. in *The Comical Revenge* there is a self-sacrificing heroine, Aurelia, who helps Bruce, whom she loves, to woo her sister. In sentiment and situation, of course, both plays are appreciably influenced by Platonic tradition.

[3] It should be noted, however, that Daniel parenthetically observes that 'a tragedy would indeed best comport with a blank verse, and dispense with rhyme, saving in the chorus, or where a sentence shall require a couplet'.

prose when we have all done. . . . For be the verse never so good, never so full, it seems not to satisfy nor breed that delight, as when it is met and combined with a like sounding accent: which seems as the jointure without which it hangs loose, and cannot subsist, but runs wildly on, like a tedious fancy without a close.'

In the same way, Restoration critics unduly denounce the opposite practice to that which they happen to favour. Though they are frequently injudicious enough to attempt to legislate in the matter for the English drama in general, they sometimes confine their opinions to what is appropriate for the heroic play, and their criticism gains in value considerably when they do so. While between them Campion and Daniel perhaps elucidate the function of rhyme in poetry better than the Restoration critics, it may be said of the latter that they concern themselves more with the immediate practical bearings of the question. In following them, therefore, we are debarred from investigating the more interesting subject of the aesthetic function of rhyme.

In the Epistle Dedicatory of *The Rival Ladies* Dryden did not limit the field of discussion to the heroic play, and his arguments in favour of rhyme ostensibly apply to plays of all kinds. This lack of specification may partly be due to the fact that the heroic play had not as yet become a stereotyped form; but it is chiefly ascribable to Dryden's eagerness to regularize and 'refine' poetic speech. His aims in this direction appear clearly during his enumeration of the various advantages which he avers that rhyme possesses over blank verse. Rhyme, he contends, besides aiding the memory and giving pointedness to repartees, 'bounds and circumscribes the fancy. For imagination in a poet is a faculty so wild and lawless that, like an high-ranging spaniel, it must have clogs tied to it, lest it outrun the judgment. The great easiness of blank verse renders the poet too luxuriant; he is tempted to say many things which might better be omitted, or at least shut up in fewer words.' [1]

At the same time, he was feeling his way towards the heroic drama, and some of his observations show that he felt that rhyme was a suitable medium for a specialized type of play. Thus, 'as the best medicines may lose their virtue by being ill applied, so is it with verse,[2] if a fit subject be not chosen for it. Neither must the argument alone, but the characters and persons, be great and noble.' And especially the following: 'The scenes which in my opinion most commend it [rhyme] are those of argumentation and discourse, on the result of which the doing or not doing some considerable action should depend.' We have already quoted instances of such scenes; one from *The Rival Ladies* itself, and also from *The Siege of Rhodes* and *Henry the Fifth*. The fashion of the characters' arguing out all the possible issues during a critical phase of the action, and finally adopting the course presented by the winning argument, was probably inherited from the French heroic romances, in which these debates figured largely, as we have seen.[3] The antithetical balance and precision of the regular distich, as Dryden perceived, made the latter the ideal vehicle for such abstract disputations,

---

[1] His desire to standardize and refine English appears also in an earlier passage in the preface, viz. 'Only I am sorry that (speaking so noble a language as we do) we have not a more certain measure of it, as they have in France, where they have an academy erected for that purpose, and endowed with large privileges by the present king'. An attempt to found a similar institution in England was made later in the same year; for in Dec. 1664 the Royal Society appointed a committee 'for improving the English tongue' which included Evelyn, Waller, and Dryden. The enterprise however, was short-lived.

[2] i.e. rhyme; as the context makes clear.

[3] They were also common in the Spanish drama. For a good example, cf. the dialogue between Clotaldo and Rosaura in Calderon's *La Vida es Sueño*, III. ii.

and eventually they became part of the regular stock-in-trade of the heroic play; so much so that they were glee-fully seized upon by parodists. The soliloquy of Prince Volscius in *The Rehearsal* (III. v),

> Honour, aloud, commands, pluck both Boots on;
> But softer Love does whisper put on none.

which ends by his hopping off the stage with one boot on and the other off, is perhaps the best-known parody of the style; but that of Huncamunca in *The Tragedy of Tragedies* (II. x) is no less effective:

> I who this morn, of two chose which to wed
> May go again this night alone to bed:
> So have I seen some wild unsettled Fool,
> Who had her choice of this, and that joint stool;
> To give the Preference to either, loath
> And fondly coveting to sit on both:
> While the two stools her sitting Part confound
> Between 'em both fall squat upon the ground.

Too often, however, dramatists looked on these debates merely as exercises in forensic ingenuity, and in many of them nothing of any consequence hangs on the issue of the argument. Samuel Butler's parody, *Repartees between Cat and Puss, in the Modern Heroic Way*, sufficiently illustrates the abstract barrenness of this type of dialogue:

Puss. Pain is the foil of pleasure and delight,
  That sets it off to a more noble height.
Cat. He buys his pleasure at a rate too vain,
  That takes it up beforehand of his pain.
Puss. Pain is more dear than pleasure when 'tis past.
Cat. But grows intolerable if it last.

The next piece of criticism on the subject of rhymed drama was Sir Robert Howard's *Address to the Reader* (prefixed to the 1665 folio edition of his *Four New Plays*), in which he attempts to confute Dryden's arguments in

The Rival Ladies preface, notwithstanding the fact that he had collaborated with him in the rhymed *Indian Queen*. Since Howard's chief and tiresomely reiterated argument consisted in pressing the claims of verisimilitude, it may be well, before quoting from it, to inquire how far the fashion of rhyme appeared to an unbiased if undependable contemporary as an unnatural intrusion into the drama. On 2nd July 1661 Pepys saw *The Siege of Rhodes* for the first time. It was one of his favourite plays, and he saw it in all about six times, and set one of the songs to music of a somewhat nondescript nature. He does not remark on its rhyme as an innovation, but was probably influenced by the fact that the piece had originally been presented as an opera. On 1st February 1664, however, he went to see *The Indian Queen*, in which the rhyme struck him as an artificial accretion: 'To the King's Theatre, and there saw *The Indian Queen* acted, which indeed is a most pleasant show, and beyond my expectation; the play good, but spoiled with the rhyme, which breaks the sense.' The next rhymed play which he saw was Orrery's *Henry the Fifth* (on 13th August 1664). He bestows high praise on it, but says nothing about the rhyme, so in the interval he had probably come to regard rhyme as the appropriate medium for the serious drama of his time.

Unlike Pepys, Howard showed an inability, or rather unwillingness, to accustom himself to the ever-increasing practice, for in his essay of 1668 his attitude to rhymed plays is substantially the same as that which he adopts towards them in his *Address to the Reader* of 1665. In the latter, he looks on the rhymed drama mainly as an importation from France, and says that he only wrote in it himself so as to follow the fashion, 'though very far off'. Blank verse, he contends, is 'as much too low for a Poem as Rhyme is unnatural for a play', a poem being 'a premeditated form of thoughts upon a design'd occasion', whereas a play 'is presented as the present effect of accidents not thought of'. He says that some may object that this is a trivial argument 'because whatever is showed, 'tis known still to be but a play', for all this, however, whatever is nearest reality is to be preferred. A happy exception he finds in the plays of my lord of Orrery, 'in whose verse the greatness of the majesty seems unsullied with the cares of composition'. But this 'does not convince my Reason, but employs my Wonder'.

Had Dryden, in his *Rival Ladies* preface, contented himself with pleading for rhyme on behalf of the heroic play only, the question of which medium was nearer to nature would have been irrelevant, since the heroic play started with an assumption of artificiality to a degree unknown in the English drama before or since. Dryden's failure to delimit the discussion enabled Howard to bring forward the above general objections to rhymed drama, though of course Howard's own position is untenable, since the choice of a medium depends on the kind of play which is required. Unfortunately verisimilitude, as we have seen, was one of the articles of the neo-classic creed to which Dryden subscribed, and in consequence he bestowed more care on Howard's argument than it deserved. In the *Essay of Dramatic Poesy* he goes so far as to supply Crites with an amplified and more forcible version of Howard's argument, and then endeavours to confute it in the speech of Neander.[1] In this he is hardly successful.

[1] In the interval between the *Address to the Reader* (1665) and the *Essay of Dramatic Poesy* (1668) a quarrel had arisen between the two authors—possibly over the honours of *The Indian Queen*—and in the *Epistle Dedicatory to the Essay of Dramatic Poesy* there is a contemptuous allusion to Howard's lack of skill in rhyming (see p. 103, n.), while in the essay itself Neander bestows ironical compliments on the person from whom Crites derived his anti-rhyme arguments.

Crites having pointed out on behalf of blank verse that Aristotle had prescribed that it was best to write tragedy in the kind of verse which was nearest prose, Neander is driven to assert that blank verse is not verse at all, but measured prose.[1] 'Measure alone, in any modern language, does not constitute verse.' Blank verse 'is but a poetic prose; and as such, most fit for comedies, where I acknowledge rhyme to be improper'. It may well be that this was one of Dryden's contentions about which he felt misgivings, when in his Dedication of the essay he said, 'I confess I find many things in this Discourse which I do not now approve; my judgment being not a little altered since the writing of it', and when in describing his method he remarks, 'Sometimes I stand desperately to my arms, like the foot when deserted by their horse; not in hope to overcome, but only to yield on more honourable terms.' Some of Neander's statements, however, are worthier of attention, particularly when they throw light on Dryden's scheme of prosody; thus he points out that the way to secure an approximation to living speech and make rhyme comply with Aristotle's dictum, is to avoid the excessive use of the closed couplet, to vary the position of the caesura, and on occasion to use the 'Pindaric way' of varied measures as employed in *The Siege of Rhodes*. To these we may add the Alexandrine and the triplet, with both of which Dryden successfully varied the staple distich.

But his strongest argument in favour of rhyme appears when he temporarily abandons the verisimilitude question, and urges the need for a new kind of drama (new both in content and in form), which should not attempt to imitate Elizabethan models. For, as regards the Elizabethans, 'There is scarce an humour, a character, or any kind of plot, which they have not used. . . . This therefore will be

[1] *Prose mesurée.*

a good argument to us, either not to write at all, or to attempt some other way. There is no bays to be expected in their walks.' He proceeds to show that rhyme is justified for the contemporary drama not only owing to the need for a fresh medium, but also because 'our age is arrived to a perfection in it, which they never knew'. But although he recognizes that each age must select the form most suited to its artistic expression, he generously admits that 'to imitate nature in that perfection which they did in prose [sc. blank verse], is a greater commendation than to write in verse exactly'. Finally, fortified by these conclusions, he returns to the question of what is nearest to nature, and contends that the selected medium should be that which is 'nearest the nature of a *serious play*: this last is indeed the representation of nature, but 'tis nature wrought up to a higher pitch. The plot, the characters, the wit, the passions, the descriptions, are all exalted above the level of common converse, as high as the imagination of the poet can carry them, with proportion to verisimility'. It is easy to see that these characteristics of the 'serious play' best fit the heroic play, and if we allow the substitution of the words, the above peroration appears as a fairly precise expression of his aims.

Sir Robert Howard's reply, the *Address to the Reader* prefixed to *The Duke of Lerma* (1668), is principally directed against Dryden's views on the Unities. On the subject of rhyme he adopts a somewhat sulky attitude and says little that is fresh. He will not pretend to say why he wrote his play 'some scenes in blank verse, others in Rime, since I have no better reason to give than chance, which waited upon my present fancy'. Perhaps suspecting (unjustifiably) that Dryden was enamoured of rhyme more for its own sake than for its suitability to the contemporary drama, he affirms that he himself would rather read good rhyme than either blank verse or prose, but maintains that that is beside the point, and that rhyme, however flexible it may be made, is not so near 'the converse of men and women' as blank verse. Moreover, ''tis not the question whether rhyme or not rhyme be best or most natural for a serious subject, but what is nearest the nature of that it represents'.

Dryden's answer, the *Defence of an Essay of Dramatic Poesy* (1668), shows a further withdrawal from the verisimilitude *impasse*. While he disclaims being 'so ridiculous as to dispute whether prose or verse be nearest to ordinary conversation', he says he still thinks he will have gained his point if he can prove that rhyme is best or most natural for a 'serious subject'. Accordingly he reverts to the unassailable argument (which it was unfortunate that he had not pursued all along) that the amount of heightening must vary according to the subject chosen.

' 'Tis true, that to imitate well is a poet's work; but to affect the soul, and excite the passions, and above all to move admiration,[1] which is the delight of serious plays, a bare imitation will not serve.'

'Prose' is not to be used in serious plays because 'it is too near the nature of converse:[2] there may be too great a likeness; as the most skilful painters affirm, that there may be too near a resemblance in a picture'. Thus he effectively disposes of the fallacy of excessive adherence to realism. By a happy image he succeeds in suggesting the nature of the appeal of the heroic couplet in the theatre —'Rhyme . . . has somewhat of the usurper in him: but he is brave and generous, and his dominion pleasing.' The

---

[1] The 'heroic' emotion.
[2] Cf. *The Rehearsal*, IV. ii:
Johnson. But pray Mr. Bayes, why is this scene all in verse?
Bayes. O, Sir, the subject is too great for Prose.

strength of its appeal was evident from the success which
the heroic drama was then gaining, and this success was
probably responsible in the essay for Dryden's increasing
impatience with abstract principles and his inclination to
appeal to the popular verdict.[1]

Howard's argument had been so extensively dealt with
by Dryden that the former found it fruitless to continue
the controversy. Others, however, came to his aid, but
they were more concerned with raising their voices on his
behalf than with advancing fresh points of view. Richard
Flecknoe's letter of 20th September 1668 to the Hon.
Edward Howard, which Pepys found 'mighty silly, in
behalf of Howard', is a scurrilous pamphlet, throughout
which Dryden is referred to as 'the Squire'. The Hon.
Edward Howard, who had mildly disapproved of rhymed
plays in his preface to *The Usurper* (1668), argued against
them more emphatically when he came to the support of
his brother in his preface to *The Women's Conquest* (1670).
He makes no attempt to come to grips with the essential
part of Dryden's argument and merely reiterates the plea
for a natural mode of dialogue. In his own play he uses
rhyme only for the Masque scenes, and for the concluding
lines of acts and of some of the scenes, 'which places are
periods where the audience may best expect a weighty and
sententious close'. He condemns out of hand the sustained
use of the closed couplet, which, he maintains, almost

---

[1] Cf. p. 63. Since the above was written, a leading article on the
subject of the Dryden-Howard controversy has appeared in *The Times
Literary Supplement* of 19 Dec. 1929, in which the point is brought out
that the disputants really had different types of drama in mind.
Howard, we may surmise, was less eager for verisimilitude than for
the freedom from restrictions which had prevailed in the drama of
the previous age. He was equally hostile to rhyme and to the rules.
Dryden, on the other hand, was well aware that the heroic play for
all its adopted conventions was far less realistic in its aims than
Elizabethan tragedy had been.

invariably renders the language of a play stiff and ponderous. He considers that the importation of rhyme was accidental, having been determined by the fact that D'Avenant used it in *The Siege of Rhodes* (which he assumes was written as an opera, not as a play), and fears lest its continuance should rob the serious drama of all vitality. Thus Orrery's productions, he says, may be more justly termed 'poems' than plays.

Though his work appeared somewhat later than that of the above writers, and though he was not implicated in the Dryden-Robert Howard controversy, we may conveniently include Edward Phillips here, as one of a group of unduly prejudiced critics. In his account of Dryden as a dramatist in his *Theatrum Poetarum* (1674) he attributed his 'French way of continual Rime' more to 'the modified and gallantish humour of the time, than to his own well examined judgment'. Similarly Milton, in his prefatory note to *Paradise Lost*, had complained that poets were carried away by custom, and had remarked, 'Long since, our best English Tragedies have rejected rhyme'.[1] It was, however, the unsuitability not of rhyme but of the regular couplet for dramatic dialogue that Phillips emphasized; and in his Preface he suggests a remedy, somewhat in the style of Dick Minim:

'And for the verse, if it must needs be Rime, I am clearly of opinion, that way of versifying which bears the name of Pindaric, and which hath no necessity of being divided into Strophs or Stanzas, would be much more suitable for Tragedy than the continued Rhapsodie of Riming Couplets, which whoever shall mark it well will find it appear too stiff, and of too much constraint for the liberty of conversation, and the interlocution of several Persons.'

[1] It is noteworthy that in his Dedication to the *Juvenal* (1693) Dryden considers it necessary to excuse Milton's fondness for blank verse on the grounds that he possessed neither grace nor facility in rhyming.

Here again we may discern an indebtedness to Milton, in particular to his observations on the choric measures employed in *Samson Agonistes*.

The Defence of an Essay of Dramatic Poesy showed Dryden determined to press on with rhymed plays, confident that they would win increasing popularity, whatever the critics said. At that date he had written only two serious plays in rhyme, namely, *The Indian Queen* and *The Indian Emperor*; and there were probably many who, like Pepys, applauded these plays on account of their scenery but remained unconvinced of the appropriateness of their rhyme. By the time he next returned to the topic, however—in the *Essay of Heroic Plays* (1672)—he had scored instantaneous successes with *Tyrannick Love* and the two parts of *The Conquest of Granada*. He had won a decisive victory for rhyme, and the fact that during this period the great majority of plays of other dramatists are rhymed is largely to be attributed to his example. These considerations are doubtless responsible for the altered tone of his criticism. Whereas in his previous essays he had introduced a certain amount of persuasiveness into his arguments, in the *Essay of Heroic Plays* he sounds the triumphant and arrogant note of one of his own conquering heroes. 'Whether heroic verse ought to be admitted into serious plays is not now to be disputed: 'tis already in possession of the stage; and I dare confidently affirm that very few tragedies, in this age, shall be received without it.' And, 'It is very clear to all who understand poetry, that serious plays ought not to imitate conversation too nearly.' But in spite of his advantageous position, he refrains from dogmatizing, and he prefers to conclude with a tolerant gesture: 'But I am willing to let fall this argument: 'tis free for every man to write, or not to write, in verse, as he judges it to be, or not to be, his talent; or as he images the audience will receive it.'

In the epilogue to *The Rehearsal* (acted Dec. 1671), Buckingham had tried to alienate the taste of the audience from rhyming plays. But the public showed no signs of satiety, and rhyme continued to hold the stage for another six years. Even at the end of this period, however, it was not so much rejected by the audience as abandoned by the dramatists in the hopes of securing a new lease of life for the heroic play. In general the essential characteristics of the heroic play were retained, but Elizabethan *motifs* were grafted on, and the new product demanded a medium with a wider range of expression than the heroic couplet. Blank verse was adopted, and with more confidence than in the early years of the Restoration, for extensive practice in the use of the couplet had given dramatists the prosodic resourcefulness and control which had so long been needed. The blank verse of *All for Love* is perfectly suited to its purpose; less flexible than that of *Antony and Cleopatra* (and appropriately so, since Dryden, unlike Shakespeare, was working within a classical form) it has at the same time an easy alternation of conciseness and copiousness which befits the many fluctuations of emotional interest of the story.

All for Love is generally regarded as the landmark of the return to blank verse, but Settle's *Pastor Fido* (1676) and Ravenscroft's *King Edgar and Alfreda* (1677) were blank-verse plays which preceded Dryden's production. Yet if they set the example, Dryden had previously pointed the way. A possible early indication of Dryden's dissatisfaction with rhyme is provided by his *Marriage à la Mode* (c. May 1672) in which the comic scenes are in prose, but the staple of the serious portion is blank verse. There are only two rhymed passages in the play; one being a protracted love-scene in II. i, and the other occurring at a point where the love and honour conflict becomes un-

usually prominent and heroic, and when on the result of
the amatory debate between Leonidas and Palmyra 'the
doing or not doing of some considerable action depends'—
in this case a rising in arms in order to dethrone the usurper
Polydamas, Palmyra's father.[1] Yet the fact that the major
portion of the main plot is not heroic, but pseudo-romantic,
is probably sufficient to account for the preponderance of
the blank verse. It is the casting-off of rhyme in the interests
of the heroic play itself with which we are chiefly concerned;
and we may note that the closeness of the affinity which
existed between the heroic couplet and heroic sentiment is
shown by the fact that though (during the whole period)
there were many heroic plays in blank verse, there were
very few serious plays in rhyme which were non-heroic.

A clearer indication of the heroic play's change of direction is afforded by Dryden's *Aureng-Zebe* (1675), in which,
though the motivation is of the conventional type, there
is a pronounced tendency towards naturalism, for which
the avoidance of bombast and violent action, and the freedom of the rhymed verse with its frequent recourse to
enjambement, are responsible. In the prologue, Dryden
admits to a distaste for 'his long-loved mistress, rhyme',
and gives the following reason for his change of attitude:

> Passion's too fierce to be in fetters bound,
> And nature flies him like enchanted ground:

[1] In the same piece of dialogue we have a good example of what
may be termed heroic repartee—the verbal wit of the Comedy of
Manners in a more pompous apparel. Palmyra urges that a virtuous
death is preferable to a state of happiness secured by wrongful violence.

Palmyra. I'll keep my promise, though I lose my life.
Leonidas. Then you lose love, for which we both contend;
For life is but the means, but love's the end.
Palmyra. Our souls shall love hereafter.
Leonidas.   I much fear
That soul, which could deny the body here
To taste of love, would be a niggard there.

What verse can do, he has performed in this,
Which he presumes the most correct of his;
But spite of all his pride, a secret shame
Invades his breast at Shakespeare's sacred name:
Awed when he hears his god-like Romans rage,
He, in a just despair, would quit the stage;

He had wearied of the artificiality of the unduly elevated style, and was convinced that if in addition to exciting the heroic passion (admiration) the aim was to represent human passions, blank verse was undoubtedly the ideal medium. Nor can this be held to be inconsistent with his previous reasoning, for he had always laid most stress on the desirability of employing the medium most suited to the particular kind. This point of view reappears in the vindication of his change of allegiance, in the Preface to *All for Love*:

'In my style I have professed to imitate the divine Shakespeare; which that I might perform more freely, I have disencumbered myself from rhyme. *Not that I condemn my former way, but this is more proper to my present purpose.*'

A cursory perusal of Dryden's contribution to the rhyme and blank verse controversy might merely lead to the supposition that the latter statement was an evasion of the issue.

In view of what we have already said concerning the experimental turn which the heroic drama took, it is significant that in the majority of plays rhyme and bombast subsided together. The love and honour background, the symmetrical grouping, the conventional characterization for the most part remained, but a quieter tone prevailed, and the dialogue gained in fluency without losing elegance. In this peaceful interregnum the pathetic and the Shakespearian types of play became prominent, and the best work of Lee and Otway appeared. But in spite of these interesting developments, the conventional heroic drama was not dead but in abeyance, and ready to reappear at a favourable opportunity. That it did so, we have already seen. A group of rhymed plays appeared towards the close of the century.[1] It is possible, however, that these plays were composed several years before they were printed. It has recently been demonstrated[2] that Settle's *The Ambitious Slave*, which was published in 1694, is not, as it appears to be, an exceptionally late example of the heroic style, but was written in 1681, and owing to various circumstances was delayed in its production. The rhymed plays in question may similarly have been held over from an earlier period; in style they seem naturally to belong to the time when the conventional heroic play temporarily reasserted itself. But though rhyme and bombast may have reappeared together, the revival of the former was not so marked as was that of the latter.[3]

[1] e.g. Crowne's *Caligula*, 1698 (heroic and bombastic), Charles Hopkins's *Boadicea, Queen of Britain*, 1679 (heroic-pathetic), Orrery's *Herod the Great*, *c.* 1694 (heroic), and Robert Gould's *The Rival Sisters*, 1696 (domestic).

[2] Hotson, *The Commonwealth and Restoration Stage*, pp. 275–7.

[3] See p. 160.

Note. For the sake of completeness we may mention Thomas Shipman's enthusiastic defence of rhymed plays which occurs in the prefatory epistle to his *Henry the Third of France, stabb'd by a Fryer* (1678), though it is unlikely that this essay had much influence at the time. Shipman shows no signs of acquaintance with the Dryden-Howard debate, nor apparently was he aware that the rhymed drama was on the wane when he wrote. The above play is his sole contribution to the drama, so perhaps he was scarcely *au fait* with theatrical matters. He contents himself with urging that rhyme has more emotional capacity, and is pleasanter to the ear than blank verse. 'A Paper of verses in Rhime, where the conceit is new, the humour springing, and the penning elegant, must needs take more in the repetition than any studied Prose. And a speech on the Stage (be its concerns what it will) must be far more harmonious and pleasing in Rhime, and more congenial to the soul.' His devotion to rhyme leads him into making strange assertions: 'Milton's *Paradise* is a work noble, strong and fanciful, but had his humour of contradiction softened it into his own sweet Rhime, what a Poem had it been!' His own talent for rhyme, however, is not conspicuous, and the verse of his play suffers from an excessive use of enjambement and of the triplet.

CHAPTER SIX

ANALYSIS OF SELECTED PLAYS

IN the Introduction it was remarked that the first few heroic plays were more correct and restrained in tone than their immediate successors, owing to the fact that the influence of French example and theory was then at its strongest. The following examination of a few representative plays in the light of the neo-classic criteria which we have been discussing will, we hope, reveal something of the progress of the heroic drama away from its early restraint to the freer atmosphere favoured by most English critics of the Restoration. We shall not be concerned, except incidentally, with the literary or dramatic qualities of these plays; our object is methodically to test them by the external standards of their time in order to gauge the better what weight these standards carried.

1. *THE SIEGE OF RHODES*

We have previously commented on this play from time to time, and a brief treatment of it will suffice here. The play in its complete form was first published in 1663, and our investigations are based on this text. In this edition [1] Roxolana (the wife of Solyman), who has a prominent rôle in the second part, is for the first time introduced into Part I, in order to increase the play's coherence. From the point of view of the plot, the first part can hardly be considered a separate entity, for though at its conclusion Alphonso's suspicions as to Ianthe's infidelity are allayed, and the two become reconciled, we are left with the city still besieged by Solyman's forces and the fate of the hero

[1] i.e. the third quarto. Earlier editions were *Q* 1 1656 and *Q* 2 1659.

and heroine remains uncertain. In considering the unities of time and place, however, we must treat the two parts separately, for since Part I (in its present form) is more operatic in character than Part II, it is less concerned with the rules than the sequel. Thus the unity of place may be said to be preserved in the second part, for though there are many changes of backcloth (depicting 'The Town Beleaguer'd', 'The Grand Master's Palace on Fire' &c.) the scenes represented are all confined to the island of Rhodes. In Part I, however, there is an abrupt change from Rhodes to Sicily in the middle of the first act, without any indication of an alteration of scenery. In Part I, again, the unity of time is violated, for Villerius informs us (in the Second Entry) that

> The foe three moons tempestuously has spent
> Where we will never yield, nor he relent.

The second part, on the other hand, shows a conscious effort to adhere to the twenty-four hour limit, for there are periodic references to the time of day, from which it may be inferred that the action begins in the morning, with Ianthe's departure for the Turkish camp, and ends at about the dawn of the following day.

With regard to the unity of action it will be recalled that Dryden considered that the play as a whole 'lacked Fullness of Plot and Variety of Character'. Compared to later heroic plays this is certainly true, for though there is ostensibly a large canvas the many vicissitudes of the siege are all subordinated to the somewhat confined love-jealousy-honour theme. At a certain point of the play it looks as if the action will be complicated by the hopeless love of the Admiral for the heroine,[1] but this episode is allowed to fade from sight when it has served its purpose

[1] Part II. i, ll. 288–301.

of furthering the plot (i.e. the Admiral shares Alphonso's jealousy at Ianthe's prolonged absence at the Turkish camp, and encourages him to resort to force rather than diplomacy). As regards tragicomedy, the play is uniformly serious in tone, and rightly so, since the presence of the comic element would ill accord with the stilted grandiloquence of the love and honour theme. There is a poor attempt at jocularity in the soldiers' choruses in Part I which is probably the outcome of a need for variegated music. Owing to the infallible magnanimity of the enemy commander, there is never any doubt that the play will end happily. Poetic justice, too, is secured, for as soon as Alphonso has finally overcome his jealousy, Solyman bestows Ianthe on him, and accompanies his gift with a moral declamation which obviously issues from the author of *Gondibert*.

Influenced, no doubt, by French example, D'Avenant carefully abstains from the exhibition of stage deaths and fights. Yet he is anxious to convey some of the stir and excitement of the many battles which take place, and accordingly there are several scenes in which the principal combatants rush in from the fray with drawn swords, and announce the progress of the fight. During two of these scenes [1] 'A Symphony expressing a Battail is play'd', while in a battle-scene in the first part,[2] Alphonso proclaims his martial ardour in *Stilo Recitativo*, an incident which received some ridicule in *The Rehearsal* (V i). It is true that from the Prologue to Part II it might be inferred that D'Avenant was not averse to violent action on the stage:

> Oh Money! Money! if the Wits would dress,
> With ornaments, the present face of peace,

[1] Pt. II, V, scenes iii and iv.
[2] Fifth Entry.

And to our poet half that treasure spare,
Which faction gets from fools to nourish war;
Then his contracted scenes should wider be,
And move by greater engines, till you see
(Whilst you securely sit) fierce armies meet,
And raging seas disperse a fighting fleet.

but his desire was probably for scenic devices, and space large enough to admit pageantry, rather than for the exchange of blows itself. As regards bombast, we have previously noted that the extreme rants did not make their appearance in the heroic drama till at a later date. The rhetoric of the *Siege of Rhodes* is pompous and stilted without being extravagant, and appears most often when passages of stichomythia are mechanically worked up to a climax.[1] In general, the more figurative the language becomes, the more frigid is the effect produced. In Pt. II. V. vi, Ianthe, a prisoner, has just heard of the Rhodians' defeat and is in anguish lest Alphonso shall be among the slain. Roxolana enters and taunts her—

How fares my rival, the Sicilian Flow'r?

and Ianthe's reply

As wet with tears, as roses in a show'r.

forcibly brings to mind Dryden's pronouncement that 'no man is at leisure to make sentences and similes when his soul is in agony'. Finally, for the rhyme, it may readily be seen that the use of varied lengths of line imposes an unwelcome restraint on the author, and is responsible for awkward passages such as:

We were too proud no use to make
Of Solyman's obliging proffer;
For why should honour scorn to take
What honour's self does to it offer?[2]

[1] Cf. especially Pt. II, IV. iii, ll. 55–66.
[2] Pt. I, Fourth Entry.

On the other hand D'Avenant's use of the decasyllabic couplet is skilful, and it is noteworthy that he tends to resort to it whenever amatory debates or soliloquies expressing a divided mind are required.

No amount of following of accepted precepts, or of independence of them, will convert a mediocre play into a good one. Little is to be expected of the man who in the operatic version of *Macbeth* of 1674, could perpetrate such alterations as:

Macbeth. He, after life's short feavor, now sleeps; Well:
Lady Macbeth. Come on, smooth your rough brow, etc.

The plot of the *Siege of Rhodes* is not without dramatic possibilities, but, under D'Avenant's treatment, the result is sterile and lifeless. The observance of the rules undoubtedly gives the play a certain compactness, and may in general be considered to prove beneficial rather than otherwise to dramatists who are not of the first rank.

2. ORRERY'S *HENRY THE FIFTH*

(*acted* 1664)

Downes informs us that on its first production 'this play was splendidly cloath'd; the King in the Duke of York's Coronation suit; Owen Tudor, in King Charles'; Duke of Burgundy in Lord of Oxford's; and the rest all new. It was excellently perform'd, and acted 10 days successively'. Pepys found 'the whole play the most full of height and raptures of wit and sense that ever I heard'. It evidently enjoyed more than a *succès d'estime*, and deservedly so, since, for all its heroic follies, it has a distinction of style and a skill in the contrivance of situations which the *Siege of Rhodes* lacks. Moreover, in spite of the characterization being for the most part of the conventional heroic type, something of Henry's pleasing impulsiveness and boyish courage is allowed to filter through his neo-classic mask. For all its theme, and its occasional somewhat blatant patriotic utterances, the play owes far less to English history-play tradition than to the drama of Corneille, which it resembles in many a turn of phrase and point of technique. It is possible that Orrery was also familiar with Corneille's *Trois Discours*, since his careful avoidance of precise reference to time and place may well be due to his having adopted Corneille's plan of idealizing these circumstances. On the other hand the fact that he had to deal with an historical scenario might by itself be responsible for his use of this device. No stage-direction concerning place occurs anywhere in the play, nor even is the general place 'France' named, though the whole action takes place in that country. A closer inspection reveals that the first act takes place in the open air, being occupied with events immediately preceding and following the battle of Agincourt, while the majority of the third act, in which King Henry visits Princess Katherine of France incognito, must necessarily take place in the latter's apartment. There are frequent changes between English and French head-quarters within the act; but these are brought about merely by a group of English characters leaving the stage, and a party of French entering, without any indication of a change of setting. In the same way all reference to time is withheld, clearly in order to avoid the improbability which would arise from crowding the campaign and its various intrigues into a period of twenty-four hours. The avoidance of references to time and place has the advantage of permitting the leisurely development of a somewhat complicated plot. As regards the relation of the latter to the unity of action, there is considerable adroitness in the way in which the fairly numerous supernumerary characters—the Queen, Dauphin, Burgundy, Chareloys, &c.—while apparently acting solely out of selfish or political considerations are thereby so engaged as to further or retard the love and honour interest of the three main characters. Many of them, it is true, might be away without seriously impairing the central theme. But they serve to increase the historical illusion, which, though a minor aspect of this play, yet saves it from utter artificiality. Viewing the Henry—Katherine—Tudor story as the main action, the only characters who do not somehow contribute to it are Bedford and the Princess Anne, whose love-story is an unconnected episode. Anne, however, plays the part of *confidente*[1] to Katherine, and, as soon as she is no longer necessary in that capacity, she is married off to Bedford.

The play bears very little resemblance to Shakespeare's *Henry the Fifth*; its tone is uniformly serious and courtly, and the common people are entirely excluded from the stage. Another marked difference from Elizabethan tradition consists in the almost invariable use of narrative for battles and deaths; the battle of Agincourt (Act I), Bedford's victory at sea (Act V), and the slaying of Burgundy (Act V) are all related by witnesses of these events. The only exception is the duel which takes place between King Henry and the Dauphin in Act III, when the former discovers the latter hiding in order to overhear his conversation with Katherine. Yet this is no concession to vulgar love of spectacle, but is introduced chiefly to provide another example of the King's magnanimity; for Henry, having disarmed the Dauphin, returns him his

---

[1] Another indication of French influence. De Chastel stands in the same relation to the Dauphin. They are not so named in *Henry the Fifth*, but in the list of dramatis personae in Orrery's *Tryphon* (1668) Hermione is styled 'Confident to Cleopatra' and Irene is 'Confident to Stratonice'.

sword on condition he undertakes never again to invade his sister's privacy.

Bombast of the type usually associated with the heroic drama is lacking in this play; in its place we have high-flown sentiments of honour; and characters striving to outdo each other in fantastic generosity. With regard to the latter we may specially notice the grand contention in the fourth act between the bosom friends Henry and Tudor. The situation, as usual, is artificially worked out and there is little attempt to secure a resemblance to normal human behaviour. Tudor, being asked by the King the reason of his melancholy, tries to dissemble the real cause, but when the King insists in knowing further he describes his trouble in general terms, thus—

> She, Sir, who does my heart subdue,
> Is by my Friend ador'd with passion too:
> And, which is worse, his passion he did tell
> To me, 'ere mine I durst to him reveal.
> And, worser yet, that Friend does me employ
> T'assist his Love, whilst I mine own destroy.
> I lose my Mistress if I condescend
> To this; not doing it, I lose my Friend.
> But, which is worst of all, I'll not deny,
> He does deserve her so much more than I
> That should she, for my sake, make him despair,
> She must be more unjust than she is fair.
> And whilst she does admit of my address,
> The wrong I do destroys my happiness.

after the recital of which dilemma we are not surprised that the King remarks

> 'Tis difficult. What hast thou fix'd upon?

Eventually the King's importunity prevails on Tudor to confess that he, too, loves Katherine. This precipitates an abnegatory contest wherein Love and Honour are indeed 'to be weighed in drachms and scruples'. The King exclaims:

> My Rival thus in Love thou shuns't to be,
> Yet thus in Honour dost out-rival me.
> I to no Monarch e'er that glory gave;
> Much less my Subject shall that glory have.

He then decides that each shall plead the other's cause in Katherine's presence and accept her choice between them. This takes place in the following act, but when Tudor speaks he resigns his claim to Katherine's hand out of modesty, a course which does not impress her favourably. Tudor then pleads for pardon.

Katherine. At once you my disdain and pardon have
Tudor. But you, to love you have denied me leave.
Katherine. He who makes Love at a true Lover's height
  Does n'er ask leave, but takes it as his right.

The King perceives he has the victory, but cheers Tudor's drooping spirits with

> Whilst, Tudor, you for me your claim deny,
> I gain the Field and you the victory:
> Yours is the nobler, mine the happier share,
> I'm the oblig'd, but you th' obliger are.

In the same connexion, it is interesting to note that Pepys considered that the play had 'but one incongruity, that King Harry promises to plead for Tudor to their mistress, Princess Katherine of France, more than, when it comes to it, he seems to do; and Tudor refused by her with some kind of indignity, not with a difficulty and honour that it ought to have been done in to him'. One would have thought that by the fifth act Pepys would have surfeited of honour; and recognized, as regards 'difficulty', that some mitigation of the self-renunciation casuistry was necessary if the dramatist was to extricate his characters from their hopelessly involved position. Orrery's nimble use of the heroic couplet and its suitability for 'scenes of argumentation and discourse' can be seen in the passages quoted above. It is true that the necessity of finding a rhyme is sometimes responsible for unnatural inversions,[1] such as:

> That prince whose flags are bowed to on the seas,
> Of all Kings' shores keeps in his hand the keys.

but if, as is generally held, *Henry the Fifth* was his first play, Orrery deserves praise for setting so good an example with his refined though somewhat severe style of versification.

3. ORRERY'S *MUSTAPHA*
(*acted* 1665)

Downes records that this play, too, was highly successful on its first production. *Mustapha* is noticeably less restrained in treatment than *Henry the Fifth*, and Orrery was evidently tiring of some of the exacting French standards when he wrote it. Unfortunately his departures from orthodoxy do not bring with them any increase in vigour or in resemblance to truth, and we have language as colourless, characters as thin and abstract, and situations as aloofly handled as before. Unlike its predecessor, this play ends tragically. Roxolana the empress plots against her step-son Mustapha in order to secure the succession for her own son Zanger. The two half-brothers are devoted friends, and even when they both fall in love with the captive Queen of Hungary, mutual magnanimity soon succeeds to jealousy. Eventually Solyman is persuaded to decree Mustapha's death, and after the latter has

---

[1] Dryden remarks that this is 'the only inconvenience with which rhyme can be charged'.

perished Zanger, who has sworn not to outlive him, puts
an end to himself with the words:

> But now o'er love I have the conquest got;
> Though love divided us, yet death shall not.

But the absence of poetic justice does not raise the play to
the tragic level, and no sense of fatality or suspense can
be engendered by a series of incidents which are chiefly
disposed so as to exhibit unfailing loyalty to rigid and
artificial rules of conduct. As in *Henry the Fifth*, there is no
trace of comedy. The common people and the troops are
kept in the background, and those of them who appear on
the stage are either mutes or do not speak. When they are
heard, it is from behind the scenes.[1]

To turn to the Unities. Since there are no stage direc-
tions regarding Place, we are left to infer from the text
that the setting of the play is alternately the town of Buda
and the Turkish lines outside, with frequent changes
within the act.[2] Unlike *Henry the Fifth*, in which such
references are withheld, there are two allusions to time in
this play,[3] which make it clear that the action is confined
to a period of twenty-four hours. The rule is observed,
however, at the cost of a preposterous crowding of incidents in the fifth act. If, as has been suggested, Orrery
knew the *Trois Discours*, it is possible that he allowed
himself this licence in view of Corneille's statement that

[1] Thus, IV, s.d. 'a Mutinous noise is heard'.

[2] In the same author's *The Black Prince* (1667) and *Tryphon* (1668)
the scenes are named.

[3] In Act IV the Cardinal says to the Queen:

> Madam, last night I did advise your stay
> But now I come to hasten you away.

and in Act V Solyman, speaking of his resolution to put Mustapha to
death, says:

> Already his dark evening is begun:
> He shall be sure to set before the sun.

the fifth act was privileged to compress time beyond the normal owing to the audience's eagerness towards the end of the play for the dénouement. The end of Orrery's play, however, presents a confused succession of sensational incidents such as Corneille would have hardly condoned. Thus, while Solyman is trying Roxolana for her life, Haly enters with the news that

> The Janizaries, by their Aga led
> Accuse the Empress, and demand her head.

Solyman despatches a force to meet them; and only twelve lines later Haly returns with the announcement that the rebellion is quelled and that its leader is a prisoner. There are other incidents which also lead nowhere, and the accumulation of them induced Dryden, who usually favoured prolixity of subject matter, to remark that 'the play should have ended with the death of Zanger, and not have given us the grace-cup after dinner of Solyman's divorce from Roxolana'. The unity of action, therefore, is scarcely maintained; for though the main theme of *Mustapha*—the love of two friends for the same woman— is virtually the same as that of *Henry the Fifth*, in the former play the plots and counter-plots of Roxolana, Rustan, and Pyrrhus, concerning the succession, confuse the issue and result in a diffusion of interest, which is avoided in the latter.

The introduction of violent action on the stage constitutes another of Orrery's departures from his former correctitude, for the hitherto meek Mustapha's sudden resistance against the mutes who had come to strangle him, which Chappuzeau found ludicrous,[1] is melodramatic spectacle for its own sake,[2] and the same may be said of

---

[1] Cf. pp. 140-1. The S.D. is 'the Mutes draw their scemitars and assault him; he draws too, and kills two of them'. (Act V.)

[2] Unlike the duel in *Henry the Fifth*.

Zanger's stabbing himself and falling at his father's feet, which occurs soon afterwards. As regards the diction, we have the same stilted sentiment and logically worked-up *tirades* as before, but there is also a foreboding of the more flamboyant style in some of Solyman's martial vaunts, e.g.,

> Did I in Winter Camps spend forty years;
> Outwear the weather, and outface the sun
> When the wild Herds did to their coverts run;
> Outwatch the jealous and the Lunatick,
> Outfast the penetential and the Sick,
> Outwake long Patience, and outsuffer Fear,
> Outmarch the Pilgrim and the Wanderer,
> And there, where last year's Ice was not unthawed
> (When in thick furs, bears durst not look abroad)
> I, with cold armour covered, did maintain
> Life against showers of arrows and of Rain?
> Have I made Towns immured with mountains yield
> Sent haughty nations blushing from the Field?
> And must I, at one cast all that forego
> For which so oft I desperately did throw?
> They steal my laurels to adorn my son.[1]

Orrery's skilful manipulation of the couplet is as evident in this play as in *Henry the Fifth*, and the rhyme imposes no irksome restraint on him when he requires easily-flowing dialogue—as for example in the scene between Mustapha and Zanger in the fourth Act, where the former confides his presentiment of approaching death to the latter and bequeaths the Queen to him as his 'life's last gift'.[2]

---

[1] II.

[2] The scene ends with the brothers walking off the stage embracing, while Mustapha declares:

> To ours alone the perfect praise is due
> At once of being Friends and Rivals too.

This was guyed in *The Rehearsal* (II. ii.), where the two Kings of Brentford proclaim as they leave the stage:

> Then, spite of Fate, we'll thus combined stand;
> And like true brothers, walk still hand in hand.

The rhyme appears most artificial in the monologues of conflicting emotions which end three of the acts; in these the author chiefly seems to be congratulating himself on having brought the plot to a further stage of intricacy. A good example occurs at the end of Act III, when the Queen soliloquizes over her dilemma:

> With noble Zanger Mustapha contends
> They strive as Rivals, and they yield as Friends.
> I injure one if I the other choose:
> And keeping either I the Sultan lose. . . .
> Those would by pious craft restore our loss
> These scorn the Crescent should redeem the Cross.
> Zeal against Policy maintains debate;
> Heaven gets the better now, and now the State, etc.

Distichs of neatly-phrased sentiments, too, are out of place in the mouth of a dying man. Zanger (in Act V) stabs himself and falls at the feet of Solyman, and having extracted a promise from his father to restore the Hungarian Queen to her throne, he expires with the following words:

> Sir, for your gift in thankfulness I bend;
>
>   [*Bows to him.*
> In death I serve my Mistress and my friend.
> He'll live in your esteem, she in her Throne,
> Now all I had to do on Earth is done.
> Lo, at your feet, dear Friend, your brother lies;
> And where he took delight to live—he dies.
>
>   [*Dies.*

4. DRYDEN AND SIR ROBERT HOWARD'S
THE INDIAN QUEEN
(*acted* Jan. 1663/4)

This was Dryden's first venture in the heroic drama. In estimating Dryden's share in the play, Scott was probably right in attributing the Montezuma and Zempoalla scenes, together with the incantation scene in Act III, to his handiwork. Dryden always had a strong partiality for supernatural scenes, while Montezuma and Zempoalla are types of character which frequently recur in his plays. Settle in his slighting remarks on *The Conquest of Granada* pointed out that 'this Huffcap [Almanzor] had been seen before in the guise of Maximin, the Indian Emperor, and Montezuma . . . you are therefore a strange unconscionable thief: thou art not content to steal from others but dost rob thy poor wretched self too'. Owing to its 'variety of action' it is likely that the plot also was of his choosing; it was drawn from Gomberville's heroic romance *Polexandre*, in which the magician Ismeron (the 'conjuror' of the incantation scene) figures.

At the outset, we recognize the individual note which Dryden introduced into the heroic drama. The Inca has refused to bestow his daughter Orazia on Montezuma his victorious general. The latter at once flares up into angry defiance, and when the captive Mexican Prince Acacis endeavours to sooth his wrath, he replies:

> Bid children sleep, my spirits boil too high;
> But since Orazia's father must not die,
> A nobler vengeance shall my actions guide,
> I'll bear the Conquest to the conquered side.

Having decided to go over to the enemy, Montezuma offers to set Acacis free, but the latter refuses owing to honourable scruples, and there ensues the following stichomythic debate:

Mont. You are my Prisoner and I set you free.
Acacis. 'Twere baseness to accept such liberty.
Mont. From him that conquered you it should be sought.
Acacis. No, but from him for whom my Conqueror fought.
Mont. Still you are mine, his gift has made you so.
Acacis. He gave me to his general, not his foe.

Mont. Be cousened by the guilty honesty
    To make thyself thy country's enemy.

This passage may be taken to typify Dryden's rejection of the over-lofty sentiment of the romances (and early heroic plays) in favour of a more vigorous and impulsive brand of heroism. As Montezuma says of Acacis on a later occasion:

    How gentle all this Prince's actions be!
    Virtue is calm in him, but rough in me.

But however much the tone of the *Indian Queen* differs from that of Orrery's plays the rejection was not complete all at once. Acacis who throughout the play is ever ready, almost eager, to suffer or die on the least provocation, was evidently intended to arouse esteem and sympathy. Not until *Tyrannick Love* does the exemplary hero disappear from the action, just as it was not until the creation of Maximin that the most flamboyant bombast was heard. The most vivid characters in the play are undoubtedly Montezuma and Zempoalla; these two allow their loves and ambitions to override moral restraints, and indulge most freely in inflammatory rants.[1] It has been justly remarked of Dryden's forcefu¹ ·characters that, if they are accepted as existing at all, they may reasonably be expected to behave as they do.[2] But though they may seem more alive than the leading characters of other heroic dramatists, they are none the less still unlike human beings. Zem-

[1] As a specimen of Zempoalla's termagant style we may instance her indignation on hearing that Montezuma refuses to yield up the prisoners he has captured for her:

    I'll hear no more; go quickly take my guards,
    And from that man force those usurped rewards;
    That Prince upon whose ruins I must rise
    Shall be the Gods', but more my Sacrifice. (Act II.)

[2] Pendlebury, *Dryden's Heroic Plays.*

poalla's public avowal of sudden love for Montezuma in Act III:

> Kill him—hold, must he die?—why let him die;
> Whence should proceed this strange diversity
> In my resolves?—Does he command in chains?
>   What would he do
> Proud slave, if he were free, and I were so?
> But is he bound, ye Gods, or am I free?
> 'Tis love, 'tis love that thus disorders me.
> How Pride and Love tear my divided soul!

though absurd if judged by ordinary standards, is at least consistent with her own extravagant make-up.

To turn to the Unities. Direct allusion to Time is withheld throughout the play; and wisely so, since the prodigality of incident [1] would require at least a week for its encompassing. As regards Place, we have previously noted that this play was one of the first to employ realistic instead of illustrative scenery; [2] but though the scenes were precisely depicted on the stage, they are left unlocalized in the text, and there is no indication as to whether the action takes place in Mexico or Peru. The scene frequently changes from the Mexican to the Peruvian forces, sometimes within the act. In a sense, therefore, we may say that both time and place are idealized. As for the action,

---

[1] Comprising *inter alia* the defeat of the Mexicans, Montezuma's desertion to the Mexicans, Montezuma's defeat of the Peruvians and capture of the Inca and Orazia, Traxalla's capture of the Inca and Orazia, Montezuma's attempt to recapture them and his being captured himself, his escape from prison and duel with Acacis, the deaths of Acacis and Zempoalla, and successful invasion of Montezuma's mother.

[2] The note of realism extended, to some extent, to the costumes. Zempoalla's dress was a robe and crown of feathers, which was presented to the King's Theatre by Aphra Behn, who had (according to her account in *Oroonoko*) received it from the natives of Surinam.

it is safe to assert that no previous heroic play had such intricacy of plot as the *Indian Queen*. Externally, most of its strands are connected, but the play is far from being an organic whole. Two incidents, moreover, may be definitely described as episodic: the incantation scene in the third Act, which is purely spectacular, and the *deus ex machina* arrival of Queen Amexia which concludes the play. In connexion with the latter we may notice that Acacis has to put himself to death simply in order that the happy union of the lovers may be effected. The moment he has done so, the *dénouement*[1] inconsequently follows.

The play is entitled 'a Tragedy'; presumably because at its end there remain 'but two of the considerable characters left alive'. Yet it has a happy ending, for the lovers survive to be wedded, and furthermore poetic justice is to some extent maintained, for the villainous Traxalla and the usurping Zempoalla deserve the fates they meet with. The death of Acacis, on the other hand, is neither deserved, nor (which is worse) is it tragic; it would come into Aristotle's category of the 'merely shocking'.

Except for pitched battles, scenes of violence are invariably brought on to the stage; indeed the authors go out of their way to exhibit them. Thus at the beginning of Act II we must needs be shown the Inca and Orazia actually in flight, and Montezuma overtaking and capturing them; similarly, in Act III, Montezuma and Acacis burst in upon the Mexican court, fight, and are captured. There is a good deal of violent action in Dryden's subsequent heroic plays, but hardly so extensively as here, and it is highly probable that its prominence in this play is to be

[1] Which reveals Montezuma's true parentage and thus enables him to marry Orazia.

ascribed to Howard, who, as we have seen, vigorously defended such exhibitions in his *Address to the Reader* of 1665. For the most part these affrays are purely spectacular, and have little psychological interest, but the duel of the two friends Acacis and Montezuma in Act IV, and the suicides of Acacis and Zempoalla in the last act are endowed with a certain amount of pathos, and so have some excuse for their representation.

The play is rhymed throughout, and the couplet is the staple medium, though there are occasional quatrains. The effects secured by the rhyme vary considerably in quality, as may be illustrated by quotations from the beginning of the fourth act. 'The Scene opens and discovers Montezuma sleeping in Prison.' Traxalla enters with Orazia, and bids her decide between yielding herself to him, and Montezuma's death. The latter at once offers to die to free her, but Orazia refuses, and confesses her love for him. Traxalla, enraged, draws and offers to stab Montezuma, but at that moment 'Enter Zempoalla hastily and sets a Dagger to Orazia's breast'. This tableau of mutual perils suggests the well-known scene in *The Critic*,[1] and may possibly have helped to inspire it. Then follows a dialogue of symmetrically conflicting sentiments which shows the couplet at its artificial worst:

Traxalla. Can fair Orazia yet no pity have?
'Tis just she should her own Preserver save.
Zempoalla. Can Montezuma so ungrateful prove
To her that gave him life, and offers love?
Orazia. Can Montezuma live, and live to be
Just to another, and unjust to me?

---

[1] (Act III) *Puff*. 'There's situation for you! there's an heroic group!—you see the ladies can't stab Whiskerandos—he durst not· strike them, for fear of their uncles—the uncles durst not kill him, because of their nieces.—I have them all at a dead lock!—for every one of them is afraid to let go first.'

Shortly afterwards, however, we have a truly effective
study of a formidable unscrupulous woman wrestling with
love and wounded pride:

Zempoalla (to Montezuma). . . . Yet thou ungrateful man,
   Let thy approaching ruin make thee wise.
Mont. Thee and thy love and Mischief I despise.
Zemp. What shall I do? Some way must yet be tried—
   What reasons can she use whom Passions guide?
   . . . Rash stranger, thus to pull down thy own Fate.
Mont. You, and that Life you offer me, I hate.
Zemp. Here Jailor, take—what title must he have?
   Slave—slave—am I then captive to a slave?
   Why art thou thus unwilling to be free?
Mont. Death will release me from these chains and thee.

Here the free movement of natural speech gains also the
precision which is conferred by the couplet.

5. DRYDEN'S *THE RIVAL LADIES*
(*acted c. June* 1664)

Though this is not a heroic play, and may best be termed
a pseudo-romantic tragicomedy, we may include a short
account of it in order to show that in the hybrid species
there was a tendency towards a greater laxity in the matter
of the rules than in the heroic drama proper. The plot is of
the Spanish intrigue type; it possesses hardly a vestige of
probability, and is aimed chiefly at keeping the audience
in a continual state of flutter as to what will happen next.
Don Gonsalvo 'A young gentleman newly arrived from
the Indies', frees Hippolito (Honoria disguised as a man)
from the attacks of robbers in a wood, and engages her as
his servant. She at once falls in love with him, as does
Angellina, who, flying from an unwelcome match with
Don Manuel, also attaches herself to Gonsalvo as a man-
servant. Gonsalvo throughout the play unsuccessfully

woos Julia (Don Manuel's sister), whose affections are bestowed on Don Roderigo. Manuel eagerly and the rival ladies reluctantly assist the cause of Gonsalvo, but the latter refuses to betroth himself to Julia against her will. Innumerable adventures are allowed to happen, until a remark of Gonsalvo concerning his parentage reveals that his rival (Roderick) is his brother and that the devoted Angellina is his sister. Gonsalvo now shows no hesitation in yielding Julia up to his brother, and in transferring his love to the faithful Honoria. There are one or two mildly amusing scenes, but the play is both trivial and amorphous, and one is inclined to believe that Dryden's cynical attitude in the prologue was unaffected:

> But blame your Selves, not him who writ the Play;
> Though his Plot's dull, as can be well desir'd,
> Wit stiff as any you have e'er admir'd:
> He's bound to please, not to Write well; and knows
> There is a mode in Plays as well as Cloaths.

To turn to the Unities; we gather that a night passes between Acts I and II, since at the end of the first Act Gonsalvo and his followers seek a night's lodging at an inn, but apart from this, allusions to time are avoided. In this play even more than in the *Indian Queen* the observance of the time rule would have resulted in incongruity. Dryden's only sign of conformity to the unity of place is that, following Corneille's advice, he has designated the general place at the beginning of the play, *The Scene*, *Alicant*; but the precincts of Alicant appear to be extensive, since they are made to include 'A wood' (I. i.), 'the Seacoast' (IV. iii.), and 'On board a Pirate Carrack' (V.). Contrary to Corneille's precept, there are frequent changes of scene within the act. As regards the unity of action, it is a natural characteristic of the Intrigue Drama that the actions of the principal characters should all link up with one another. In Act V, Angellina, expecting death, reveals her identity and declares her love for Gonsalvo, which elicits from Manuel a remark which shows the absurdity of the geometrical pattern of the plot:

> We're now a Chain of Lovers linked in Death;
> Julia goes first, Gonsalvo hangs on her,
> And Angellina holds upon Gonsalvo
> As I on Angellina.[1]

Complexity of action naturally detracts from clearness of aim, and it is by no means certain whether Gonsalvo's unsuccessful wooing of Julia, or the rival loves of the two disguised women, is intended to supply the main interest. In spite of the inter-connexions of the intrigue plot, the unity of action is not always preserved, for in I. ii. an irrelevant farcical element is introduced, when Don Roderick's servants prepare the wedding feast and indulge in obscene chatter, while later a poet enters with an epithalamium and is beaten off 'with a Staff of his own rhymes'. There is also an occasional touch of comedy in the main portion of the play, as in IV. iii, when the rival ladies on discovering each other's sex and identity 'draw, and fight awkwardly, not coming near one another', until Manuel enters and separates them. Dryden's application of the term tragicomedy to this play, however, would seem to be conditioned as much by the fact than none of the principal characters are killed, as by the slight comic element which it contains.

There are many fights on the stage, chiefly between Gonsalvo and Don Roderick and their adherents, Dryden's principle apparently being 'nothing succeeds like excess' in a play of this sort. There is only one fatality, which occurs in the first scene of all, when Gonsalvo during his

---

[1] Fielding ridiculed this situation in a footnote to *The Tragedy of Tragedies*.

encounter with the robbers 'seizes the sword of one of
them, runs him through, then, after a little resistance,
disarms the other'. Spectacle and violent action are
not ineffectively combined in the Masque scene, where
Angellina, having secretly advised Julia to play the part of
Proserpine, Roderick rises in a chariot as Pluto and
endeavours to abduct her in earnest. In doing so his dis-
guise falls off, and a fight ensues between Masquers on one
hand and Gonsalvo and Manuel on the other.

We have previously discussed the rhyme of this play,
but in conclusion a comparison between two blank-verse
passages may be offered: one from the present play, in
which Dryden was courting his new 'mistress', and one
from *All for Love* in which he had wearied of her and
abandoned her. In the third act of *The Rival Ladies* Júlia,
havin sent for Roderick to come and rescue her, is torn
between modesty and fear, and argues thus with herself:

> I sent for him; yet if he comes, there's danger;
> Yet if he do not, I forever lose him.
> What can I wish? And yet I wish him here!
> Only take the care of me from me.
> Weary with sitting out a losing hand,
> 'Twill be some ease to see another play it.
> Yesterday I refused to marry him,
> To-day run into his arms unasked, &c.

The passage would gain both in pointedness and vigour
if it were in rhyme; the chill logic and the balanced antithetical structure demand the closing snap of the distichs
to complete them. But if we turn to a speech of Cleopatra
in *All for Love* (II. i)—

> I am no queen
> Is this to be a queen, to be besieged
> By yon insulting Roman, and to wait
> Each hour the victor's chain? these ills are small:

For Antony is lost, and I can mourn
For nothing else but him. Now come, Octavius,
I have no more to lose! prepar thy bands;
I'm fit to be a captive: Antony
Has taught my mind the fortune of a slave.—

it is evident, not only that the medium has been mastered, and that conflicting sentiments can be as well expressed in blank verse as in rhyme, but that the alteration of medium is due to a greater intensity of thought and feeling. Thus Dryden by his own example abrogated his earlier theory.

6. DRYDEN'S *TYRANNICK LOVE, OR, THE ROYAL MARTYR*

(*acted c. June* 1669)

From the point of view of the present inquiry, this play is of special interest, since it shows a greater vigour and individuality of treatment, and at the same time a closer attention to the rules than any we have yet considered. These attributes are not incompatible, for superhuman characterization, bombast, and increased remoteness from ordinary life (which were largely the outcome of the attempt to imitate the heroic poem) are hardly affected by observance of the unities and the like. The play shows what we have called in the Introduction the second stage in the relation of critical theory to practice; it may be placed in the category of 'plays affected by French theory as interpreted and slightly modified by the growing school of English criticism'. The latter is in the present instance represented by Dryden's recently-written *Essay of Dramatic Poesy* and the *Defence of the Essay*, and *Tyrannick Love* shows clear traces of their influence. In his preface, Dryden draws attention to the fact that, though the play was hastily written, 'yet the scenes are everywhere unbroken[1] and the Unities of Place and Time more exactly kept, than perhaps is requisite in a Tragedy; or at least, than I have since preserv'd them in "The Conquest of Granada".' The *Conquest of Granada*, besides being in two parts, is unusually full of complicated incident, and therefore the unities could hardly be maintained in it; but that Dryden still considered the unities 'requisite in a Tragedy' is shown by the fact that in his next heroic play, *Aureng-Zebe*, they are as closely adhered to as in *Tyrannick Love*.

The plot is well known, and a brief summary of it will serve. Maximin, the tyrant emperor, wishing to reward his successful general Porphyrius, offers to bestow on him his daughter Valeria, who is beloved by Placidius. She loves Porphyrius, whose affections, however, are secretly engaged by Berenice, the wife of Maximin. The captive princess St. Catherine is brought in, and Maximin immediately conceives a passion for her, which conflicts with his hatred of her religion. She converts many of the Romans to Christianity, including Berenice. Maximin is elated at his wife's defection, since it enables him to order her execution without fear of a revolt; St. Catherine scornfully rejects his love, and in fury he has her martyred. Berenice, in pious loyalty to her husband, forbids Porphyrius to take up arms against him; nevertheless Porphyrius attempts forcibly to prevent her death. Maximin then orders that they shall be executed together, whereupon Valeria in despair commits suicide. This so enrages Placidius that he stabs the emperor, who returns the blow, and they perish together; leaving Porphyrius to reign as emperor, happily united to Berenice. The play is decidedly better constructed than Dryden's earlier productions; and

---

[1] *Liaison des scènes* is in fact scrupulously maintained, which is seldom the case in the heroic drama. *Aureng-Zebe* (1675) is another play which makes use of this device.

in its conduct of the exposition and catastrophe it bears out the principles advocated by Corneille in his *Discours du Poème Dramatique*. Thus the first act contains the germ of all the succeeding action, and in it all the principal characters are directly or indirectly made known to the audience. Corneille urges the importance of arousing suspense, and maintains that it may be best secured by postponing the catastrophe for as long as possible and by preventing it from being too clearly foreseen. During the last act of *Tyrannick Love* the sense of impending disaster increases; Maximin becomes more and more tyrannical, the position of the various sets of lovers becomes more hopeless, and St. Catherine becomes increasingly defiant towards Maximin and more intent than ever on being martyred. Furthermore the reversal comes at an unexpected moment, when the tyrant is apparently in his strongest, and the lovers in their most dangerous position.

As regards the Unities: direct allusions to time are present in this play, unlike *The Indian Queen* and *The Rival Ladies*. From the unsuccessful request made to Maximin in Act I to postpone the assault on Aquileia 'but only for this day', and from the prophecy of the 'Astral spirit' Damilcar in Act IV (uttered apparently at 7 p.m.!) to the effect that the conclusion of the emperor's love affair will come to pass within a few hours, we may conclude that the action is well within the twenty-four-hour limit. That in consequence there is an unnatural compression of incidents can hardly be denied, and we may instance the rapidity with which St. Catherine converts one important character after another to her faith, and the bewildering succession of executions, murders, and suicides in the last act. But while the observance of the time rule does nothing in itself to promote verisimilitude, it is probable that had the rule been neglected the play would have been as burdened with complicated incident as *The Indian Queen*.

The general scene is confined to straiter limits than usual: 'The Camp of Maximin, under the Walls of Aquileia.' In the preface Dryden defends the play against those who had complained of its profanity (as expressed in the vaunts of Maximin), and points out that Maximin is amply punished 'even for his impiety to his false gods'. Further, he remarks, 'as if I had foreseen this objection, I purposely removed the Scene of the Play, which ought to have been at Alexandria in Egypt (where St. Catherine suffered), and laid it under the walls of Aquileia in Italy, where Maximin was slain; that the Punishment of his Crime might immediately succeed its execution'. It may be surmised, however, that it was chiefly the demands of the unity of place which occasioned the alteration. With one exception the scenes are laid in various parts of the royal camp, and the 'discoveries' (as, for example, 'the Scene opens and discovers Berenice on a scaffold') are not departures from the rule, since they are all scenes which might credibly be viewed through the aperture of a pavilion. There is nothing in the play, however, to account for the sudden appearance of an 'Indian Cave', which is the setting for Act IV. Here the conjuror Nigrinus summons up his astral spirits who, having prognosticated the outcome of the love-affairs of Maximin and Placidius, provide an interlude of song and dance. But 'Indian Cave' is merely a generic term for some unlocalized scene suitable for supernatural exhibition, and it is unlikely that the scene was regarded as infringing the place rule. Half-way through the act occurs the stage-direction, 'the Angel ascends, and the scene shuts',[1] but *liaison des scènes* is still maintained; for Nigrinus and Placidius remain on the

[1] The action presumably took place at the rear of the stage.

stage and two fresh characters enter to speak with them. As for the unity of action, there is a closer nexus than usual between the affairs of the principal characters, and once the play has got started there is no tiresome re-shuffling of interests. Even the Indian Cave scene, which is principally introduced for the sake of spectacle, cannot be considered as wholly episodic, since it serves to strengthen Maximin's resolve to pursue his guilty passion.

The play might be considered tragic owing to retribution which overtakes the dominant character, were it not for the fact that the motivation is too crudely melodramatic to render Maximin credible as a human being. As regards Violent Action, Dryden has relegated to behind the Scenes what La Mesnardière would call a *spectacle horrible*, namely, the martyrdom of St. Catherine; but to atone to this there is in the last act a general carnage on the stage which is carried to the point of grotesqueness, as in the actual monstricide, which involves the spectacle of the expiring emperor sitting on the prostrate Placidius and stabbing him, in between outbursts of bombast. The bombast and superb arrogance of Maximin are of course the most striking feature of the play, and Dryden no doubt expected his audience to be lost in horror-struck admiration of his headlong tyrant. In the earlier portion of the play his blustering self-aggrandisement often appears merely fatuous, as in the threat which he addresses to Albinus, whom he suspects of bringing the news of his son's death:

> Stay; if thou speaks't that word, thou speaks't thy last:
> Some God now, if he dares, relate what's past:
> Say but he's dead, that God shall mortal be.

—a passage which was perhaps echoed in *The Rehearsal* (IV. ii):

Prince Prettyman. Durst any of the Gods be so uncivil
> I'ld make that God subscribe himself a Devil.

But after his monstrous actions have begun to accumulate, these flamboyant passages convey his indomitable spirit more convincingly, as when, on seeing St. Catherine's guardian angel descend and shatter the wheel intended for her torture, he exclaims:

> . . . And, one by one, her Miracles I'll tire.
> If proof against all kind of Deaths she be,
> My Lov's Immortal, and she's fit for me.

Indeed, the words which Dryden spoke of Almanzor[1] might almost be taken as applying also to Maximin: 'I design'd in him a roughness of character, impatient of Injuries: and a Confidence of himself, almost approaching to an Arrogance. But these Errors are incident only to great Spirits, they are Moles and Dimples which hinder not a Face from being Beautiful, tho' that beauty be not regular.'

In *Tyrannick Love*, as in Dryden's other heroic plays, the couplet naturally lends itself to passages of debate and altercation. These, as usual, appear at their best when 'some considerable action' depends on the issue of the argument. Thus the amorous debate between Porphyrius and Berenice (Act II) as to whether Porphyrius shall secure Berenice's hand by killing her tyrant husband, is skilfully wrought and shows how emotions can be confined within a regular pattern without losing their value. Best of all, perhaps, is the scene in which Valeria and Porphyrius try to outdo each other in self-accusations before the dully impatient Maximin. Porphyrius is really indifferent to Valeria's affection, but the latter, in order to save him, maintains that it was she who rejected his advances:

> He raves, Sir, and to cover my Disdain,
> Unhandsomely would his Denial feign.

[1] In his Dedication of *The Conquest of Granada* to the Duke of York.

And all means failing him, at last would try
T'usurp the Credit of a Scorn, and Die.
But—let him live—his Punishment shall be
The Grief his Pride will bring for losing me.

Here, though her attitude is feigned, her words are also designed to convey to Placidius her real feelings—the reproaches of the slighted lover. The chill and protracted argument, on the other hand, which takes place between St. Catherine and the heathen philosopher Appolonius in the second act, and on the result of which nothing immediate depends, is both tedious and undramatic. The heroic couplet is not used continuously, for besides occasional triple rhymes and Alexandrines,[1] short unrhymed lines occur intermittently which serve to give some freedom of movement to passages of an emotional nature. Dryden satisfactorily accounts for these diversities of measure in the preface: 'I have not everywhere observed the equality of Numbers in my Verse, partly by reason of my haste; but more especially because I would not have my Sence a Slave to Syllables.'

7. LEE'S *SOPHONISBA, OR, HANNIBAL'S OVERTHROW*
(*acted* 1675)

In the Introduction it was remarked that as English dramatic criticism began to free itself from French influence, so the heroic play gradually widened its scope, and no longer dealt exclusively with heroic motives and situations. Though this departure from stereotyped forms was not fully evident until the period when rhyme was rejected, yet there are indications of it in the early work of Lee and Otway, whose serious plays (together with those of Dryden) are in general marked by a greater

[1] Alexandrines are generally used to round off passages of an exalted tone, as in St. Catherine's last speech.

individuality of thought and treatment than those of the other Restoration playwrights. Lee's plays are remarkable for their consistently tragic endings, for their sombre atmosphere—illumined occasionally by flashes of genuine poetry—and for their more natural way of treating scenes of passion than was customary in the heroic school. Lee undoubtedly owed something to the example of Webster and Ford, and his drama may be described as an amalgam of the Drydenesque and Fordian type of play. In his earlier (rhymed) period the Dryden strain predominates, but in it a certain originality of aim and freedom of technique is perceptible, as an examination of the present play will show. The plot may be briefly summarized as follows: Hannibal, who has been falsely dealt with by Carthage, and whose mistress Rosalinda is a prisoner of Scipio, resolves to stake all on a last encounter with the Roman army in spite of unfavourable auspices from the priests. Massinissa, King of Numidia, who is in the service of Rome, loves Sophonisba, a Carthaginian lady who has lately been married to her captor, the Carthaginian Syphax. Scipio regards Sophonisba as an enemy, but permits Massinissa to assault Cirta, the head-quarters of Syphax. Massinissa slays Syphax in battle, and on being persuaded by Sophonisba that she has not been unfaithful to him, he marries her in defiance of Scipio's wishes. Meanwhile Rosalinda has smitten the heart of Massinissa's young nephew Massina, but does not return his love. Massina obtains Scipio's permission to escort her back to the Carthaginian camp; but on their arrival Hannibal is stricken with jealousy of the young prince, to dispel which Rosalinda rejects Massina, who, overcome with grief, kills himself in their presence. Soon afterwards the battle of Zama is fought, which results in a decisive victory for Scipio mainly owing to the prowess of King Massinissa.

Rosalinda is killed fighting in man's apparel, and Hannibal, though crushed, retires meditating revenge on Rome. Scipio, while full of gratitude for Massinissa's heroism in the battle, insists on his giving up Sophonisba as a prisoner. To prevent this indignity Massinissa undertakes to put her to death himself, and after a touching farewell the lovers drink poison together. Scipio is so impressed by his ally's nobility that he decides to conclude a peace with Carthage and retire into private life.

If the play does not bear much resemblance to life, this is less on account of heroic exaggeration than of its persistent theatricality. It retains many of the heroic characteristics, such as the love and valour theme, the two contrasted pairs of lovers, and the despairing lover who takes his own life. The characters are no more than types, but they are clearly differentiated from each other, which is more than can be said of most heroic plays. Thus, while Sophonisba is expert in the arts of allurement, Rosalinda is consistently the strong-willed, resolute Roman lady, and while Massinissa is impetuous, Hannibal is stern and inflexible throughout the play. Lee's skill in the contrivance of situations is another thing which distinguishes him from the majority of his fellow-dramatists. The scene of jealousy which precedes Massina's suicide, the mutual self-sacrifice of the lovers in the face of Scipio's obduracy at the end of the fourth act, are crises which arise naturally out of the action, and are not arbitrarily imposed on it. Moreover, the author has an ability to create an atmosphere of tragic foreboding, as is shown in Sophonisba's premonition of approaching death, and in the gloom which Massina's suicide casts over the reconciliation between Hannibal and Rosalinda.

While Lee does not ignore the rules, he does not allow them to stand in his way when theatrical effects are within reach. He entitles the general scene of the play 'Zama',[1] but this is inaccurate, for in the middle of the third act we are suddenly transported to 'The City of Cirta' in order to behold Massinissa's victorious entry and reunion with Sophonisba. Apart from this, a loose unity of place is maintained, though there are many changes of scene within the acts from the Carthaginian to the Roman camp and vice versa. The play contains one allusion to time, when Hannibal in the fourth act resolves to bring about the final encounter with Scipio 'with to-morrow's dawn'. If we suppose the twenty-four-hour rule is to be observed, the confinement of the action of the first four acts to one day taxes probability to some extent, and it may have been due to the author's consciousness of this that he made Massinissa remark, concerning the Cirta expedition, 'Was ever Victory so swiftly won?' (III). The unity of action is clearly kept; and we may recall Lee's solicitude for this rule, in his preface to *Oedipus* (1679). There is no subplot, but the parallel stories of the two pairs of lovers provide diversity of interest without involving confusion. The unfortunate love-affair of Massina may be said to retard the action slightly, but this episode was probably included in deference to heroic convention. Massinissa and Sophonisba are supplied with confidents who, having no concerns of their own, yet help to keep the play moving.

With regard to violent action: up to the end of the fourth act none but 'justifiable homicides' are shown on the stage, for Massina's suicide and Massinissa's killing of Scipio's officer who had tried to wrest Sophonisba from him have an emotional and psychological value in the situations in which they occur. In the final act, however, Lee's fondness for theatrical effect gets the better of him,

[1] Lee prefixes a general locality, usually a name of a city, to all his plays.

and various engagements during the battle of Zama are fought out on the stage, in the Elizabethan manner. Unlike Lee's first play *Nero* (1674), *Sophonisba* is comparatively free from bombast. It is true that hyperbole is carried to excess in the scene of Massinissa's rapturous reunion with Sophonisba—

> Nectar, and Flames, the Sweets of Hibla grow,
> About her Lips ambrosial Odours flow.[1]

But passages of this sort are few, and it may be said of most of the rhetorical outbursts that their emotional content justifies the amount of heightening employed.

The verse is successfully varied with triple rhymes, Alexandrines, short unrhymed lines, and occasional quatrains. The couplet, however, imposes no restraint on the free movement of Lee's dramatic dialogue, as may be seen, for example, from the following passage, where Scipio confronts Massinissa with the choice between death and yielding up Sophonisba:

Scipio. Canst thou both Promises and Threats refuse?
Mass. Death, or what's worse, you only bid me chuse.
Scipio. Bring forth thy Love, and Life thou shalt enjoy.
Mass. Is that a Life? Your purpose act; destroy:
Turn all your Javelins Points against this Breast;
But let it not of Love be dispossest. &c.

The couplet shows itself to advantage in two prominent jealousy-debates: one between Hannibal and Rosalinda, in which the former is jealous in spite of himself, and the other where Massinissa tries to maintain his suspicious obstinacy but is wheedled out of it by Sophonisba.[2] The second is the more effective of the two, probably because more depends on the issue of it than of the other.

Though the theme is tragic, the play lacks the pervading

---

[1] III.   [2] Both in Act III.

intensity and singleness of aim of tragedy. It is not conceived as a whole, and relies for its effect on the appeal of individual scenes. Moreover, the emotion which it seeks to arouse is still admiration, whether the frustration of lovers' hopes or the insubstantiality of worldly renown are depicted. Nevertheless, *Sophonisba* helped to widen the somewhat narrow limits of the heroic drama, for which alone Lee deserves special recognition.

CONCLUSION

IT may be confidently affirmed that none of the foregoing plays are so bound by the neo-classic rules as to be sterile and lifeless on that account alone. In this respect what applies to them may be considered as true of the rhymed heroic drama in general; between 1660 and 1678 the rules in England were never so unreservedly respected as to render possible the production of a play like D'Aubignac's *Zénobie* or of an heroic poem like Chapelain's *La Pucelle*, in which correctitude was considered all-important and every other artistic consideration negligible in comparison.[1] For the most part the rules exercised a wholesome restraint on the heroic plays of our period; for the latter had in them something to restrain. The overflowing vigour of a play such as *The Conquest of Granada*, for example, partly manifests itself in the profusion of incident employed; yet the checking of this tendency in *Tyrannick Love* by the application of the unity of action results in a more homogeneous, better-balanced production, without any loss of vitality. Not often do we meet with a play which ignores all the neo-classic precepts, though this is more common than to find one in which they have been carried out to the letter. Of the seven plays we have discussed in detail one only (*The Indian Queen*) shows a complete disregard of the rules, and this probably represents fairly the proportion of non-conforming to conforming plays over the whole rhymed period. Moreover, individual exceptions apart, it is clear that the heroic play gradually moves away from its early adherence to the strict standards of the French theorists to a state, not of lawlessness, but

[1] Between 1678 and 1700, however, there were two plays of this type, viz. Rymer's *Edgar, or the English Monarch* (unacted, 1678), and Filmer's *The Unnatural Brother* (1697).

of freedom within limits; the limits being, perhaps, most clearly defined by Dryden in his *Defence of the Essay*.

The return to blank verse and the exploration of new themes, however, was accompanied by a readoption of neo-classic orthodoxy; this was due to the fact that a fresh school of French law-givers, with Rymer as their English spokesman, happened to make their influence felt just at the time when the popularity of the heroic play was becoming endangered by the dull repetition of its excesses. Dryden's *All for Love*, besides being one of the best plays of the new type, also shows most clearly the tendencies that were at work. The love and honour conflict so dear to contemporary taste was inherent in the plot, but the variety of Shakespeare's creative genius afforded many suggestions for the novel treatment of familiar situations, and the glowing intensity of his poetry provided a model for a more naturalistic way of treating scenes of passion. At the same time the strictest requirements of the unities were complied with, without, however, resulting in any undue sense of constraint. For a time the serious drama developed on these lines, the Shakespearian and the pathetic types of play rising into a deserved prominence. But the conventional heroic play was so closely united to the spirit of the age that, after a brief breathing-space, its reappearance was inevitable; and towards the close of the century we find many plays of the old type being written, slightly modified by the newer elements. This reversion to type was attended by a relaxation of the rules, as can be seen in a play representative of the class, Dryden's *Don Sebastian* (1689).[1]

---

[1] Dryden observes in the preface that he has 'not exactly kept to the three mechanick Rules of Unity' because 'the Genius of the English cannot bear too regular a Play'; moreover 'the English will not bear a thorow Tragedy; but are pleas'd, that it should be lightned with Under-Parts of Mirth'.

These conclusions which our survey has enabled us to reach may not be of the first importance; but it is hoped that the process of arriving at them has been more illuminating, in exhibiting the interactions of applied criticism, abstract theory, classical example, the taste of the age, contemporary satire, and the like. Perhaps at no period was the English drama subjected to such a complex medley of influences as during the Restoration. We are always, however, aware of the two chief contending forces: incoming neo-classicism and the independent temper of the national drama. The product of the two, the heroic play, shows a kind of logical audacity which may be best termed the baroque spirit.

We tend to judge heroic plays by the standards of tragedy; largely because of the difficulty we experience in entering into the contemporary point of view. Unless, however, we can approach the latter, the heroic play is bound to appear to us somewhat as an inexplicable monstrosity, even when we have analysed the type and accounted for the various elements of which it is composed. But it was the synthesis of these elements which captivated and held spellbound a cultivated portion of seventeenth-century society. For them at all events the heroic play was *sui generis*; it was a law unto itself in virtue of its peculiar appeal. As Mr. T. S. Eliot says of Dryden's dramas: 'From the point of view of either the Elizabethan or the French drama they are obviously inferior; but the charge of inferiority loses part of its force if we admit that Dryden was not quite trying to compete with either, but was pursuing a direction of his own.'[1] Moreover, in his criticism, as we have previously seen, Dryden has left us in no doubt as regards the claims of the heroic play to be considered a distinct dramatic species.[2] Certainly it has as

---

[1] *Homage to John Dryden.*   [2] See pp. 174–5.

much right to be considered a separate and self-contained form of art as has baroque architecture, in which there has recently been a marked revival of interest, and there are decided correspondences between the two forms. Baroque art generally may be said to result when a culture endowed with an unusual store of exuberant vigour accepts but strives against an established art-form, almost breaking its bounds in the process of expressing itself within them. We have seen this in operation in the case of the heroic play;[1] in baroque architecture it shows itself in such typical features as the undulating entablatures, broken and curved pediments, and sculptured figures in contorted attitudes which so profusely adorn the façades of buildings of the period in Spain and southern Italy. The style, which permitted the utmost amount of grandiose display within a more or less conventional framework, was the product of the Counter-Reformation, and was adopted by the Jesuits in order to popularize Catholic orthodoxy. The architect set before him the same aim as the heroic dramatist, which was, in Dryden's words, 'to endeavour an absolute dominion over the minds of the spectators'. And, indeed, such examples as the great *Seminario Conciliar* of Salamanca, or the western front of the Cathedral of Murcia, astonish the beholder with their vainglorious magnificence in much the same way as do the best heroic plays of the bombastic type. The inherent weakness of both forms consisted in an over-reliance on the element of surprise; so that, when the novelty of its first triumph had worn off, the heroic play tended to deteriorate into a thing of spectacle, and similarly baroque architecture degenerated into the Chur-

[1] It is noteworthy that, with the possible exception of music, the heroic drama was the only form in which baroque art gained a secure footing in England. The work of Vanbrugh perhaps represents the nearest approach to an English baroque style of architecture.

rigueresque or rococo. On the one hand we have the spectacular excesses of a play like *The Empress of Morocco*, on the other the riotous confusion caused by the lavishness of applied ornament—the flowers, shells, scrolls, and medallions which bespangle the pillars of the Sacristy of the Cartuja at Granada.

BIBLIOGRAPHY

I. WORKS OF LITERARY HISTORY AND CRITICISM

[Texts of dramatists and critics previous to the eighteenth century are only included when they appear in modern editions and are accompanied by introductions and notes.]

ARNAUD, Charles. *Les Théories dramatiques au XVIIe siècle. Étude sur la vie et les œuvres de l'Abbé d'Aubignac.* Paris, 1887.

BELJAME, Alexandre. *Le Public et les Hommes de Lettres en Angleterre au dix-huitième siècle* (1660–1744). 2nd ed. Paris, 1897.

BETTERTON, Thomas. *The History of the English Stage from the Restoration to the Present Time.* 2 vols. 1741.

BIOGRAPHIA DRAMATICA. 3 vols. London, 1812.

BOILEAU, Nicolas. *Art Poétique.* Edited with notes and introduction by Ferdinand Brunetière. 7th ed. Paris, 1911.

BRAY, René. *La formation de la doctrine classique en France.* Paris, 1927.

BROWN, F. C. *Elkanah Settle, his life and works.* Chicago, 1910.

BUTCHER, S. H. *Aristotle's Theory of Poetry and Fine Art.* With a critical text and a translation of the Poetics. 1895.

C. H. E. L. Vols. vi, caps 5, 9, vii, caps 11, 12, viii, caps 1, 5, 6, 7, 11, 16.

CAMPBELL, Lily B. *Scenes and Machines on the English Stage during the Renaissance.* Cambridge, 1923.

CANFIELD, D. F. *Corneille and Racine in England.* Columbia Univ. Studies, 1904.

CHAMBERS, Sir E. K. *The Elizabethan Stage.* 4 vols. Oxford, 1923.

CHARLANNE, L. *L'Influence française en Angleterre au XVIIe siècle.* Paris, 1906.

CHASE, L. N. *The English Heroic Play.* New York, 1903.

CHILD, C. G. *The Rise of the Heroic Play.* Modern Language Notes, 1904.

CIBBER, Colley. *An Apology for the Life of Mr. Colley Cibber.* Edited by R. W. Lowe. 2 vols. 1889.

CLARK, Barrett H. *European Theories of the Drama*. Cincinnati, 1919.

CLARK, William S. *Dryden's Relations with Howard and Orrery*. Modern Language Notes, XLII, 1927.

The Sources of the Restoration Heroic Play. Review of English Studies, Jan. 1928.

COURTHOPE, W. J. *History of English Poetry*. Vols iii & iv. 1910.

CROWNE, John. *The Dramatic Works*. With prefatory memoir and notes by J. Maidment and W. H. Logan. 4 vols. Edinburgh, 1873–4.

DANIELS, W. M. *Saint-Evremond en Angleterre*. Versailles, 1907.

D'AUBIGNAC (Hédelin, Abbé d'Aubignac). *La pratique du théâtre*. Edited with preface and notes by Pierre Martino. Paris, 1927.

D'AVENANT, Sir William. *The Dramatic Works*. With prefatory memoir and notes by J. Maidment and W. H. Logan. 5 vols. Edinburgh, 1872–4.

Love and Honour and The Siege of Rhodes. Edited by J. W. Tupper. Boston, 1909.

DOBRÉE, Bonamy. *Restoration Comedy*, 1660–1720. Oxford, 1924.

Five Restoration Tragedies. Ed. with Introduction. 'The World's Classics'. 1928.

Restoration Tragedy, 1660–1720. Oxford, 1929.

DOWNES, John. *Roscius Anglicanus*. Ed. by the Rev. Montague Summers. 1928.

DRYDEN, John. *Works*. 18 vols. Ed. Scott and Saintsbury. 1882–93.

Essay of Dramatic Poesy. Ed. by T. Arnold; revised by William Arnold. 1903.

ELWIN, Malcolm. *The Playgoer's Handbook to Restoration Drama*. 1928.

FLEAY, F. J. *A Biographical Chronicle of the English Drama*. 2 vols. 1891.

FRIEDLAND, L. S. *The Dramatic Unities in England*. Journal of English and Germanic Philology, 1911.

GARNETT, R. *The Age of Dryden*. 1895.

226 BIBLIOGRAPHY

GENEST, John. *Some Account of the English Stage, from the Restoration in 1660 to 1830.* 10 vols. Bath, 1832.

GOSSE, Sir E. *Seventeenth-Century Studies.* 3rd ed. 1897.

HAM, Roswell G. *Dryden versus Settle.* Modern Philology, May 1928.

HARBAGE, A. *Thomas Killigrew.* Philadelphia, 1930.

HILL, Herbert W. *La Calprenède's Romances and the Restoration Drama.* Chicago, 1910.

HOTSON, Leslie. *The Commonwealth and Restoration Stage.* Harvard, 1928.

HUME, Martin. *Spanish Influence on English Literature.* 1905.

JOHNSON, Samuel. *Lives of the English Poets.* Ed. G. Birkbeck Hill. 3 vols. Oxford, 1905.

JULLEVILLE, L. Petit de. *Le Théâtre en France.* Paris, 1889.

KER, W. P. *Essays of John Dryden.* 2 vols. 1900.

LANCASTER, H. C. *Le Mémoire de Mahelot, Laurent, et d'autres décorateurs.* 1920.

A History of French Dramatic Literature in the Seventeenth Century. Part I, The Pre-Classical Period, 1610–34. 1930.

LANSON, Gustave. *Corneille.* 4th edition. Paris, 1913.

LEMAÎTRE, Jules. *Corneille et la Poétique d'Aristote.* Paris, 1888.

LOWE, R. W. *Thomas Betterton.* 1891.

LYNCH, K. M. *The Social Mode of Restoration Comedy.* New York, 1926.

MANTZIUS, Karl. *A History of Theatrical Art.* Translated by von Cossel and Archer. 6 vols. London, 1903–21.

McAFEE, Helen. *Pepys on the Restoration Stage.* Yale, 1916.

MILTON, John. *Samson Agonistes.* Edited by A. W. Verity. Cambridge, 1892.

NETTLETON, G. H. *English Drama of the Restoration and Eighteenth Century.* New York, 1914.

NICOLL, Allardyce. *British Drama.* 1925.

The Development of the Theatre. 1927.

History of Restoration Drama. 2nd edition. 1928.

ODELL, George C. D. *Shakespeare from Betterton to Irving.* 1921.

OTWAY, Thomas. *The Complete Works.* Edited by Montague Summers. 1926.

PALMER, John. *The Comedy of Manners.* 1913.

PENDLEBURY, B. J. *Dryden's Heroic Plays.* 1923.

RIGAL, E. *Le Théâtre français avant la période classique.* 1901.

ROLLINS, Hyder E. *A Contribution to the History of the English Commonwealth Drama.* Studies in Philology XVIII, 1921.

The Commonwealth Drama; Miscellaneous Notes. Studies in Philology XX, 1923.

SAINTSBURY, George. *Dryden.* 'English Men of Letters.' 1881.

History of Criticism and Literary Taste in Europe. 3 vols. 1900–4.

A History of the French Novel. Vol. 1. 1917.

SCHELLING, Felix E. *Elizabethan Drama, 1558–1642.* 2 vols. Boston and New York, 1908.

SHERWOOD, M. *Dryden's Dramatic Theory and Practice.* Yale Studies, 1914.

SMITH, David Nichol. *Shakespeare Criticism.* A selection, with an introduction. 'The World's Classics'. 1916.

Shakespeare in the Eighteenth Century. Oxford, 1928.

SPINGARN, J. E. (edited by). *Critical Essays of the Seventeenth Century.* 3 vols. Oxford, 1908.

SPRAGUE, A. C. *Beaumont and Fletcher on the Restoration Stage.* Harvard, 1926.

STUART, D. C. *Stage Decoration and the Unity of Place in France in the Seventeenth Century.* Modern Philology, vol. x, 1912–13.

THALER, Alwin. *Shakspere to Sheridan.* Harvard, 1922.

THORNDIKE, Ashley H. *Tragedy.* 1908.

TILLEY, A. *From Montaigne to Molière.* 2nd ed. 1923.

VERRALL, A. W. *Lectures on Dryden.* 1914.

WILSON, John H. *The Influence of Beaumont and Fletcher on Restoration Drama.* Ohio, 1928.

WOOD, Paul S. *Native Elements in English Neo-Classicism.* Modern Philology, Nov. 1926.

The Opposition to Neo-Classicism in England between 1660 and 1700. Publications of the Modern Language Association of America. March, 1928.

II. WORKS BEARING ON THE LIFE AND THOUGHT OF THE RESTORATION PERIOD

BREDVOLD, L. I. *Dryden, Hobbes, and the Royal Society.* Modern Philology, vol. xxv, May 1928.

BRUNETIÈRE, Ferdinand. *La Société précieuse au XVIIe siècle.* (Études critiques sur l'histoire de la littérature française. Deuxième série). Paris, 1893.

CHANCELLOR, Beresford. *The Lives of the Rakes,* vol. ii. 1924.

COUSIN, Victor. *La Société française au XVIIe siècle d'après le Grand Cyrus.* 2 vols. Paris, 1886.

CUNNINGHAM, W. *The Influence of Descartes on Metaphysical Speculation in England.* 1876.

DENT, Edward J. *Foundations of English Opera.* Cambridge, 1928.

DESCARTES, René. *The Meditations, and Selections from the Principles of Philosophy.* Translated by John Veitch. With preface, essay, and notes by L. Lévy-Bruhl. Chicago, 1905.

EVELYN, John. *The Diary and Correspondence of John Evelyn.* Ed. William Bray. 4 vols. 1870.

HAMILTON (Antoine) Count. *Memoirs of the Comte de Gramont.* Translated by Peter Quennell. With an introduction and commentary by C. H. Hartmann. 1930.

ORNSTEIN, Martha. *The Role of Scientific Studies in the Seventeenth Century.* Cambridge, 1928.

PARRY, C. Hubert. *The Music of the Seventeenth Century.* In the *Oxford History of Music,* vol. iii, 1902.

PEPYS, Samuel. *Diary.* Ed. Henry B. Wheatley. 9 vols. 1893-9.

POWICKE, Frederick J. *The Cambridge Platonists.* 1926.

SAINT-EVREMOND. *The Letters of Saint-Evremond.* Edited by John Hayward, with an introduction and notes. 1930.

SPRAT, Thomas. *The History of the Royal Society of London.* 4th ed. 1734.

STEPHEN, Sir Leslie. *History of English Thought in the Eighteenth Century.* Vol. i. 3rd ed. 1902.

INDEX

eloquence in love–scenes and scenes of grief, 151–2.

Sarasin, favours happy ending, 72–3; condemns comic admixture, 73; on method of complying with unity of time, 90; strictly interprets unity of action, 91; on unity of place as observed in *L'Amour Tyrannique*, 121; condemns violent action, 137.

Scaliger, introduced principle of verisimilitude, 87.

Scott, Sir Walter, on *Indian Queen*, 197.

Scudéry, G. de, regards heroic romances as prose epics, 8 n.; on Rules of Aristotle, 65; *L'Amour Tyrannique*, 71–2; unity of time observed in, 90; unity of place observed in, 121.

Scenery, transition from illustrative to realistic, 127–9.

Seats on the stage, in the French Theatre, 116.

Serlio, theatrical settings of, 115 n., 123.

Settle, Elkanah, *Empress of Morocco*, 51, 146, 223; Ed. Phillips on, 156; *Pastor Fido*, 180; *Philaster*, his version of, 50–1.

Shadwell, Thomas, upholds the Unities, 106; upholds *liaison des scènes*, 106; on unity of place, 131; on bombast, 159; *Squire of Alsatia* (Prologue to), 24 n.

Shakespeare, 47 n., 48, 57, 182; taught Betterton, 46; *Antony and Cleopatra*, 112, 180; *Henry the Fifth*, 20; *Macbeth*, 53, 56, 112; *Midsummer Night's Dream*, 53; *Richard III*, unity of action imposed on by Cibber, 113; *Tempest*, 53.

Sheridan, R. B., *The Critic*, 202.

Shipman, Thomas, defence of rhymed plays in prefatory epistle to his *Henry III of France*, 183 n.

Stilo recitativo ridiculed in *The Rehearsal*, 186.

Successive scenes, 117, 122 n.; French admiration for, 126.

Suckling, Sir John, 47 n.; *Aglaura*, platonic element in, 12, 13.

Supernatural in the heroic play, 53, 210.

Tasso, Torquato, 68 n.; 154.

Tate, Nahum, *Lear* (adaptation of), 35, 56, 70 n.

Teatro Olimpico, 116–17.

Theatrical conditions, influence of, on the drama, 58–64.

Thought, contemporary, influence of, 27–39.

Thurloe, Secretary of State, 43–4.

Torelli, designer of stage settings, 54 n.

Tragicomedy, 69–86; application of the term to Dryden's *Rival Ladies*, 205.

Translations of the Corneilles and Racine, 15–19.

Tuke, Sir Samuel, *Adventure of Five Hours*, 55; reference to unity of time in prologue to, 98; scene changes in, 128, 131; on unity of place, 131.

Unities, The, 87–135 *et passim*.

Unity of place, general interpretation of, in England, 131.

Vanbrugh, Sir John, 222 n.

Verisimilitude, principle of, 106; introduced by Scaliger, 87; impaired by the Unities, 93; stubbornly upheld by Sir R. Howard, 172–3, 175–6.

Violent action, avoided in French plays, introduced in English, 18, 52; views of critics on, 136–46.

Vitruvius, 115 n.

Waller, Edmund, 191.

Wren's Theatre Royal, Drury Lane, 126 n. 128.

Wright, James, *Historia Histrionica*, 58.

Wycherley, William, *Country Wife*, 61.